CW01425668

The Art of the Subject

The Art of the Subject

Between Necessary Illusion and Speakable Desire in the Analytic Encounter

Mardy S. Ireland

Other Press
New York

Production Editor: Robert D. Hack

This book was set in 11 pt. Berkeley by Alpha Graphics of Pittsfield, NH.

10 9 8 7 6 5 4 3 2 1

 For information write to Other Press LLC, 307 Seventh Avenue, Suite 1807, New York, NY 10001. Or visit our website: www.otherpress.com.

Library of Congress Cataloging-in-Publication Data

Ireland, Mardy S.
The art of the subject : between necessary illusion and speakable desire in the analytic encounter / by Mardy S. Ireland.
p. cm.
Includes bibliographical references and index.
ISBN 1-59051-033-X (alk. paper)
1. Psychoanalysis. I. Title.
RC504 .I74 2003
616.89'17—dc21 2003004930

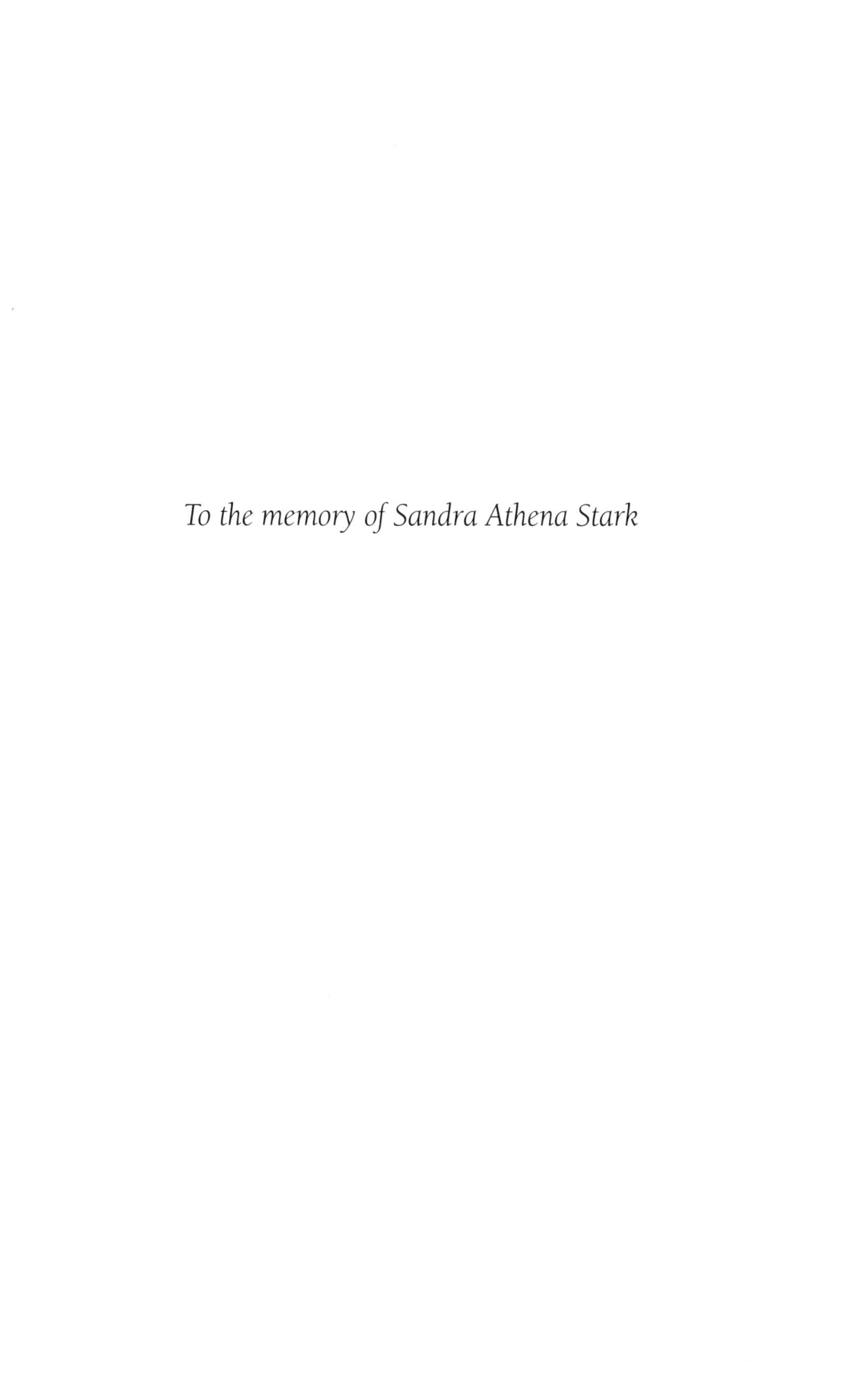

To the memory of Sandra Athena Stark

Contents

Acknowledgments

My gratitude to my former analysts, mentors, supervisors, colleagues, and all the individuals with whom I have worked in my practice, for all that I have learned from my experience with them.

My special thanks to Judith Feher-Gurewich for believing in the concept of this book and to Kate Scannell for facilitating the creation of the necessary writing space to complete it.

Many, many thanks to Teri Quatman as my personal editor and translator. And finally, my appreciation to everyone at Other Press, especially Stacy, my editor, and the art designers, who made this text an *external* reality.

1

Making Waves: The Analyst as Disturbance in the Clinical Field

> ***Disturbances in the field are the most difficult to correct and the most dangerous threat to the continued survival of a species.***
>
> **(An unknown ecologist)**

This phrase from environmental ecology, "disturbance in the field," was spoken by someone in my practice in reference to a recent visit to his home of origin. It is a phrase that echoes frequently in my mind because it serves to remind me how much, as an analytic practitioner, I become a disturbance in the psychic field of each person who seeks psychoanalysis or analytic psychotherapy. The task of dealing with the difficulty my disturbance provokes, the danger I pose, the hope I evoke, becomes central to the analytic work. For instance, my words in one moment may evoke an all-too-familiar echo of judgment that the patient must defend against by a reflexive rebuttal or a denigrating verbal attack. In another moment, with the same person, my silence may be experienced as a dangerous spear aimed to pierce him or her—which must be eluded through massive emotional withdrawal. And perhaps at yet another point, there may be moments when the mere sound of my accent or the rhythm of my voice, and not my words, evokes the experience of being wrapped up in a profoundly longed-for blanket of warmth and safety, or, in contrast, the experience of being enlivened by the presence of desire.

Daily I am reminded that psychic change occurs in analysis or psychoanalytic psychotherapy via the refraction of one person's suffering, and the personal narrative surrounding that suffering, through those of another. This refraction, I believe, passes through both the theory(s) the analyst uses to think about what happens within the analytic encounter and the practitioner's[1] subjectivity as well, creating a disturbance in the analyst's field that must be processed to further the analytic work.

Integral to this refractive process is the analyst her/himself as psychoanalytic instrument. Psychoanalytic theory has, from its inception, affirmed the fundamental singularity of the individual. More than any other clinical perspective, it has sought to address the suffering and problems unique to each individual, spoken and enacted. Yet the field of psychoanalysis took a fair amount of time to form ideas regarding the singularity of the analyst as a psychoanalytic instrument.

Today the analytic encounter includes two "subjects" within the analytic dyad, who generate a co-created third space—the "analytic third"—providing the medium of the analytic experience from which many of the analyst's interpretations are harvested in one way or another.[2] Interpretations of the "here and now" transference are central to, though certainly not exhaustive of, the analyst's harvesting.

Within this field of work Donald Winnicott proffers a model of psychoanalysis as a lived experience between two subjects from which the analysis of one subject proceeds. In this model, the notion of an analytic third—a creation of the particularities of both members of the analytic dyad—implies that it does make a difference who the person of the analyst is, especially when working with more disturbed individuals and/or with infantile mental states of mind in the neurotic.[3]

A different emphasis as to the analyst's position and where the analyst's attention should be directed has been developed by Jacques Lacan and his followers—perhaps the least known of the multiple psychoanalytic schools of practice in the United States. Within this perspective, language and speech are emphasized as the "third term" structuring the analytic dyad, orienting and referring the analyst's attention to the analysand's unconscious discourse as the primary field of work. The analytic third (as a co-creation of two analytic subjects and which includes particularity of the analyst) is not intended as an explicit focus of spoken interpretation, nor as a major vehicle moving the analysis.

In this book, I attempt to set into motion a theoretical and clinical engagement between the two psychoanalytic fields represented by Donald

1. For purposes of consistency, analyst/clinician/practitioner will be designated by analyst.

2. See the work of André Green (1985a) on the analytic object, and of Tom Ogden (1994) on the analytic third.

3. However, self-disclosure by the analyst is neither assumed nor precluded.

Winnicott and Jacques Lacan. While it could be said that Freud mapped the workings of the unconscious-conscious mind, Winnicott and Lacan, in contrast, have explored the making and unmaking of the human mind. Freud's thought and practice addressed itself to a broad array of symptoms and conflicts of everyday life. Winnicott and Lacan, in addition, explore the territory related to the very construction of, and reliable functioning of, the subject as a psyche-soma (mind and body).

The theory and clinical technique represented by the Winnicottian and Lacanian schools of psychoanalysis are often thought to be inherently incompatible—such that to employ one clinical perspective would be to preclude the use of the other. In fact, a common critique concerning their incompatibility contends that a Winnicottian treatment focuses too much on matters related to the psychic construction of the infantile body-ego (and early fusional relationships). The Lacanian approach concerns itself with the Symbolic function, how symbolization constitutes the very essence of human subjectivity, and how human desire comes into being. Thus the Winnicottian approach has been criticized by the Lacanians for not sufficiently taking the Symbolic into account. On the other hand, the Winnicottian perspective strives to include both pre- (and non-) verbal and affective elements within the analytic matrix, so Winnicottians have criticized Lacan for overemphasizing the verbal domain while underemphasizing the importance of affect and other nonverbal elements. They have further criticized the Lacanians for not adequately taking into account the role of the object, and the significance of the analytic dyad's co-constructed object-relational matrix as forerunner of the oedipal subject. So, while it may be true that Winnicott and Lacan make an odd couple, it has been my preference to bring them into relation with one another, rather than participating in a polemic that excludes the work of one or the other. I believe that the dialectic created in their complementarity and supplementarity can deepen and broaden the working space available to us as analysts and psychoanalytic practitioners.

WINNICOTT AND LACAN: THE ODD PSYCHOANALYTIC COUPLE

It is not a stretch to say that on the North American psychoanalytic scene, Winnicott occupies the place of the familiar "One," while Lacan marks the place of the lesser known, if not outright strange, "Other." The works of

Winnicott and the British school have made significant inroads into North American psychoanalysis during the last twenty or so years. Many of Winnicott's seminal ideas are familiar to, if not fully understood by, numerous psychoanalytic practitioners. Such familiarity is clearly not the case with Lacan and his ideas. Although Lacan has long been a known figure in certain venues within American universities, he occupies only a recent, fledgling, and in many ways contested, presence on the United States' clinical psychoanalytic scene.

Put most simply, Winnicott elaborates the developmental trajectory of the infant in the process of becoming human. For Winnicott (1962a), who is working to articulate the minimal developmental conditions necessary for establishing symbolization, the capacity to feel alive and to live creatively is directly related to the quality of "environmental provision" from the beginning of life beyond the womb (p. 62). Provision is first, Winnicott (1974) says, or there can be no "real" human life to be enlivened by play, desire, or creativity, only a life dominated by "unthinkable agonies" (p. 104). With good enough provision (and assuming development proceeds in an ordinary way), an ego/self can be constructed, and instincts integrated, and as a result the problems of day-to-day living can "all feel real to the infant who becomes able to have a self that can eventually even afford to sacrifice spontaneity, even to die" (Winnicott 1956, p. 304).

In contrast to Klein, Winnicott brings us into the thinking and experience of the mother as a subject (something that Klein's rich elaboration of mother as internal object does not do). He positions the mother in relation to the emergent psyche-soma of the infant, whereas the father receives scant attention. Where Klein is also concerned with symbolization and seems to make the conceptual leap from instinct to drive as fantasy, Winnicott remains interested in how the instincts become localized and imaginatively elaborated via symbolization. His work focuses upon the realm of Freud's (1915, 1915a) concept of primary (primal) repression (sometimes called the unrepressed unconscious [Green 2000]) and that of establishing the me/not me boundary or contact barrier (Freud 1915)[4]—both of which are of particular interest in this text. Winnicott (1945, 1947, 1954, 1971) further examines the role of primary aggres-

4. This is the aspect of the unconscious that holds those nuclei to which later conscious, but unacceptable (and therefore secondarily repressed), thoughts are attracted. This makes the space inside of the subject to be; contact barrier is the attainment of Klein's depressive position or Lacan's (1953b) moi of the mirror stage.

sion in psychic development as the source of primary creativity, and in contrast to Klein, focuses upon how the environment must meet the initial spontaneous gestures of the baby as emerging subject. In this vein, he elucidates the necessary process of the infant's co-creation (with mother) of a space in which to live, to create, to discover—both intrapersonally and interpersonally. This co-created space exists first as an intermediate (transitional) zone, but over time it gives the developing infant an avenue to external reality (as well as to creative, internal reality). In summary, Winnicott delves deeply into the subjective experience of the mother–infant couple in its process of birthing a human subject.[5] Thus, maternal concerns of attunement, optimal failure, waiting, recognition of the spontaneous gesture of primary creativity, and so on, inform the analyst's/clinician's stance.

In complement, Lacan works to elaborate the structuring elements of what we call the human condition itself. For Lacan (1952–1953, 1953a), there is no conception, no birth, no libidinal life, without the desire of the Other—the Symbolic network in which the human infant is immersed. This immersion in the Symbolic order actually begins with the mother's desire to bear a child. For Lacan a treasure chest of symbols preexists every baby's conception; prenatally, an expectation is already established that she/he (the baby) will assume a set of consensually preestablished symbolic meanings—that is, words, rules, and laws that will place real limits upon his/her body, feelings, thoughts, and life possibilities. And where Winnicott is concerned with the process of a human being's becoming "real," Lacan offers via his interlocking registers of the Real, the Symbolic, and the Imaginary what this "real" concerns. Assuming, then, that structure supersedes development, such "paternal" concerns as defining and accepting limits (as necessary elements of human living), engaging in speech as a creative act, assuming one's unique pattern of desire, and so on, inform the analyst/clinician's stance.

One way into the territory of the dialectic between Winnicott and Lacan is to imagine the way in which an analyst/clinician's experience parallels that of a particle physicist. Take a moment and imagine that you could see zillions of atoms and their constituent parts. Depending upon your observing position, these atoms might seem either to be a cloud of particles or a series of waves. With this in mind, now consider that in each

---

5. He eschewed putting it into a frame of reference where it might be described from a third perspective.

analysis (or psychoanalytic psychotherapy) the analyst might at times encounter the analysand as if she/he/the analyst were being enveloped in a swirl of emotional, cognitive, and visceral particles. At other times, the analyst might experience herself as receiving the analysand as though via a series of waves, which, by virtue of their sheer regularity, seem to constitute a more symbolizable, organized pattern. While there may be individuals in analysis who appear more consistently to exhibit as either particles or waves, it is more common that each analysand manifests, at different moments across sessions, particlelike or wavelike properties. In fact, sometimes these shifts occur even within the confines of a single session. In either analytic mode of encounter (when the patient is either a swirling cloud of particles or an organized series of waves), the moment is mediated by the analyst's subjectivity in a manner not dissimilar from how in the act of scientific observation, the scientist is a mediating factor in his/her own experiment. Winnicottian thinking and clinical sensibilities can be depicted more by the metaphor of psyche as an experience of dispersed particles, and the treatment as what enables their organization. The thinking and sensibility of the Lacanian field is better represented by the metaphor of the psyche as embedded within preexisting wave patterns (setting degrees of freedom concerning love, desire, thought, etc.), within which each individual must find/create a place.

Despite their differences in focus, Lacan and Winnicott converge around a certain kind of space that resides at the center of the human subject. Each perspective addresses the question of how one can live a satisfactory life, given lifelong uncertainty and an opening and closing of possibilities, which are contextualized and provoked by a certain kind of emptiness/potential space at the core of what it means to be human. This space is experienced in multiple ways in the ongoing flow of life's sequential moments. One may feel this gap or space as a vague sense of something missing, or as desire, or as loneliness, creativity, good solitude, a restless wanting, anxiety, relaxation, sadness, and so forth. But when a person's life doesn't flow, so to speak, the range of possibilities inherent within this space become constricted and rigid—generating, perhaps, a paranoid fear of something unknown, or an unbearable isolation. For some, the space at the core of being human is experienced as a vapid black vortex, for others a white space of annihilating deadness, or a cave filled with terrorists. Or worse, where there ought to be many possible experiences there is only a single repetitive freeze frame of acute agony which for that person defines what it means to be human. For that individual, there are no potentialities within this space, only destructive certainties.[6]

CLINICAL IMPLICATIONS OF THE DEVELOPMENTAL VERSUS THE STRUCTURAL APPROACH

It should be recognized that Winnicott's maternal and Lacan's paternal concerns are not inherently at odds with one another, but there may be a sense in which Winnicott focuses too much on the maternal matrix and Lacan too much on the paternal phallus from their respective vantage points. My aim in the following chapters is to present Winnicott and Lacan as quite separate voices, meeting so as to create a parallactic space[7]—one formed by the many paradoxes their two theoretical and clinical perspectives offer.

Their two forces, as it were, can meet sometimes (in my mind) with the help of Bion, who can be used to facilitate a movement between the dialectical positions represented by Winnicott and Lacan. Let me name just a few ways in which Bion has contributed to my thinking here, and I'll leave the remainder to the subsequent chapters to further this dialectical discourse. Whereas Winnicott highlights the importance of necessary illusion, Bion, in his theory of thinking (1962a), denotes illusion's potential destructiveness to the mind and psyche-soma. He proffers a model of how the proto-subject of the baby is able, or not able, to transform Winnicott's sensory/ holding environment into psyche. In the fact that Bion's (1963) containment is an internal process (involving the symbolic) versus Winnicott's sensuous holding, Bion moves along toward Lacan, as does his (Bion's) notion of preconception where there preexists a form that the emergent mind meets and recognizes (Bion 1962b). At the same time, by Bion's designating that there must be requisite emotional experiences for preconceptions to be realized, Winnicott peeks again over the horizon. Bion's (1967) offering of a framework (and clinical

6. In my work as a clinical supervisor at Boyer House Foundation, such experiences and states of mind are common among the severely disturbed individuals who are in treatment there. Boyer House Foundation is an assisted-living program that includes psychoanalytic psychotherapy in its multimodal treatment approach.

7. A parallax is an apparent change in the direction of an object, caused by a change in observational position that provides a new line of sight.

narrations) for understanding how fragmented the world and mind can be when symbolization cannot be adequately established or maintained, supplements both Winnicott and Lacan. Bion adds feeling and thinking flesh to the place where Lacan locates the materiality of language (see Chapters 3 and 5, this volume) and to what Lacan calls the Imaginary. Bion focuses upon the meeting of symbolic processes with severe trauma, a meeting that also interests Lacan (see Chapter 9, this volume). But Bion's focus is more in the territory of psychic traces, signs, and symbolic equations versus Lacan's privileging of the linguistic symbol. Bion's accent upon movement via ongoing oscillations in psychic transformation (or its destruction) is an insistent message that the analyst must be able to access both maternal and paternal functions in order to further analytic work. Bion's (1970) notion of the necessity for the analyst to have a working "faith" in aiming toward "O"—the realm of unspeakable fullness of the Real—is not so far afield from Lacan's paradoxical insistence that the human subject lives within the gap co-created by the signifier and its limits.

The engagement proffered in the following chapters is this analyst's reflection on how two psychoanalytic (developmental and structural) perspectives invite and enable the analytic encounter. This engagement is not meant as a synthesis or an integration, but as a complementary and supplementary meeting of two separate and fertile psychoanalytic minds—each bringing a particular aesthetic and clinical sensibility to psychoanalytic practice, each enriching and deepening the work of the other—to be heard and viewed through the presentation of one analyst/author's work, as a mediating third.

I will be describing a working analytic space in which Lacan and Winnicott are brought together to form a creative coupling—sometimes facilitated by the transforming influence of Bion. In doing so, the ideas of Lacan, which are less familiar or clinically described, will be actively highlighted and interpolated into the more familiar psychoanalytic discourse within the United States, that of the British school—the middle school of Winnicott and to a lesser extent Klein. As a beginning, Chapter 2 considers a descriptive metaphor for helping the reader grasp intuitively Lacan's (1952–1953) three interlocking registers of the Real, Symbolic, and the Imaginary within a description of the analytic encounter. From Chapter 3 onward, both theory and clinical material are presented as these issues have presented themselves in my practice. Somewhere between Winnicott/developmental and Lacan/structural perspectives as vantage points, a parallactic space has taken/is taking shape over time in my practice. The subsequent chapters are a chronicle of my sojourn. I invite the reader to make her/his own sojourn through these pages. It is my hope that, as on any journey to a foreign city, the reader will leave changed by this experience.

The parallactic analytical space I will be describing is one composed of three terms (plus one): the analysand, the analyst, and the analytic third, plus the symbolic webbing that marks the limits and possibilities for the first three elements. In this parallactic space, the conflict between a developmental versus structural model in psychoanalysis may indeed be transformed into a working dynamic paradox.

2

A Parallactic Space of Analytic Practice

Analysis is an experience of the particular.
(Lacan 1953)

One depiction of a parallactic psychoanalytic space engendered by the engagement between Winnicott and Lacan is the figure of the mobius strip. The mobius is a topographical form that appears to have two surfaces, and when viewed from a certain position appears to make two spaces, but when viewed from another appears to have only one surface and one space.[1]

The mobius (Fig. 2–1) illustrates the paradox inherent in the relationship between the Symbolic network and the inner world of the psyche/mind, and between the Symbolic order and the biological body or soma. A Symbolic network not only defines the parameters of human subjectivity, but also in part delineates the substance of human interaction—shared emotions, fantasies, and discourse. The mobius, through its paradoxical visual form, shows how the simple question of what is inside or outside one's psyche-soma, or where the other in conversation stops and one's self actually begins, is neither simple, nor is it answered satisfactorily by a singular perspective (Winnicottian or Lacanian). Thus, this paradoxi-

1. The mobius strip is a mathematical equation discovered in 1858 by August Mobius. If you take a strip of ribbon, hold it by its two ends, and then twist the ribbon once and join the two ends of the ribbon together with a piece of Scotch tape, you will have made a 3-D mobius. As you observe this three-dimensional mobius figure, you will have easier access to the illusion that there are two "spaces" delimited by the ribbon. This 3-D mobius figure could be described by Lacan's three dimensions as being bounded by the Symbolic, bounding the Imaginary, and perfused with the Real.

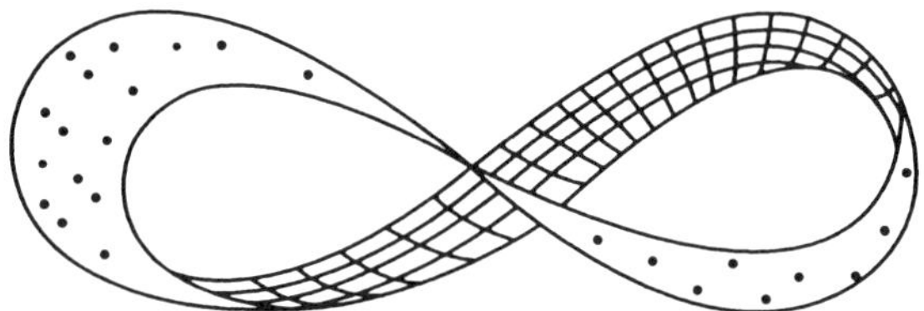

Fig. 2–1. 3-D Mobius

cal figure of the mobius lends itself to illustrating the complexity of human subjectivity that is at play within any human encounter, but especially within an analytic encounter, where this complexity is the primary focus of attention.

As is theorized in modern physics, space and time are interlocked and inseparable dimensions. So too are the three interwoven dimensions of human subjectivity—dimensions to which Lacan has brought a rich discourse. While different psychoanalytic schools may describe, emphasize, and even harvest the interactions of these three dimensions differently from one another, these dimensions are operative in every analytic encounter. What follows, then, is a description of these three interlocking dimensions as conceptualized by Lacan, with a view to highlighting salient similarities and differences as they are represented within the more familiar Winnicottian persepctive. So let me begin with the Symbolic.

THE SYMBOLIC ORDER

The Symbolic network structures and conveys most of our human experience. This Symbolic network reaches into every nook and cranny of society, even to the womb itself. For example, words exchanged between the pregnant mother and father can produce effects on the fetus that are apart from the ordinary homeostatic needs of the fetus. The fact that human beings alone are immersed in a Symbolic network, and it is a network in which they must find their way, is critical. The Symbolic makes a place for you (i.e., your name) in the family and in the wider society. Your name in itself, however, means nothing. Your name only takes on meaning in relation to other symbolic elements—be they fantasy(s) of some sort, or statement(s) about your identity and place in the world. For Lacan (1955–1956) the Symbolic order means language and speech, while for Winnicott and the British School, other forms of psychic representation are included in this Symbolic network as well.

In language, there are both signifiers and signs. The difference between the sign and the signifier is one of consequence in the analyst's day-to-day work. A signifier is a unit of something (i.e., word, gesture) that can carry ambiguous/multiple meanings (e.g., as President Clinton once said, "It depends on what the meaning of the word 'is' is . . ."); a sign is a unit of language whose reference is fixed in relation to its object (e.g., a door always means a wooden portal versus the many other meanings it could take on). In the Symbolic, there is no one-to-one correspondence between the signifier (the word or gesture) and any object or meaning to which it refers (Lacan 1964). In contrast, with a sign, there *is* a correspondence (e.g., in an airplane, a picture of a person with a seat belt fastened means one and only one thing: Buckle up!). In this respect, then, the sign (of which the image is an example) is more static in its meaning, whereas the signifiers in a sentence are free to move, and thus may have multiple meanings depending upon the surrounding signifiers, and this meaning can only really be formed when one reaches the period at the end of the sentence. Lacan (1953d, 1955–1956) posits a precarious relationship between the signifier and its signified—slippage, if you will. As such, the signifier gives the analyst a degree of clinical leverage in her/his making of interpretations and in their potential impact. It is often the case that a person seeking analytic treatment is psychosomatically stuck/identified to a word or phrase (thus making the word/phrase a sign) and has been unable to benefit from the dynamic movement and multplicity of meanings that words as signifiers hold in potential.

THE IMAGINARY ORDER: THE INNER OBJECT WORLD AND THE PSYCHE-SOMA

Imagine that we all carry with us clouds of protosymbolic particles that are our earliest psychic registrations of infantile sensory experience and instinctual drives. In the mobius figure this might look like there were particles floating in the space (or spaces) of the mobius. Now each of these protosymbolic particles is in fact made up of two smaller subatomic particles held together by an emotional charge, or affect. For example, picture the hydrogen atom, with one proton and one electron. The electron is held in place with respect to the proton by a particular charge. In this picture, the electron corresponds to traces of the infant's (not yet formed) self-experience; the proton, to traces of the infant's experience of mother; and the charge, to the affect that links them in that moment of experience (i.e., *+*). These protosymbolic particles can be thought of in at least a couple of ways. One way is that these particles are the most primitive psychic registrations of a person's infantile sensory experience—as in those somatic traces left by the sensory sounds of letters versus the meaning of those letters when put together. Another way of conceiving of these protosymbolic particles is that they could be a bit more elaborated as in an image or pictogram. These slightly more elaborated psychic registrations of experience or protosymbolic particles can be thought of as the beginning of fantasy and/or a form of primitive thinking using nonlinguistic representation (i.e., phonemes functioning as signs—e.g., ba = bottle, Bion's [1962b] alpha elements cohering to make a contact barrier). Why are these protosymbolic particles important? These early protosymbolic elaborations are pivotal to the infant's making of a viable psyche-soma and establishing the relative psychic investment in the ego/self and in relations with others, and we carry these with us into adulthood where they continue to influence who we are with ourselves and others.

These early psychic traces or nonlinguistic representations are not quite fully symbolized as would be worded experience, but they do represent a step away from unmediated experience (see Chapter 6, this volume). The infant (via symbolic containment by the mother) slowly transforms primitive sensory experience into a psychic body—a transformation that only takes place in relation to an "other" and that may be more or less adequate. The adequacy of this psychic body in an Imaginary realm helps determine how reliable the psychic boundary is between inside (me) and outside (the other, or not me), and how stable that boundary remains (see Chapters 5 and 6, this volume). The human being's inner sense of his/her own body (which can never be seen in its entirety but is imaginatively pictured as such) comes together first via a psychic transformation of sensory experience around the body openings, and later spreads across the surface of the entire body—as a body-ego, according to Freud (1914), on the basis of a primary identification through parental holding and handling of the infant. These protosymbolic particles—psychic traces that are at least partially elaborated—are what make up the inner object-world and/or Lacan's Imaginary realm of experience.

The register of the Imaginary is associated with how one's original sense of body ego or narcissistic integrity is formed through an identification with an external other (the mother who is both object and locus of symbolization). In the development of the infant, the visual image of an other assists the infant in *imagining* the sense of body integrity that the infant does not yet feel. In the Imaginary, narcissistic integrity is maintained by identification with sameness. There is no third position from which two different people—you and I—can be recognized at the same time. It is always either/or, you or I, black or white. Thus, when the only possibility of recognition is either one or the other, aggressivity (Lacan 1953d) becomes a built-in component of the relationship—even if the relationship is established on positive grounds—because it can shift suddenly the moment either person does not want to be exactly the same as the other anymore. Importantly, since it is in the realm of the Imaginary that the earliest form of representation of one's self/ego and of the other is established, Winnicott would say that the psychic conditions of the Imaginary bear greatly upon analytic work with individuals suffering severe disturbance in their sense of self or in relationships with others. Though it is easy to equate the Imaginary with the image or fantasy (because these are working elaborative elements within it), the Imaginary is really a psychic space or inner theater created by the intervention of the Symbolic upon the biological (Real) body of the infant insofar as his/her needs are symbolically interpreted by an other.

THE REAL: THE SPACES OR GAPS IN A SYMBOLIC NET

The Real refers to human experience that is unmediated by our symbolic capacity. It is, in other words, all that is in excess of, lies outside of, or is beyond what the symbol can represent. Experience that is symbolically unmediated is normally rare, as in those moments when a person is at one with her/his body and nature, but has no self-awareness of that experience. The Real also includes a dimension of the impossible—for example, elements of acute or cumulative trauma that can never be completely drained away by our symbolizing it, however much it helps to do so.

We are, in some sense, as human beings, cut away from the Real—from the ongoing fabric of nature. This would be akin to each one of us being a strip of ribbon cut from nature's fabric and then being fashioned into a mobius strip. Even if we were able to fit ourselves back into the ongoing fabric of nature, we would never seamlessly fit; there would always be a bit of a gap. This is a gap that is never overcome or sealed permanently. The presence of this gap or perceived sense of something missing in the human being is what paradoxically enables humans to have the capacity for symbol making, and all that follows (for better or worse) from this symbolic capacity.

The Real also includes the noticed and unnoticed ongoing bodily drives of hunger, assertion/aggression, sex, and so on, which move through us. Additionally, human beings can "fall into" unmediated Real experience, be that via momentary ecstasy (e.g. sexual orgasm) or trauma—for instance, if another automobile were not to stop for a stop light, and you, as the driver of your car, barely escaped being hit head on, you would experience a moment of falling into the Real. (Should this unmediated moment become prolonged or too repetitive, it would lead to psychic states of primitive agony; see Chapters 6 and 9, this volume.) Ordinarily, the Symbolic network and its structures shield us from experiences of the Real that are too traumatic, providing a psychic integrity and holding for us. However, as holes or spaces within any weave might suggest, we can at times fall into the hole of the traumatic or ecstatic Real.

Since no one knows exactly when and how symbolic functioning entered the animal kingdom, we might assume the existence of a mythical moment in the history of human time, when the human species was cut away, like our ribbon, from immersion in the continuous fabric of pure instinctual life and was made into a mobius figure. It is not that the human ribbon, so to speak, is devoid of instinctual experience, but that in being cut apart from total immersion in instinctual or bodily experience, a bit of something of the Real was lost. In its stead, the human body must become "redoubled" in the sense that the human infant has to construct a psychic body ego that is in effect superimposed upon his/her biological body. This superimposed psychic (in the Imaginary) body has Real effects upon the actual body. (The most extreme example would be a person with a severe personality split who manifests a physiological disorder in one ego state, and yet has no such disorder in the other ego state.)

THE IMAGINARY, SYMBOLIC, AND REAL WITHIN THE ANALYTIC PROCESS

When a person presents for analysis or analytic psychotherapy, what evolves in the analytic encounter is a structure akin to the triangular configuration (see Chapter 3, this volume) of the infant–mother matrix. This evolution in the nature of the analytic relationship occurs by virtue of a number of elements: the symbolic definition of what it means to consult an authority and ask for help, the regularly scheduled frequent meetings, the kind of free associative discourse that is promoted. All these factors combine in a manner that unconsciously replicates aspects of the infant–mother dyad, and so reconstitutes this set of psychic positions.

From the beginning of an analytic encounter and increasingly over time, the subjectivity of the analyst and the analysand is subject to distortion. This distortion depends upon the movement and force of all those protosymbolic particles (in the Imaginary) of both the analysand and the analyst upon the analytic dyad.

In any analysis there is a constant dynamic movement of the patterns of such psychic particles between the analysand and analyst, whereby their two patterns mix with, connect, and repel each other, moving back and forth between them, the patient seeking unconsciously to maneuver the analyst to match a familiar unconscious Imaginary pattern concerning her/his ego and the other. The protosymbolic particles within the analysand metaphorically flow into the interior of the analyst, through a process of verbal and nonverbal exchanges, only to be subsequently returned to him or her. This cycle will be repeated again and again in the treatment, such that with each influx to the side of the analyst, there may begin to form a sort of organization to the mix of atoms, and a cumulative effect begins to accrue. In this accumulation, the analyst allows her-/himself to become saturated with the transferential experience until, as Bion noted, a "selected fact" (Bion 1962b, p. 72) seems to emerge, enabling symbolic elaboration to begin to take shape within the analyst. It is like Braille slowly emerging to the touch, which becomes something that eventually can be read and understood, ultimately (hopefully) leading to an interpretation. Lacan has visualized the three interlocking dimensions of the Symbolic, the Imaginary, and the Real as a borromean knot (see Fig. 2–2). No thread may be cut without the knot becoming undone.

THE ANALYST AND ANALYTIC ACTS

No matter how tight a weave is, there are gaps. So too with our symbolic network. The gaps in the Symbolic weave refer to those bits of an infant's experience not captured by symbols (because not all of the infant's needs are met by the mother's (or father's) interpretation of a need or demand).

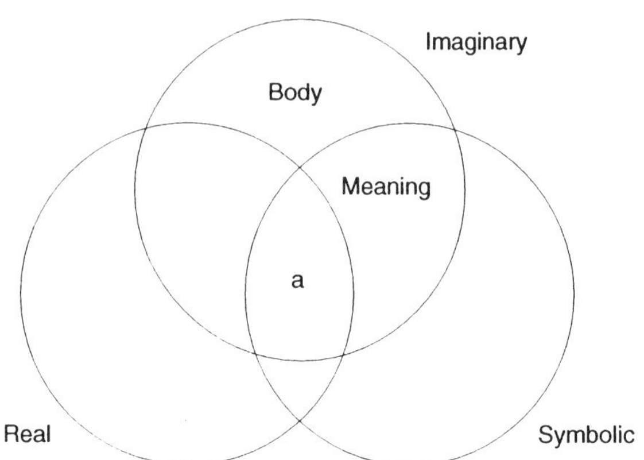

Fig. 2–2. Borromean Knot

The ongoing paradox in this state of affairs is that there is a shared human fantasy of a paradise lost that is in fact only retroactively constructed illusion—which is related to the gap created when infant need must be symbolically interpreted by a mother. From a structural or Lacanian perspective, "the object" most referenced in the analytic work is this Real gap originating from the foundational impact of the Symbolic order upon human beings. The loss of mother as the primal object during the infant's separation-individuation process is different from the bit of the Real (object) that is lost, thereby leaving a gap within the subject as a result of the effects of symbolization.

In the field of the analyst's acts, the British school or Winnicottian analyst does not operate outside the purview of the Symbolic order—otherwise no effective interpretations could be made. Likewise, the Lacanian analyst cannot maximize the use of the "Symbolic" to interpret and intervene if she/he is not fully in play within the dynamic forces of the protosymbolic particles of the Imaginary or inner object world—the Imaginary.

From a Winnicottian perspective, the inner-object world and its development is the primary axis orienting the analytic work; thus, the object most often referenced in the work will be the primary object (usually a mother) from whom the developing child must separate. The primary task of the Winnicottian analyst is to assist the analysand in making use of what is going on in the analytic matrix to learn about how her/his unconscious patterns affect her/his conscious life—for worse and for better. The analyst here makes interpretations concerning the psychic organization of the analysand through an ongoing processing of her/his (the analyst's) own subjective experience. This processing often begins as spontaneous reveries, affective undertows, somatic experiences such that the analyst begins to think, "Why is this happening at this moment?" The "analytic third" is a concept for elaborating and thinking about the patterns of psychic particles comprising the inner object relations, and how this "other scene" affects the analysand's functioning in the various spheres of her/his day-to-day life (e.g., hindering or facilitating one's ability to love, to mourn, to work, to desire, etc.). In the parlance of the "analytic third," the working emphasis is on transferences between the analysand and the analyst, and on what of the co-created "analytic third" can lend itself to be interpreted or made use of by the analysand.

In contrast, it is precisely because of the moving transference/countertransference dynamic that a Lacanian analyst focuses on the analysand's language in its particularity. This privileging of the language of the analysand is, in some measure, a direct attempt to diffuse the (inevitable to a certain extent) contamination of the countertransference, or, in other words, the transference of the analyst to the analysand. Here the analyst makes intentional use of what is called the principle of the "double inscription" of language (Lemaire 1977, p.131). This refers to how language is inscribed at the conscious level of mind or Symbolic as signifiers, but at the primal unconscious level it is experienced as Real *letters* that carry the palpable effects of language upon the body as affective and/or visceral ripples in the psyche-soma. Thus, by the analyst's tracking and using common sounds of letters and phonemes within the analysand's speech, there can be an evocative replaying of aspects of the infantile music of speech to which the analysand's psyche-soma unconsciously responds. The analyst also counts upon the fact that words/signifiers are polyvalent, that is, that they can mean many things, depending upon the context of their use. With this multiplicity in mind then, interpretation at times leans on the side of evocation versus explanatory genetic interpretations, leaving the analysand more room to create his/her own new meanings (Nasio 1992).

The Lacanian analyst thus uses interpretation to facilitate the analysand's own encounter with how something fundamental about her-/himself (and all human life) has been misrecognized (Lacan 1952–1953), avoided, missed, denied, and so on by unconsciously engaging others—including the analyst—and her-/himself, in an Imaginary drama of completeness. Or how paradise was lost or is being denied to her/him. This drama takes the form of unconscious (perhaps preconscious also, at times) contingencies comprising a fantasy-laden landscape: "If only this . . . , then my inner sense of loss—e.g., inadequacy, something missing, loneliness, material deficits, existential anxiety—would cease and this loss/gap/uncertainty in me would be healed." This imaginary drama hampers the analysand's ability to recognize and bear the fundamental truth that something of experience, of self, and of the other/object, by definition, is not represented and can never be "filled in," so to speak. Insofar as this fundamental truth is obscured by the imaginary drama of transferences, the analysand lives life as though it were an egregious fate etched by an Other—mother, father, bad analyst—but never by her-/himself. But if the analysand can subjectively assume her/his circumstances with respect to how she/he has been uniquely inscribed within a symbolic network, speaking can, on certain occasions, become a creative and ethical act of embracing and forging a singular destiny.

THE INTERPOLATION OF MULTIPLE TEMPORALITIES IN THE TIME OF AN ANALYSIS

The analytic encounter occurs within a complex field: (1) the unmediated elements of two Real physical bodies meeting together in a room, (2) the dynamic force and movement of an Imaginary inner object world of protosymbolic particles moving between two subjects, and (3) the "Symbolic" frame of the psychic boundaries of both analysand and analyst and of their contract to work together.

Linear time consists of the ongoing series of appointments and the actual time that elapses within each session. When the analyst has fluid access to her/his symbolic thinking, time seems to flow in a session, and one's sense of linear time is not disrupted; it is a background constant. There is a sense that the intersubjective mix is being lived in actual time.

But, while each session is linearly connected to the previous session, each individual session simultaneously exists in its own time. Within each session—sometimes across any number of sessions—moments of ahistorical, frozen, or distorted time can occur. This is the time of transference enactments. The greater the distortion in the analyst's subjectivity within a session, the more difficult it will be for the analyst to ascertain what is going on, how what is going on is related to prior sessions, and how to intervene (see Fig. 2–3). In fact, when there is a great deal of distortion in the analyst's

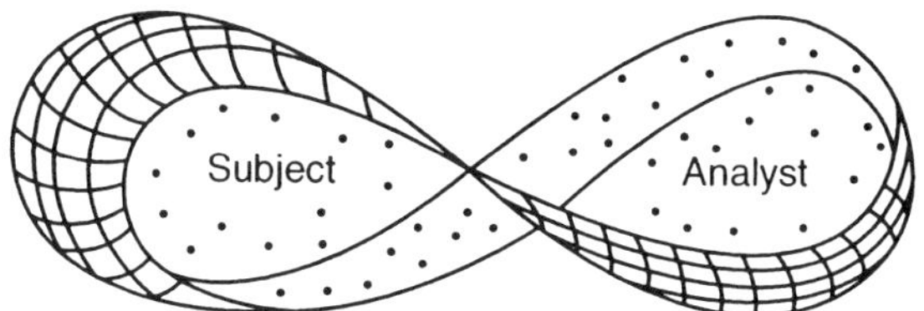

Fig. 2–3. Analytic Encounter

subjectivity, and/or this distortion becomes fixed, time seems to stop. Thus there is more than one time zone in analysis.

At such times, the progress of the analytic work will depend upon how well the analyst can bear with these distortions of shape and frozen movement, such that when symbolic processing ultimately does become possible, these distorted experiences can be made meaningful and useful to the analysand—in yet a different time zone, retroactively (Green 2002, Lacan 1964).

Since the analyst has put her-/himself in the analytic mixer, the patterns of psychic particles of both members of the analytic dyad participate in co-creating an analytic third. However inchoate this third may feel, for however long it may last, it falls to the analyst to be alert to any emergent discernible patterns that may become readable. To read or decode the analytic third that is created in the analytic encounter, the analyst draws upon the well of his/her own life experience, personal analysis, what is already known about the analysand, and her/his clinical and theoretical sensibilities, in order to eventually form something—be it in the form of spoken interpretations or some other therapeutic intervention. What is thus read might be spoken or not, depending upon the circumstances within the particular treatment. Over the duration of an analysis or treatment, it is assumed that the analysand will increasingly be able to assist in the work of interpretation as the distorting effects of the transferences on both subjects lessen. If some portion of an accumulating return cannot be spoken about by the analyst in a timely enough manner so that it will be useful for the analysand, the treatment will be likely to end unsatisfactorily. The analysand will feel that he/she is once again stuck in a repetition of how the world (and the word) has failed him/her.

Of course, as the analysis progresses, there will always also be portions of this accumulation that go unspoken about, but this does not mean that this metabolized accumulation is of no benefit for the analysand. This benefit can be thought of as facilitating the complexity of the analysand's waking unconscious associative thinking process, such that she/he is experienced by others (as well as her-/himself) as having gained more psychic ballast or subjective depth. (See Bion on dream-work alpha in *Cogitations* [1992].)

PRESERVING THE SYMBOLIC FRAME OF THE PSYCHOANALYTIC WORKING SPACE

Fundamental to preserving the possibility of the analysand's learning from his/her encounter with the unconscious is the analyst's maintaining of a viable working analytic space. This possibility hinges upon establishing and maintaining the Symbolic frame.

Concerning this working analytic space, let me take the reader on a brief side-trip into the extreme circumstance when a symbolic framing is missing altogether. The psychotic person inhabits this kind of space such that he/she is pressed in on and/or invaded by all sorts of things that are very Real for him/her (Lacan 1955–1956). Words are neither able to contain nor to express the person's experience. Often, the psychotic's words seem to refer to anywhere, everywhere, or nothing at all—to the listening other who hears the psychotic's words, but cannot understand. As a result, in the psychotic individual, internal fantasy is often confused with external reality, because he/she does not have a stable enough identity, nor a secure enough link to the Symbolic order of the world (Bion 1956, Lacan 1955).

In the psychotic person's tumbled and unmoored speech we hear the disturbing testament of how the human infant becomes "truly human" only through being sufficiently severed from a pure instinctual life. Through a mother's "good enough" interpretation of infant need: (1) a psyche-soma and symbolic identity can and will be constructed by the child, and (2) this identity will become reliably linked within the preexisting symbolic order of the family and society. If this does not happen, as in the case of the psychotic individual, the voice and words of others are frequently felt as too Real, too persecutory, because, with no reliable psychic boundary, all discourse is potentially an intrusion or assault on his or her body and mind—even when the voice and words are spoken from inside one's own skull. For the psychotic person, "Sticks and stones may break your bones, but words, and beliefs expressed in words, can surely kill you."[2]

HOW THE ANALYTIC CIRCLE BECOMES A WORKING PSYCHOANALYTIC SPACE

When an individual walks into an analyst's office to seek treatment, he/she is in a sense moving into the analyst's circumscribed circle of Oneness—an office of Real objects put together in an Imaginatively personal way, by an individual who has a Symbolic identity as one who can enable a particular kind of discourse. This is a time of pregnant possibility. If, and when, the moment comes that both individuals decide to work together, the analyst's circumscribed circle will become transformed into the working analytic space like the metaphorical and paradoxical mobius figure, a working space that the analyst will assume responsibility for preserving. Although it takes a mutual decision to begin any analytic treatment, it is the analyst, in his/her asymmetric role of being representative of the Symbolic order of things, who must make and sustain the analytic configuration. (In the mobius metaphor, this would be to make sure the mobius figure does not fall apart into a mere strip of ribbon.) The point at which the analyst takes her/his place in one of the two inextricably linked spaces of two human subjects, she/he will be putting her/his own psychic particles in play to be used, while simultaneously holding the frame of the Symbolic. This use includes allowing her-/himself to receive the transference of past significant relationships as well as making her-/himself available as a new object to be creatively encountered and used in the present by the analysand.

The metaphorical procedure of making a circle become an analytic working space remains essentially the same in each case, but at the same time, if, when, and how this is done will always be a singular event, reflecting the particularity of the one seeking treatment and the other of the

2. For many in the United States, on September 11, 2001, the Symbolic safety net usually taken for granted was punctured such that psychic reality was not unlike that of a psychotic individual. For her or him, the world is a place in which the threat of intrusion by an unknown dangerous Other lurks everywhere, all the time. Neither his/her mind nor body is a safe place within which to live.

analyst. Accepting someone into treatment, whether that be a psychotherapy or an analysis, and agreeing to put one's self into play as I have described, is a daunting and humbling undertaking—one that does not get easier over time. It is that way every time.

The analytic paradox, as I have experienced it, is that I, as an analyst, have set for myself the task of living in two psychoanalytic residences—moving back and forth between the clinical and theoretical figures of Winnicott, who elaborates the importance of the external object and the Imaginary space of the inner object world, and Lacan, who marks the importance of Symbolic processes and the necessary gap implied—as well as keeping in mind the Symbolic's co-creative relationship with the Real of what lies beyond the symbol's reach. The analyst who seeks to work within such a dialectic must foreground and background each position while the analytic work unfolds over and through time, while striving to remain mindful of the difference between the two. And when in doubt about the oscillation of foreground/background, the analyst then must return to residing in the space between them in whatever manner this can be clinically occupied at the time.

The analyst's task is not unlike that of a mother. Likewise, the analyst's task is not unlike that of a father. Both positions and functions are necessary within any analytic encounter. The measure of how much one analytic position versus the other is utilized within any particular treatment depends upon a heterogeneity of human factors. In the following chapters, my aim is to bring you, the reader, further into experiencing some of these human factors as lived within the analytic encounter. In my thinking and clinical work, I explore the possibilities of working within a frame in which these two theoretical poles provide a shifting or oscillating foreground and background with respect to one another: the analytic dyad as particles to waves and waves to particles.

3

Refractions of the Mother–Infant Discourse: the Symbolic Third and the Link to Analyzing Primitive Mental States

> ***Attention to the moment is requisite to its observation and thought is limited by the richness of this observation.***
> **(Bion 1992b)**

INTRODUCTION

The fetus hears the one-two rhythm of its mother's heartbeat. Imagine for the moment that the space between these heartbeats is an incipient Third, the place for the baby's identity, not yet realized but anticipated. When things go well enough, even before birth, a place of thirdness already exists in the mind of the mother. It is hoped that within the time of her pregnancy, what Lacan called the Imaginary and the Symbolic registers of experience will work together in the mother's unconscious fantasies and conscious thoughts regarding her yet-to-be-born infant. These fantasies and thoughts begin to make a place for that child's identity to emerge and reside.

When things go well enough, mother consciously imagines her child having his/her own place in the family. She carries both unconscious and conscious fantasies about her child's future identity and role in society beyond the family. She may wonder what characteristics in her child will, and will not, be like herself and the father. When, however, there is not a true enough degree of psychic separation operating in these fantasies to leave room for the child to be discovered as a different and separate "other," the child will, in effect, remain psychically unborn, despite being separated from the Real of the mother's body. From the beginning, the interconnected structures of the Real, the Symbolic, and the Imaginary preexist and, to a degree, map certain life coordinates for that unborn child.

For the "good-enough" mother, the loss she feels with each successive degree of psychic and physical separation from her baby can be borne or endured successfully. At some level, it can even be welcomed by her. When things go well enough, "a Symbolic Third" develops as an interstice within the mother. This third, combined with the ever-increasing psychic and physical space between mother and baby, provides a frame that is seamless, invisible—much like the space between heartbeats.

To be good enough, the intersubjective field of mother and infant must always be a triadic rather than a dyadic structure. It is that the mother's symbolic functioning must first hold the infant in relation to the world. By being securely held in the Symbolic, the infant becomes enabled to (slowly) transform her/his sensory experience into psychic traces and semiotic elements, and thus to begin the making of her/his own body-ego and mind. (In terms of a mobius figure, the body-ego would be represented by the infant's generating a unique pattern of atomic particles on one surface of the ribbon, and then beginning to fill in the spaces.)

The near or total failure to develop a Symbolic Third within the mother–infant dyad will foster psychosis in a child (Bion 1967, Lacan 1955–1956); a partial failure or an unstable establishing of Symbolic thirdness within the dyad may nurture psychosomatic formations and/or distorted character structures (McDougall 1989, 1995). The presence of an adequate Symbolic Third in the infant–mother couple (assuming development proceeds in an ordinary way) will yield a child into an adult with the ordinary assortment of psychological symptoms and neurotic conflicts.

Thus, under ordinary, good-enough circumstances with mother, an infant psychically installs the mother inside himself over time within the context of the child's own calls/appeals to the mother. As part of the infant's process of construction and internalization, there will necessarily be included aspects of mother's own psychic world and of her personal modes of thinking and feeling (Green 1999). Also included within this construction will be a "working fantasy" that will ultimately be constructed of what the baby perceives the mother might want or lack. This fantasy is constructed both in moments when the mother is absent from the baby, and when she, in her normal discourses and movements, exhibits interest in an "other" that is outside the orbit of her interest in the baby. Mother has to be consistent and inconsistent enough to imply the existence of her desire versus projecting total completeness.This becomes perceived in the baby's psyche as a want, a desire, or a lack in the mother.

Over time, links between mother and the traces of the child's earliest experiences with mOther, are made. In this linking, mother becomes transformed. She is given her own individual and unique form, but at the same time she is afforded a measure of flexibility: room is reserved for her to make changes (Green 1999).

Likewise, from the earliest moments of a woman's self-perceived pregnancy, the Symbolic Third is actuated on behalf of her unborn child. This is the context in which the mother, via her present and future interactions with the infant, begins to weave a certain quality into the infant's emergent psychic organization. This "quality" concerns the nature of the infant's predominant organizing defenses—ranging from the most primitive to the most sophisticated—that the infant, and later the child and adult, will employ—that is, foreclosure, negation, splitting, disavowal, and/or repression. The quality of these defenses is related to the space afforded for the Symbolic Third. If the space for the Symbolic Third in the infant–mother dyad is completely closed down, such foreclosure may lead to psychosis. In contrast, a space in the dyad that is either too little or too big creates conditions where splitting and disavowal may remain prominent in the psychic organization, thus leading to character disorders. Finally, if a space for the Symbolic Third is present enough, the child is enabled to create a viable fantasmatic inner world that has as a part of it a unique template of sensory pleasures. Along with her/his unique schematic of sensual pleasure, this whole inner world will fall under the veil of repression during the oedipal passage. Later, however, this repression will invariably (but not necessarily disastrously) be disrupted by the eventual enlivening of this developing subject's desire. In Lacanian parlance, desire must have its[1] say.

A RATIONALE FOR INFANT OBSERVATION TRAINING

Some analysts and theoreticians reject the contribution of infant observation per se to clinical psychoanalysis. Peter Wolf (1996, p. 386) dismisses infant observational evidence as being based only upon "enumerative induction, hypostatized analogies, and circular reasoning," and sees it as not relevant to understanding unconscious ideas. Lacan (1953) discounts infant observation because in his view, entry into symbolic speech retroactively reorganizes all infantile experience anyway. André Green (2000) argues that observation does not contribute as much to understanding the workings of the unconscious mind as does clinical work with severely dis-

1. *It* because there is no representation of sexual difference in the unconscious.

turbed patients—a position similar to Winnicott's. Since these three theorists all inform my own analytic position, it is important to say here that I believe the value of infant observation to be primarily in the way it immerses the clinician in powerful and primitive experiences that later, in a particular kind of group setting, can be thought about or played with from various theoretical perspectives. This experience, then, as a whole is very valuable in linking felt experience to theoretical concepts in a manner different from that which is available in the ordinary clinical encounter. The combination of intense affective experiences from the infant observations, when brought and held within a symbolic space of mutual respect and curiosity, is a potent forum for a kind of analytic thinking that contributes an undefinable depth to one's clinical work.

Paradoxically, I would say that the superimposition of the work of both Lacan and Green upon the framework and process of infant observation provides a clarification and elucidation of their respective theoretical contributions. For instance, Lacan's articulation of the Symbolic Third, within his three interlocking registers of the Real, the Imaginary, and the Symbolic, describes factors observable in mother–infant relations. But it is equally important for its utility in organizing the subjective experience of the observation within the observer's own self. Lacan's (1952–1953, 1973), Harari's (2001), and Green's (1999) differing thoughts on the relationship of affect and representation are useful, not only along the axis of the observed affective development of the infant in the infant–mother matrix but also on the axis of the observer's lived experience, which at times leaves the observer struggling during, and after, an observation to give form to potent affective experiences.

Concomitantly, Green's (1998) "work of the negative" is part of the infant's work of making mental/psychic representations from her/his sensory motor and affective experiences. Psychic representations will come to regulate relations within the infant's developing world of internal object relations; they will also regulate the relations between the inner object relations world and the outer world of reality and external others. The usual progression of the positive "work of the negative" is thus indispensable because it provides the very ground for the constitution of human subjectivity in all of its myriad forms. Clinical work with severely disturbed patients is one way experientially to enter the field of the work of the negative and its derailment; infant observation is another avenue. One advantage of infant observation is that when the observer is able to be a member of an ongoing supervision group (with multiple infant–mother couples being observed at the same time) there is a wide exposure to primitive processes—and considerably less responsibility to be borne—than when working with a severely disturbed patient.

Thus, while both Lacan and Green explicitly eschew the value of infant observation in the training of psychoanalytic candidates, their works (particularly their combined works) paradoxically can be used to argue *for* the contribution of such training. Thus, despite Lacan's and Green's explicit reservations, I offer the following argument for infant observation training in psychoanalytic formation as representative of the spirit, rather than the letter, of their teachings.[2]

For the infant observer, the weekly practice/ritual of being in the presence of a highly charged infant–mother relationship, but absent from any means of actively intervening, demands mental work. Much of the mental work consists in the observer's being pushed to expand the available breadth/complexity of affect and levels of psychic representation within his/her own internal world. As well, the observer is pushed to expand the breadth and complexity of the regulation between his/her own internal world and external reality. Keats (1817) describes this as the attaining of "negative capability" (p. 477). Participation in infant-observation training increases one's capacities in both domains (depth/breadth complexity/ inside/outside). The observer learns to sustain waiting in uncertainty and inaction in the face of variable pressures coming from within and from external reality "to act"—even if this act is only to initiate speech. The clinician's "negative capability" has direct bearing upon analytic work in terms of psychic spaciousness, that is to say, how much of the analysand's subjectivity can be present or can emerge in the analysis.

---

2. In contrast to those disputing the relevance of infant observation to clinical psychoanalytic practice, others, most notably the Kleinians, consistently describe its positive contributions. For example, some see a correlation between infant observation and clinical constellations (Cooper 1989, Kumin 1996, Silverman 1989); others, its usefulness in terms of understanding aspects of the therapeutic relationship (Jacobson 1993, Scharfman 1989). Others have used infant observational paradigms to enhance understanding of child developmental sequences and to further inform understandings of the transference (Fajardo 1988, Fonagy 1996, Kestenberg 1977, Parens 1996). Still others have studied infant observation in the context of aiding the clinician to locate (internally) the position of observer (Crick 1997, Miller 1999). Sowa's (1999) and Hansen's (1996) work has centered on describing infant observation's contribution to enhancing the clinician's capacity to tolerate the unknown, and later to think about unformulated experience. It is in this latter arena that this chapter locates itself.

Infant observation offers a rich opportunity for a clinician to palpably (psychosomatically) experience how the interlocking elements of unmediated experience (the Real), fantasy (the Imaginary), and the Symbolic Third work together in constituting the subject in relation to mother. As a way of noting the clinical significance of both the Other of the Symbolic and the maternal object, mother as the usual primary caretaker will from this point forward be written as mOther, whereby the capital O reminds us that the mOther is the first "little other" who will stand in the place of the big Other (the Symbolic), structuring human experience. The infant observer is given the chance to witness the activity of the Symbolic Third as it orders the Real needs of the infant, and constitutes the space of the Imaginary that the child will fill with an inner object world. The observer may witness, as well, how the relative presence of the Symbolic Third shapes and limits the inherent possibilities for the infant and the infant–mother relation.

Within the context of an ongoing observation, the observer may see, hear, feel, and viscerally respond to how an infant's biological instincts and strivings are transformed via the interventions of the mOther—a mOther who must symbolically interpret what the infant's needs are and how they are to be met, thereby essentially cutting the infant away from the original cloth of instinctual nature. A symbolic network and its associated meanings preexist the infant in that the Symbolic exists in the mind of the mOther (and father) prior to birth, but at another level the infant must also come to simultaneously create and discover him-/herself within and through the Imaginary and Symbolic dimensions of representation.

One observes the co-creative relationship of the Symbolic function carving the space for a human psyche that is separate from, but in relation to, the Real (instinctual body) of nature. Further, if infant observation is continued into a second and third year, fantasy (the Imaginary) can be seen to emerge visibly, establishing and mediating the coordinates of the baby's relationship to her/his own body and to the external world. All of what has just been described is psychic territory best labeled as the unrepressed unconscious in terms of the infant.[3] For the observer it is different. This Imaginary world (of intrapersonal and interpersonal human relations) that

3. Unrepressed unconscious refers to the period in which the child has entered into a symbolic world, but has not taken a position within the Symbolic. This taking of a position within the Symbolic occurs during the oedipal passage when secondary repression or repression proper occurs.

is being organized by the infant is, of course, not yet repressed, but for the observer who has his/her own repressed and unrepressed unconscious Imaginary landscape of human relations, there are many reverberations. An example of this will be described on page 33, when as an observer I acted impulsively during an observation.

By virtue of the regularity of scheduled observations, and also by virtue of the inevitable (but behaviorally constrained) degree of psychic participation in the infant–mother (and family) relation, there is engendered in the observer a deeply felt appreciation of the complexity of the task for the infant and its family to bring a human subject into being. Such a profound level of appreciation is true even among the observers who are also parents, who, being parents, often do not expect the experience to so profoundly impact them. There is also engendered in the observer a felt appreciation for both the fragility and the resiliency of the human psyche as the observer undergoes his/her own revisitings of primitive landscapes.

A MODEL OF INFANT OBSERVATION

Although it sounds simple, infant observation is neither a simple nor a straightforward task. The psychic field of an infant–mOther couple can evoke intense countertransference experiences in the observer, but is without any sanctioned means of intervention for discharging these primitive states (Hansen 1996, Trowell 1996). It is inevitable that during infant observation the observer will encounter unexpected moments when s/he stumbles into the realm of his/her own primitive/infantile anxieties. As in analysis, these must be lived through as best they can, discharged through action when they cannot, and, it is hoped, understood later. It is perhaps too easy to forget that for all practitioners, interpretations, timely or not, provide a ready vehicle for evacuating primitive anxieties. Speech is not always the same, and infant observation helps one to attend to the many kinds of speech that can be facilitative in the analytic encounter—or not. Infant observation is a potent training ground for developing or expanding the emotional containing capacities of the clinician. It helps increase the capacity to bear, to process, and to make use of intense countertransference states occurring during analytic treatment. And it also increases one's appreciation for the symbol and what it can or cannot do to transform human experiences.

STRUCTURE OF THE OBSERVATION

The observer observes an infant and mother (and other family members, if present) once a week for an hour at a specified and regularly scheduled time. In other words, a frame is created within which an observation takes place. No notes are taken during the observation hour; it is only after the observation that the observer then records as descriptively and noninterpretively as possible the observation, from memory—much like process notes after a session. In the beginning, all the members of the group in which I participated (all experienced clinicians from different theoretical perspectives and analytic institutes) found that surrendering relatively fully to their immediate experience in the observation was difficult (Tuters 1988). During the length of an infant observation, which may extend from one to three years time, the clinician also attends a supervised group that usually meets weekly.[4] In the group setting, observations are read aloud in turn, section by section.

The work of the infant observation group is to do a close reading of the texts of the written observations of the different group members, allowing cumulative experience to form an impression while listening to the observation. In this process, "allowing" rather than "efforting" thoughts and conjectures about the states of mind of the infant and mother is a pivotal element. The impressions thus formed are often visceral, emotional, or evocative of reverie at times. Possible links between members' reactions and that of the developing infant–mother relation are explored (Bion 1970). Over time, as each observer increases in her/his capacity to be present in the observation experience without acting out in speech or behavior, more purely descriptive and detailed observation becomes possible. Additionally, the ability to recall observed material for the write-up is expanded, and obsessional (defensive) efforts to recall and analyze the observation are let go of in favor of allowing the group mind to do the thinking. It is not at all uncommon that conceptual links and understandings of emotional reactions and/or acting-out behaviors that occurred during the observation are pieced together only within the presence of the group and the supervisor.

---

4. Therefore, within the context of the ongoing participation in the observation group, one also has the comparative experience of following multiple mOther–infant pairs. In our group these meetings were monthly because the supervising analyst (Yvonne Hansen, Ph.D.) flew in to meet with us.

Group supervision thus provides a second context within which to wrestle with the emotional stirrings and incidents of "acting out" that invariably occur at times during one's observations. Here is an example.

> Once during an observation I found myself acting instinctively to remove fuzzy threads that the baby I observed had plucked from an afghan throw sitting on the back of the couch beside me and was about to put in his mouth. Since this was a period when everything went into his mouth and yet other items had not elicited this kind of acting out on my part, the group suggested I try and catch the impulse next time. At a subsequent observation, I was watching the baby sleep. I could see in the crib a wad of stringy threads that the baby had clearly unraveled from a wide ribbon attached to the slats of the crib. It lay across his chest and some of it was wrapped around his hand. As he awoke he struggled to a sitting-up position. As he did so he began to bring some of the stringy threads up to his mouth. Again I felt a strong urge, almost a panic, to intervene but I didn't. Instead I focused on my intense anxiety and the physical suffocating feeling I was experiencing; then an image appeared. I am lying on my back and a gauzy thing is being brought toward my face and I try to move away. I can't move my arms. I turn my head away. It is put over my nose and mouth. It is a terrible smell. I see swirling, loud, and vibrating colors. There is a terrorized feeling and then nothing. I realized then that these fuzzy objects had evoked my four-year-old self fighting to avoid the gauze full of ether when my tonsils were to be removed. With the presence of the group inside me, I had been able to endure the experience long enough to make a place for having the felt-thought.

In this way each group member serves as part of the containing envelope for the other observers. Thus, the group supervision process itself also contributes to the clinician's containing capacity—which is, after all, a foundational element in maintaining an analytic stance in treatment.

THE OBSERVER AS AUXILIARY THIRD

With the onset of the actual observation, the observer is immediately plunged into the experience of how a family deals psychically with his/her own presence as an auxiliary third and, by extension, how the family deals psychically with the "thirdness" represented by the baby itself. Sometimes the observer is psychically incorporated and allowed no separate identity; sometimes the observer is related to as a benign and welcome visitor; sometimes the observer is covertly or overtly treated aggressively by family members as an intruder, and so forth.

Within a less healthy mother, where there appears to be a collapsed sense of symbolic capacities, what this might look like is that she psychically draws upon the observer, as she no doubt would also draw from her infant, to psychically hold projected parts of herself. There would be little or no space in the mind of this mother for the infant, or the observer, to exist as separate individuals; both would remain receptacles or psychic extensions of herself. This may be manifest in verbal or nonverbal requests for the observer to caretake her, her infant, and/or other siblings during the time of an observation. The psychic pull can be to such an extent under these circumstances that the observer may have difficulty, or might actually be unable to consistently hold an observing stance. At times this can bring the observation to an unexpected and untimely end.

Alternatively, a mother may actually psychically draw upon the presence of the observer as a third in her home to support her own symbolic capacity, so to speak, to keep in mind the separate emergent identity of her infant. This support might come through the simple behavior of the mother telling the observer (who does not initiate conversation) about the infant's activities, developing personality, siblings' reactions to baby, and so on—all of which serves to keep the baby in her mind as a separate person. The infant may also, out of its own primary creativity (Winnicott 1953), encounter the observer as a third who can be utilized in different ways (Fajardo 1988). Thus, the intermittent presence and absence of the observer as a third can be a corrupting, compensatory, or benign influence on the infant–mother couple. Usually within any supervised group of observers, all of these experiences occur.

LACAN'S SYMBOLIC THIRD AND BION'S CONTAINER-CONTAINED

I wish now to speak theoretically, drawing from the works of Bion, Winnicott, and Lacan to further illustrate what is happening in the infant observation situation. For Bion (1962a,b), the very capacity for mentalizing experience and, indeed, for thinking itself is rooted in the degree to which the infant's experience has been contained by mother. Therefore, maternal failure to function as an emotional/mental container for processing baby's psychic callings, and ultimately for returning them in more digested form, results not only in an inability to adequately mentalize experience but can also promote psychosis or the proliferation of psychotic parts (Bion 1957, 1967). Speaking in the same vein, Winnicott (1960) observed, "There is no such thing as an infant—only a mother–infant couple" (p. 39). In actuality, from a Lacanian perspective, there is never only the mother–infant couple, because the Symbolic Third is always more or less present (Lacan 1953, 1955, Muller 1996). Mother's allowance for this Symbolic Third, if you will, sets the parameters of her own containing capacity, and this in turn sets the degrees of psychic separation and maturation she will allow and/or promote in her child.

"Negative capability" (a term Bion borrowed from Keats) is a facet of Symbolic Thirdness that is a precondition for learning from experience. "Negative capability" describes the breadth and depth of the internal space available first to bear, and secondly to think about one's experience without simply reacting to that experience through some kind of evacuative process, that is, motor or verbal discharge (Bion 1962a,b, Harris 1976, Sowa 1999). As clinicians we strive to "be with" the fullness of experience, versus foreclosing it by discharging it into action via premature interpretations. I believe infant observation enhances the capacity to do this—to bear with something intense and not understandable, to wait, and retroactively to be able to formulate these agonizing and sometimes lengthy nonverbal experiences. Such capacities are crucial when working with primitive mental states, in adult patients as well as children, because these states manifest in nonverbal and at times very difficult emotional and somatic experiences for the analyst as well as for the individual in treatment. These impassioned experiences must be lived through without action in order to enable time and space for thinking about them to emerge—time and mental space being the obvious prerequisites for the analyst to be able to formulate his/her verbal interventions (Britton 1987, Winnicott 1963).

Theoretically speaking, what I believe occurs during a period of infant observation is that the observer, over an extended number of observations and group supervisions, derives a felt experience of how Lacan's Symbolic Third functions as the critical element with respect to Bion's concept of the mother–infant as container/contained (Forbes 1977). For Lacanians, doing an infant observation brings alive the importance of the mother as an object (in addition to being the representative of the Other) for making or not making certain structural moments possible, such as that of the "mirror stage," the structural moment when the infant takes up an

Imaginary identification/body ego (Lacan 1951, 1953b). Let me now describe a few brief infant observations.

MOMENTS IN INFANT OBSERVATION

I have selected several moments from different infant–mOther couples. A caveat to keep in mind before reading further is that it is an ordinary experience for a mOther to be emotionally inattentive or unavailable at times when her baby reaches a critical moment of needing psychic holding. In infant observation, the observer witnesses moments when even the most attuned mOther is not present, such that the baby "falls apart," so to speak, because his/her own psychic resources have failed to psychically hold the emergent self (protosubject) together for even one more second. Under what Winnicott would call "good enough" mothering, these missed moments are not substantially psychically damaging to the baby. Some infants, however, have much more than the ordinary misses with mOther to contend with. For instance, infant Sam had a mOther who was overwhelmed by the demands of her infant and her other child, a 4-year-old. MOther was in an on-again, off-again hypervigilant state that left her exhausted. Infant Sam began to show possible signs of defensive holding very early on. These are notes from an observation at two weeks old.

> Mother told the sister to get away, and meanwhile was trying to help Sam, who did not latch onto the nipple right away. He sucked in a pattern of 5–6 times and then rested; at first his eyes were open, but he did not look at mother's face, but rather at the breast which was large and I thought must nearly have filled his whole field of vision.

A bottle and pacifier quickly replaced mother's breast, however, and mother's physical holding during feeding, a holding which usually serves to promote a baby's psychic skin (ego) development, was compromised by placing infant Sam on a pillow in her lap rather than against her body.

> Sam jerked, lost the pacifier, and began to cry pretty hard. When mom came back she once again gave him the pacifier, saying to settle down, settle down. Sam cried around the plug, however, so mom picked him up, turning his face toward me as she lifted him from the crib, so the moment of face-to-face greeting between mother and infant did not occur. Sam, who had stopped crying, looked directly at me but without any expression. Mom kept talking

> to him and moved toward the changing table. Just as she put him down, the sister entered the room and when she saw mother engaged with the baby she screamed, "No, no, no." Mother turned sharply to her and told her to stop that. Sam meanwhile lay quietly staring at a pattern on the wall. The sister escalated, screaming "No" and repeatedly jumping up and down. With one hand over Sam mother turned and said rather desperately but directly to me, "Oh, no! The bottle is in the warmer. It will be too hot!" I resisted the impulse to go get it and just said in a decrescendo, "Ohhh." The older sister gave it one more try screaming and jumping and very distressed, and mom snapped at her, "You know I have to give Sam his bottle, now stop it." When mom sent her out of the room, she went. I couldn't help feeling sorry for both of them and what seemed amazing was that Sam never moved his eyes off the pattern. Not once during his changing did he look at his mother.

From the descriptive style as well as the content itself, the observer is stressed in both observations as she appears to take up an imagined identification first with the baby and then with the mOther. As readers, we can even feel the psychic undertow pulling on the observer to somehow help mother be the mOther she would like to be.

It is the earliest psychic task of the infant to make a boundaried self/ego. A self that is initially only felt to be islands of experience (Stern 1985, p. 72) must be transformed into "islands of consistency" and then into boundaried body self/ego (Freud 1923). Vocalizing, the gaze, and mOther's touch—governed by the mother's particular cultural code as a part of her inner thirdness—these are the usual organizing elements the infant uses in relationship with mOther to construct this boundaried ego (Muller 1996). When mOther is not available somehow, as in baby Sam's situation, most babies will try to use their own sensations (i.e., gazing, touching, sound, movement) in a focused way in an effort to hold or pull themselves together. In the above example, the group wondered whether baby Sam had used his gaze in this way, or did he simply fall to pieces?

The psychic boundary or body ego being constructed by the infant has been described by some as a skin ego (Anzieu 1990, Bick 1968). Skin, by its nature, is supple and semi-permeable, so that as clinicians we think of psychic skin as enabling internal experience to be expressed, and external input to be taken in (Grotstein 1990). Elemental to the healthy development of a skin ego is the holding of both the infant's body and his/her emotional experience by mOther's body as well as her mind. In essence, the first skin is a shared one between mOther and baby, a skin from which the infant must gradually pull away to make the first "me–not me" boundary—to construct a body ego. The psychic body begins making its shape first by there being an accumulation of elementary particles (i.e., psychic sensory traces) around each of the body openings, as mOther holds, handles, and cares for the infant. The body openings become linked to some degree over time through a spreading pattern of these psychic particles. This pattern can be more or less adequate to its task to become a psychic container for the infant's emergent self.

Let us hear about another baby involved in this same primal task. Baby Adam, as was the case with baby Sam, is also a second child of a mOther who already had a 3-year-old son at the time of Adam's birth. From an observation at three weeks the qualitative difference in the mOther–infant couple is apparent.

> After another little round of burping, in which again Adam was quite interested in the world around him, he began to be discontented. He made sounds suggesting frustration and when moved to Susan's lap he moved his arms and legs as if to say "No." She moved him to her other shoulder and then said she thought he was getting fussy and maybe needed to nap. She talked to him, asking him what he needed as she stroked him. She got up and got the pacifier and returned to her seat placing him lying across her lap. He took to the pacifier quickly and as he sucked she ever so gently stroked one eyebrow and then the other, then down the bridge of his nose, and around to one temple—once, and then again and again. It had such a rhythmic quality that when she stopped for a moment he made a little sound urging her to continue almost. Under her gaze and touch, his eyes got sleepier and sleepier and she cradled him more at this point. He reached up and took hold of one ear and Susan said she had noticed that this seemed to be something he did when he was ready to go to sleep at times.[5]

The writing of this observer conveys an attuned quality in terms of how the baby is handled and held in this mOther's mind. If, as opposed to this level of attunement, the infant were to be physically and/or emotionally walled off, impinged upon, or precipitously pushed away by mother (as appeared to be happening with baby Sam and his mOther), then distortions and defects may occur in the psychic boundary that the infant is attempting to construct. When the infant experiences trauma from either

5. This is a good example of how one might imagine that places on the body are paired: pleasure with language, where language is not meaning, but a sound with elements of the earliest psychic activity attached to it.

internal or external sources, the baby needs to be able to project these traumatic states into the mOther, so that they can be transformed by mOther's containing symbolic capacity and taken back inside the infant. These transformed-reintrojected experiences are then used to link those islands of sensory experience concentrated around the body openings into a viable psychic skin.

Should the baby be prevented from experiencing this process of containment-transformation-reintrojection of his/her traumatic states, the infant will be unable to create an adequate background framework that makes for mental space (or his/her own negative capability) and the inner stage where his/her Imaginary world will be constructed. Neither will the psychic skin or ego be adequate to make a stable me–not me boundary. Thus, where a baby's inner world would ordinarily begin to live, instead, too large a gap or hole is left in the developing psychic skin. Through this tear, then, what has been projected by the infant to mOther to be transformed, is instead psychically returned in even more frightening and bizarre forms. Such holes will make for terrifying experiences which can reoccur throughout life under certain conditions and circumstances. These terrifying experiences may include the feeling states of falling endlessly into empty space, leaking out, despair, and so on. "Black holes," a term coined by Frances Tustin (1986, p. 39), are thus the result of severe discontinuities in the infant's experience of his/her trying to make a boundary for the self in which to live. Speaking in terms of our mobius figure, the spaces among the pattern of atomic particles would be too large. These spaces are Real places where, under certain conditions, the infant (or the adult) can actually fall into the Real in an unspeakably traumatic experience, and she/he will no longer be psychically held together.

Alternatively, or sometimes in addition to black holes, infants for whom the infantile environment is traumatically impinging and/or severely neglecting, versus being "good enough," may develop a somewhat hard and brittle "second skin" in a protective effort not to fall into one of these traumatic holes. Since this "second skin" (Bick 1968, p. 484) has a rigid and impenetrable character, although it offers psychic protection, such a skin severely limits what internal experience can be expressed and what external experience of the object world can be taken in (Anzieu 1990, Tustin 1990). In listening to the observation of baby Sam, within the context of other observations of Sam and his mother, the members of the infant observation group began to wonder whether Sam could become a child who might develop a defensive "second skin," and/or a dissociative style, due to his mOther's difficulty in remaining emotionally present and attuned. We would have to wait and learn.

From a different vantage point, a second psychic-skin formation can sometimes also be linked to a baby's precocious development. This may be especially likely if mOther is not available to receive the infant's moments of neediness, and/or overencourages or recognizes his/her pseudo-independence. In the instance of such precociousness, a baby may begin to take up an omnipotent pseudo-independent stance toward mOther, while simultaneously rejecting her/his own actual neediness for her.

The following observations illustrate critical moments in the observation of two separate infants, where the potential for second-skin formation appears to be present, and how the outcome for the infants depended upon the attuned handling or mishandling by their respective caretakers.

> As mom returned to the car to unload the groceries, Adam looked up and then crawled over to the couch and pulled himself up by grabbing the couch and my pantleg. He then moved to grab my leg and reach for my watch. He pulled the watch, all the while making yelling sounds. I said that it didn't come off. He then looked and touched my ring and made a yelling sound as if to say, "I suppose this doesn't come off either." He then moved back an arm's length from the couch and let go of all support. He stood there a little wobbly, looking into the kitchen. It was very obvious he was practicing standing. He made an upper body movement like he was going to take off walking but his legs couldn't follow the fantasy, it seemed. He then came back to the couch and came over to my legs, mouthing my kneecap. At this moment mom came back in loaded with bags, and he gave her a big smile when he saw her. She spoke to him and continued into the kitchen. After one more trip of groceries, she settled into the kitchen to put them away and then Adam crawled into the kitchen.

A bit later in the same observation:

> Adam crawled over to her and began to climb up her body, reaching her chest. He then backed down with her encouragement and crawled over to the dresser, stood up, and reached for a round knob. Then suddenly he seemed to get distressed and began to make noises of urgency and went crawling back toward mom. Susan asked if he wanted to nurse and swooped him into her arms and positioned him across her lap. He took the nipple and settled down. He reached for her hand that was on the side of his body, grabbing her thumb and fingering her fingers. Susan said in the last week she had noticed that he reached for her hand wherever it was on his body when he nursed. He did

> not nurse long but this seemed to have been the kind of contact he needed because he looked like he was feeling fine once he sat up. He then crawled away.

The group experienced, along with Adam, joy in his achievements and at the same time a longing, and need, to return to the safety and comfort of mOther—a mOther who seems capable of allowing both parts of him to exist.

Finally, here are moments from an infant observation of baby Robert, 7 months and 3 weeks old.

> He opens his eyes a little and looks at me. Then he opens them wider. The rest of his body is completely still, as if completely relaxed. He looks at me for a few moments, unsmiling but also unworried. I give him a mild friendly smile. He makes a kind of whooshing sound on exhaling his breath. I imitate him and he repeats it, still not smiling.
>
> He looks around the room and back to me a few times. He looks to his left and reaches out with his left hand. He brings the pile of blanket and sheet bunched up there over to his face, covering his face with it. He leaves his face like that, buried in the sheets for few moments, then turns his face back toward me.
>
> He looks at me for a moment and he suddenly smiles, lets out his breath, and turns his head away from me, into the bunched-up sheet and blanket. The smile seems meant for the blanket more than to engage me, and it looks to me as if he might be thinking he is nestling into his mother's chest. After a few moments he looks back at me with a calm face. He repeats this a number of times. Occasionally, while his face is nuzzled into the sheet, he says something like "uh, duht," but he does not talk while looking at me.

The observer has been watching this 7 month, 3-week-old baby sleep. The baby seems to use the movement of his body surrounding sensory elements, visual contact with the observer, and finally a form of speech, to express and emotionally collect and contain himself after awakening from some kind of dream state (indicated by rapid eye movements).

Through these different observed moments of babies Sam, Adam, and Robert, I have attempted to convey a flavor of the psychic terrain that is part and parcel of the everyday work of infant observation and participation in group supervision. In addition to one's individual observation experience, being in group supervision also immerses one into the unconscious/conscious field of several infants and their families over an extended period of time. Participation in an infant observation training experience ultimately contributes to the clinician's capacity to bear chaos and uncertainty while living through primitive emotional states, and also facilitates finding more words with which to think about clinical work once the bearing of it comes to an end.

It is not uncommon in clinical practice with adults to encounter autistic phenomena—second skin and black holes—which can appear as a repetition of infantile trauma within the transference. Quite often there is a contiguity of adult experience with infantile psychic phenomena. In such analyses or treatments, repetitions of infantile mental states present themselves in ways that cannot be spoken initially, but only evoked, through intense affect, confusional states, and somatic resonances. When this occurs the analyst enters the territory of reexperiencing her/his own "unthinkable anxieties," as Winnicott (1960, p. 38) would say. In addition to the experience of one's analysis, infant-observation training can offer the opportunity to contact one's reservoir of primitive and infantile anxieties, expand one's capacity to bear traumatic excess, and further symbolize aspects of these anxieties. Infant-observation training can also be very helpful to the clinician in bearing the transference/countertransference of infantile experience that needs its own time, not only to be brought into a net of symbolic meaning, but for a necessary waiting before such words can be spoken in the voice that can be heard.

CONCLUSION

Bion's (1963, 1967) elaboration of maternal reverie and his theory of thinking, when experienced within the context of an ongoing infant observation, can assist in linking the theoretical differences between a developmental versus a structural model of analysis (marked in this text by Winnicott and Lacan). Several infant observations were offered here in the effort to evoke how lively the experiences of the dynamic relationship between Lacan's registers of the Real, the Symbolic, and the Imaginary can be when participating in an infant observation and a group supervision. Although it is beyond my own Symbolic capacity to fully articulate exactly how this experience contributed to my formation as an analyst, it contributed in the general sphere of adding a quality to my presence in shared silences, enabling me to wait and maintain a certain faith in lending myself to the analytic process. In other words, repetitions of infantile mental states within the transference become opportunities to transform elements of a traumatic past into words that can weave meaning to these experiences. But this kind of symbolic netting must be woven within the analytic relationship—first by the analyst's living through the islands of fragmented and unlinked experiences, secondly by the analyst's bringing these experiences into his/her own mind to be thought about, and thirdly by the analyst and analysand finding words together that can bring some of this experience into the analytic discourse so as to be claimed by the analytic subject her-/himself (Bion 1967, Lacan 1953a, Mitrani 1992). The following chapters explore different clinical and theoretical issues, and yet the infant-observation experience remained present as an ongoing background element in the mind of this analyst.

4

Symbol, Eros/Sexuality, and Aggression: The Bermuda Triangle of Human Subjectivity

> ***The umbilicus of a treatment is the question of desire and how it is trapped in its birth or its movement.***
>
> **(Lacan 1953)**

INTRODUCTION

We live life every day as split beings: where our conscious words may start to lead, unconscious impulses and desires may refuse to follow. This fact of human life is tied to how our bodies must become libidinally enlivened through mediation by an Other. Mother, as the first Other, facilitates (or not) this libidinal enlivening and intersubjective possibility through her "good enough" symbolic interpretation and response to her child's infantile needs. Each individual is faced, then, with the daunting task of constructing her/his identity and sexuality upon the uneven and conflictual ground constituting her/his conscious and unconscious fields of mind.

I will begin by describing aspects of Lacan's contribution to psychoanalysis's understanding of how the human being is held within symbolization and its effects. Following this discussion will be two cases, Ms. Y. and Mr. X., whose personal and individual difficulties reflect the Bermuda triangle of human subjectivity and its necessary knotting together of symbol, eros/sexuality, and aggression. Weaving a bit, I will also pull in threads of infantile sexuality, and the body-ego world of the infant–mother matrix (characterized by Winnicott and the British school). This weaving will include more threads, if you will, from Lacan's emphasis, as his ideas are less generally familiar, and because these ideas bring in an elaboration of human sexuality and its intricate relationship to symbolic functioning that is missing in Winnicott and the British school. Of course, this weaving cannot do justice to the complexity and richness of the whole fabric of the

Lacanian cloth, but it is hoped that it will be sufficient for purposes of this chapter, and that it will arouse enough desire that the reader will go on in pursuit of more.

INTERSECTION OF THE BIOLOGICAL HUMAN BODY AND THE PSYCHIC BODY

Symbolic capacity is core to the experience of desire (sexual and otherwise) in a human being. Likewise, sexuality is core to the experience of human thinking. In other words, human beings live within the erotics of the symbol. One form of the Symbolic function is the human being's capacity for fantasy (Laplanche and Pontalis 1973). This capacity opens human sexuality into the realm of "the constitution of desire."[1] It is within the context of desire that human sexuality moves beyond biological reproduction or even genital satisfaction—into "de-territorialized zones" (Green 2000, p. 10). The sexual charge/jouissance/enjoyment that accompanies words we may speak (or hear) at times is a visceral example of just how much human sexuality is de-territorialized.

As is true of all living creatures that reproduce by twos, humans' sexuality certainly entails the biology of reproduction. But for the human being, sexuality exists at the intersection of the biological human body and the psychic body. For animals, where biological instincts might be, for human beings, *drives* are—part psychic, plus part biological. And thus all drives, including sexuality, are partial (Freud 1905, Lacan 1964). (In contrast to Freud, Lacan thought Freud's idea of partial drives fusing and organizing in the oedipal passage was more of a fantasy than a psychic reality.) Sexual desire, then, emerges in partial and multiple forms.

When circumstances go well enough in infancy, a process of maternal refraction is at work to mediate infant experience. Imagine that at each of the newborn infant's body openings, a biological instinct is emitted as a ray of light. Unlike other animals who we imagine to simply follow the light of their instincts, the human being has an additional component to contend with. For the human being there is an Other—both a subject/

---

1. Therefore the development of sexual desire owes "as much to the absence of the object as to its investment in the encounter" (Green 2000, p. 10).

person and a symbolic network[2]—interpreting the meaning of the infant's desires and calls, refracting, if you will, the light of every instinct, through his/her own symbolic visual (and *acoustic*) prism. Via this process of refraction the infant's instinctual experience is partially transformed, bit by bit, into psyche, as the infant is able to make use of what the mOther psychically returns in the elaboration of her/his own unique subjectivity. This symbolic filtering or refracting of sexuality (via mOther and father's symbolic interpretation) turns pure unadulterated instinct into libido, the fuel for the ongoing (and necessary) psychic transformation of sensory and affective experience into needed psychic currency. For better or worse, the human must contend with his/her instinctual body's being refracted by the Symbolic Third, which produces multiple component or partial drives that are not always going in the same direction. To give an example of the kaleidoscopic nature of libidinous fuel and its disparate effects, one may actually need to eat, but because of the awareness of a deadline set by an ego ideal of another kind of fullness, hunger will be suppressed or converted into anxious excess energy to work.

Thus a human being's refraction through the symbol makes possible the *most* human thing—desire—and gives us multiple ways to experience our sensory drives, such as hunger, vision, audition, and sexuality. The existence of this symbolic visual and acoustic prism adds an element and subtracts an element from human experience. The refraction of a hunger drive could be thought of as additive when, at the site of the mouth, hunger becomes refracted into multiple partial drives. One result of this multiplicity of drives would be how a richly textured description of a food dish can make your mouth water. You might even begin to desire it as you fondly recall the circumstances in which you last consumed it. And all this may occur even though you don't feel the least bit hungry.

The symbol also subtracts something in that we are limited, except in brief moments, from a total direct experience of pure animal pleasure/ jouissance. This is simply because human experience, most of the time, is mediated by an internal world of symbols—be these fantasies/daydreams or mono-/dialogues within our minds. (For example, I feel that the temperature is hotter and more humid than is usual for San Francisco, and

2. This would be, as referred to in Chapter 2, the "little other" or person of the mother, and the "big Other" or symbolic network itself. To connote both, I will use mOther in the text.

looking out the window I have a momentary childhood memory of sticky summer afternoons relieved by sprinklers and dripping popsicles. But then I bring myself back to writing.) The byproduct of the encounter between the symbol and the human being is that something is lost. This loss leaves in us an existential sense of the reality that something is always missing, for no matter what object or person we manage to obtain, this missing always returns. Often this something missing is a desire that moves us toward others—a desire that is clothed by unconscious fantasies of how there must be a special someone/something, somewhere, who will fill in that something missing within us (Lacan 1973).[3]

All human beings need to be held by the symbol to a large extent—more so than most people realize. For to actually push beyond the limits of the symbol into unmediated experience constitutes a kind of death—for instance, the psychic disappearance of yourself as a self-reflective subject during orgasm (in fact, a French term for orgasm is "little death"); or the shattering of one's psyche from an unbearable and unimaginable experience of too much jouissance, which is too much experience beyond the symbol's capacity to contain it in that moment. This is not pleasure but trauma, something that occurred for many in the United States on September 11, 2001. Likewise, in the film *Realm of the Senses*, two people are portrayed as pushing the limits of aggression's link to sexual excitement and orgasm to the extent that it leads to the actual death of one.

Human pleasure, sexual and otherwise, always resides in a paradoxical area. For the ordinary human being (not one with a psychotic or perverse psychic organization),[4] the best pleasures are found in an arena where symbolic or social limits are accepted and internalized. But at another level, desire itself is often fueled by fantasies of what it would "really be like" if there were no such limits.

---

3. A general tendency of object relations theory is to frame the categories of loss and space too much in terms of the loss of the primal object—the mOther—and not nearly enough as the byproduct of the encounter between the symbol and the human being.

4. In thinking about symptoms, Lacan is not phenomenological like the *DSM-IV*. In the Lacanian perspective the important factor is to what degree the person/subject is woven within the Symbolic network—or what is the psychic structure. The neurotic operates on the side of fantasy and accepting limits to an unlimited jouissance; whereas in the perverse subject there is a failure to use fantasy and the person puts her-/himself in the position of enacting being and remaining the object of an imagined omnipotent Other's jouissance, as if to get around the necessity for limits on jouissance. This is why in the Lacanian frame there are only three psychic structures: psychotic, perverse, and neurotic—each different in terms of the degree to which symbolization is operative.

It is the play of the symbol, in its form of fantasy upon the refracted surfaces of the conscious/unconscious mind, that ultimately makes human sex *sex*, and not simply, or only, reproduction; it is also what makes for multiple sexual aims, objects, and identities. It is not uncommon to see in one's consulting room couples where there is human reproduction but no real eroticism, couples where there is eroticism but no reproduction, couples where there may be both, and couples where there is neither.

The human being must become sufficiently processed through, and linked within, a symbolic network, or s/he will experience more than the ordinary amount of psychic and/or somatic pain and suffering (Bion 1957, Lacan 1955). For the human being, her/his psychic body is never an exact replica of the actual somatic body. The degree of difference between these two bodies can range from there being a cooperative working partnership to there being a catastrophic disjuncture that produces terrible psychic and/or somatic suffering (see Chapters 6 and 9, this volume). In this respect, the biological body and the psychic or Imaginary body operate with different logics. But, as the hyphenated word "psyche-soma" suggests, these influences can be reciprocal. For the most part, however, it is the psyche, the word that leads the hyphenated couplet, that leads the human being. Humans experience somatic and emotional pain when the psychic body or body-ego we have constructed is inadequate. Even when one's ego is adequate, suffering occurs when one is unable to maintain psychic integrity in day-to-day life (see Chapter 5, this volume). The more inadequate an individual's symbolic functioning, the more he/she will be subjected to being invaded by traumatic anxieties, perceptual or cognitive distortions, and/or somatic disorders that arise from a body and mind inadequately symbolized (Bion 1967, Lacan 1955). Individuals who live through major distortions in how their infantile needs were prismed and interpreted struggle in varying degrees: (1) to form a cohesive (which does not mean whole) and stable identity, (2) to function interpersonally and sexually, and (3) to assume a social role within their society.

THEORETICAL SECTION: THE OTHER IMPLICATED IN THE KNOT OF HUMAN SEXUALITY

Let us return to our mobius figure (Figure 2–1) mentioned in Chapter 2. Suppose that when a length of ribbon was cut from fabric to make a mobius strip, a small rectangular-shaped piece had been cut out away from one end of the ribbon. Cut in this manner, the ribbon lends itself to illustrate metaphorically the biological Real of sexual difference reflecting femaleness. In contrast, if the small rectangular piece protrudes instead, this could represent the biological Real of sexual difference illustrating maleness. Each human being (ribbon) comes most often in one of two Real biological forms, female or male. Females and males share more capacities and experiences than not, though, by virtue of the fact that both are submitted to the effects of symbolic immersion. That is to say, both sexes are cut away from seamless nature and inserted into a Symbolic network in which they must create and find themselves (Lacan 1953). In this sense, then, the oedipal complex is always composed of four terms: the child, the mother, the father, and the symbolic.

The biological Real of sexual difference (Copjec 1994, Lacan 1953e, 1972, Ragland 1991)[5] and its tie to reproduction are but one aspect of the knot of human sexuality. Sexual difference can be thought of, however, as if it were (or should be) the determinant of sexual orientation (basically a Kleinian position). Symbolic processes inherently complicate human sexuality. Sexual difference, therefore, functions as a perplexing thread in the knot of human sexuality; what appears to be biologically Real at the level of anatomy is not always so at the level of an individual's conscious attitudes or unconscious psychic reality.

Sexual difference has traditionally been a means for symbolically anchoring identity, both intrapsychically and interpersonally. The fact that new parents are always asked, "What is it, a girl or a boy?" is a concretization of this fact. Historically, intersexed infants—those who have partial sex organs of both sexes—have routinely been surgically assigned a sex at birth. Yet this traditional procedure is now being questioned for good reasons (Diamond and Sigmundson 1997, Dreger 1998). In our postmodern period, modernity's traditional meanings of masculine and feminine have been and are being deconstructed. It is thus becoming possible to have room to think about how a surgical assignment of sex at birth might permanently foreclose the opportunity for the intersexed child's psychosexuality to develop—knotted within the braided matrix of biological predispositions, a family's unconscious and conscious fantasies, and the symbolic patterns of one's particular culture.

5. Copjec critiques the position put forward by Judith Butler, where language and positions in it can be seen to negate the Real of sexual difference.

PREOEDIPAL INFANTILE SEXUALITY OF THE IMAGINARY

Human sexuality, Freud said (1905), only *leans* on the instinct of reproduction; reproduction alone is not sufficient to account for the variability in human sexuality, both in behavior and in orientation. To account for this variability Freud (1911, 1915, 1915a) looked to the effects of symbol-making on the human being. Given the refraction of sexuality by the symbol, we can expect to see more than two variants of psychosexual identities; usually, however, only certain psychosexual identities are culturally sanctioned within any given historical context.

For Freud and Lacan there is no representation of sexual difference in the unconscious (Kleinians are not so sure). At the level of the infantile body-ego and Imaginary object relations,[6] the experience of difference is rooted in what Freud (1923, 1940) described as the two moments of the drive: active and passive/receptive. These two moments of the drive are often *assumed* to be inextricably linked to the anatomy of sexual difference on the basis of a retroactive organization. This does not, however, take into consideration the third, or reflexive, moment of the drive. It is this third position—the reflexive moment of the drive (Lacan 1964)—that proffers the most space for thinking about sexuality. According to Lacan (1960), the reflexive moment of the drive describes a position wherein the object (or intention) of the drive is never to meet its (human) object per se, but it is to circle the object, returning to the subject who, in the moment of satisfaction, "comes into being." Until the moment of satisfaction, it could be said that the instinctual or biological element of the drive leads, but in the moment of satisfaction, the subject appears—because she/he is reexperiencing a satisfying moment that includes the psychic component of having been separated from total satisfaction via the symbol (and partial Real satisfaction). This is one of the best ways of knowing and differentiating one person from another person: by the particularity of their desires, in search of what can only be a partial drive (e.g., Ms. M. must have only French chocolate). Therefore, due to the effects of the symbol upon the human sexual drive, not all men, and not all women, will organize their sexual aim, object choice, or preferred moment of the sexual drive into a single, binary, heterosexual, oedipal equation.

There is for humans the tension of a psychic divide between the fluid (Imaginary) sexuality of the unconscious mind, and the social prescrip-

6. Klein and Lacan take exception and mark this territory by "early oedipal."

tions for sexuality and gender in the conscious (Symbolic) mind. Due to this divide, variations in sexual aims and sexual object choices manifest in the human being to a degree not seen in other animal species. As simple and obvious as the sexual act may seem to be, human sexuality is neither simple nor obvious because of the erotics of the symbol. As such, human psychosexuality resides in a Bermuda Triangle of psychic and Real forces. The assemblage of a working symbolic identity, sexual difference, gender role definitions and limits, and object choice is a complex configuration to navigate. What one sees on the surface may not always reflect who or what moves one from the inside. And through it all, there is the drive. Drive has the character of being a verb—it is not the subject, or the object, but it does move us toward and into the world of others, if conditions are hospitable enough (Green 2000).

Returning briefly to our mobius figure again, if we imagine that there were particles moving within the space (or spaces) of the mobius figure,[7] this would represent the content of an individual's unconscious fantasies of self with the other, formed within a fluid field of infantile sexuality. According to Lacan (1959–1960, 1972, 1973), bits of Real satisfaction reside at the core around which Imaginary infantile unconscious fantasies are spun.

At the very heart of these Imaginary unconscious fantasies is an aspect of the Real that is not the same as, but is not unrelated to, the Real of sexual difference itself. Paradoxically, this bit of Real satisfaction is the limit point of symbolization (in that it cannot be symbolized), as well as the inexhaustible source for symbolization (in that all subsequent symbolization harkens back to these bits of Real satisfaction). In keeping with our mobius figure metaphor, this aspect of the Real is denoted by the spaces between, and among, the patterns of atomic particle units making up the fantasy content. These are kernels of Real infantile jouissance (also called surplus-jouissance) around which is a fantasmatic elaboration, which the sex and gender researcher John Money (1988) calls "love maps." These love maps, first etched in infancy, are later retroactively reinscribed or rewritten on the body during the sexual maturing time of adolescence when the question of object choice is most often largely settled. They are the individual's unique triggers of sexual arousal and the template of sensual pleasure as supported by one's unconscious phantasm(s). Lacan's

7. Atomic particles = self/ego + object, related by an affective charge.

(1959–1960, 1964, 1972, 1973) concept of the "object a" (which evolved over time) became his designation for a particular aspect of the Real—the object that causes us to desire and move outward toward others. The "object a" is trickster-like or paradoxical in that it can be described as the kernels of the Real of one's sensory template that, when touched by an other, are then projected onto him or her. At the same time, the "object a" is a hole or gap—something perceived and experienced as missing in one's self (Nobus 2000). The "object a" resides at the center of where the three registers of the Real, Symbolic, and Imaginary all meet to make a knot, called the Borromean knot, that Lacan (1972) uses to describe the intricate, and necessary, relation among all three registers of human subjectivity.[8] If any one of the circles is cut, everything falls apart (see Figure 2–2, p. 18).

The "object a," then, is a Lacanian concept that is very useful in terms of retaining the complexity of human sexuality and avoiding a concretizing collapse of the Real of sexual difference into a presumed heterosexuality. Putting together Lacan's notion of the "object a," along with the psychic reality that sexual relations are mediated via fantasy within a fluidly sexual unconscious, it should not be surprising that sexual desire may potentially be evoked by someone of either sex, whether or not this desire is socially or individually deemed symbolically legitimate.

In terms of symbolic legitimacy, the notion that symbolic thinking and object choice are absolutely psychically tied can be seen as a defense against the possibility of psychic disintegration should the link between these two categories be broken. Such fear of falling apart, however, prevents exploration and has significant implications for individual creativity and social or political action. (The Pope's position that Catholics will not think about the issue of celibacy and church service comes to mind.)

OEDIPAL PSYCHOSEXUAL IDENTIFICATION WITHIN THE SYMBOLIC

Oedipal identity is a compromise formation framing how an individual's unique unconscious erotic map and personal idiom of creativity will live within a physical body that is categorized as either female or male. This

---

8. The Symbolic takes a bite out of the Real. The Symbolic has a hole because it cannot hold off of the Real. The Imaginary provides coherence in the image but also leaves out an element of the Real and thus is not complete.

individual, because of having a female or male body, must respond to cultural (symbolic) definitions and expectations regarding gender roles, whether these definitions/expectations reflect her/his psychic reality—which is masculine or feminine. S/he also must respond to erotic impulses that move her/him toward another, be that other male or female or both.

The transversing of the oedipal passage (Freud 1924a) means that a child is accepting certain limits: (1) that neither parent can be the exclusively loved and desired object because mother and father belong to each other (the superego reinforcing this repression); (2) that thus love and desire must be displaced to a partner of one's own generation; (3) that generational and gender differences prescribe different points of access, privileges, and limits within the Symbolic order of society; (4) that she/he cannot be both a female and a male; and (5) that she/he must take up a symbolic position/identification linked to certain ego ideals.

With reference to gender as a symbolically inscribed category of meaning with associated limits, there is a cultural shell game at work. The Real of sexual difference is encountered as a limit that has multiple consequences, despite the fact that some of these consequences have little to do with Real differences in capacities between the sexes. They actually have more to do with Symbolic definitions and Imaginary fantasies regarding gender that are elaborated specifically within a cultural-historical time period. The oedipal child entering school begins years of learning related to the prevailing possibilities and limits her/his society has delineated for each sex. In this sense, prevailing symbolic definitions of gender are encountered as social expectations as well as social laws—expectations that as a girl or boy one should be certain ways. These social expectations can be a source of conflict and suffering for many individuals even while they are (at least in part) a source of confirmation and a directional guide to others.

Laws and culturally encoded gender expectations are Symbolic elaborations, and as such, can and do change (e.g., men used to wear powdered wigs; women could not vote). When Symbolic laws are differentially applied to the body and mind in accordance with sexual difference, it is far less about Real differences (which themselves remain an enigma) and far more about using Symbolic structures to manage unconscious anxieties. These anxieties are linked with unconscious fantasies about an imagined omnipotent other initially generated by our relationship to mOther and thereafter father, and then generalized to others in life. Misapplications of Symbolic laws and forms are nourished by individual and group infantile fantasies wherein the woman and "things feminine" are linked to the unconscious as unknown, while "things masculine" are linked to the known, to conscious identity, to a sense of personal agency.

To refer back to the mobius figure as a grounding illustration, the Symbolic in the mobius figure makes the shape of the ribbon itself. Whether the ribbon has the designated cut rectangle as missing or protruding (to connote sexual difference as Real), the general configurations the ribbon may take are established by the ribbon itself and not by the missing or protruding rectangular appendage. It is the original cutting of the ribbon away from the whole cloth of nature that carves, in a sense, a gap in the human being, not sexual difference. This figure illustrates how profoundly the Symbolic orders our world and appears to set immutable parameters that constrain that world—certainly in terms of our consciously imagined possibilities. While the necessity for the Symbolic to provide order is undeniable, the forms the Symbolic may actually take are, in fact, not immutable; they are always subject to redefinition. In the case of sexual difference, the biological Real of sexual difference can be distorted by the combination of Imaginary fantasies with Symbolic laws to make possible the seemingly justifiable control of one sex by the other. Along this same vein, for those whose oedipal knotting of sexuality, sexual difference, and gender do not mirror the current most dominant Symbolic definitions of gender and normative adult sexuality within a culture, there can be psychic suffering linked to a lack of social recognition or actual persecution (e.g., Butler 1990, 1993, Foucault 1976, Young-Bruehl 2000). Lacanian theory offers considerable assistance in generating mental space within the analytic field concerning the complexities inherent to the oedipal knotting. It also helps to open up the language for the analyst for speaking to psychic position versus sexual activity. For example, in the case of Ms. Y. (to be presented in this chapter), it was important to differentiate a wish to penetrate the other from a wish (as symbolic equation) to being a man having a penis. Likewise, it was important with Ms. Y. and Mr. X. (also discussed in this chapter) to differentiate their inhabiting of a psychic position from that of their enacting interpersonal aggression/dominance.

LACAN'S REVISION OF OEDIPUS

In addition to the way in which Lacan's concept of "object a" helps free desire's movement from a mandatory hetero- or homoparadigm of sexuality, Lacan (1955) offers an important revisioning of Freud's Oedipus.

Lacan's revision of the oedipal passage, castration complex, and oedipal identification can all be read as "politically neutral," in that they are free from assigning symbolic legitimacy to certain psychosexual identities while withholding it from others.

Lacan reframes castration as the splintering and yet constitutive effect that the symbol (language) has upon all human experience (Lacan 1953, Mitchell and Rose 1982, Ragland 1987). He reformulates the oedipal passage as one wherein the individual psychically relocates his/her psychic identification from the Imaginary to the Symbolic (Nobus 2000).[9] Lacan sees the male or female body as a *referent* for masculine or feminine identification. But anatomy is not seen as necessarily *determining* identification, because in fact both male and female children are taking a position vis-à-vis the father, who stands as the representative of the Symbolic. Oedipal psychosexual identification is seen by Lacan as the child's taking up of a symbolic identification or position within language—becoming a subject of the symbol in one of two positions, either in a masculine or feminine position.

The masculine position, according to Lacan (1972), is an identification that is more tied to the symbol; or, put another way, the masculine could be thought of as the threads of a symbolic net. The masculine is thus a position that carries more weight in the Symbolic order. Because this oedipal position is more attached to the symbol, the masculine subject may have a particularly strong need to affirm a personal identity by powerfully reinforcing the links between the mind and the somatic body.[10] Therefore, the person in this position may approach the loved and desired other through physical/erotic contact first or early on in the relationship. Through sexual access to the body of another, the masculine identity seeks replenishment and reminding that the symbol must first be anchored in the lived body, before taking flight on the wings of the symbolic. This reinforcing of links can be very problematic for someone in a masculine identification in a sexual relationship with a woman. The bit of the lost Real, which is

9. This means the child gives up identification with "being" the imaginary phallus of the mOther, to taking up an identification with "having" the symbolic phallus, or not. In truth, no one has the phallus, or doesn't have it, in the sense that phallus is a privileged signifier intended to mark the entry into language and the taking up of a position within it.

10. Besides the Real of testosterone, this is another reason for the significance of sports in men. Also because the Imaginary body-ego is formed in relation to the mOther, a woman, there is the wish to reinforce the link between Symbolic identification and the Real of sexual difference of having a male body.

the kernel of infantile satisfaction causing desire, is virtually always clothed in the unconscious fantasy of woman as mOther. It is a virtual certainty, then, that in the absence of a genuine discourse with the feminine (or masculine) subject within the female sexual partner, there can be no actual encounter with the subjectivity of the other person or her form of jouissance. There can only be a maternal reunion. This is a common complaint heard among women about their relationships with men, that they aren't talked to by their male partners and don't feel seen by them.

The feminine position, though also clearly subjected to the Symbol, remains—more than the masculine position—tied to the anchoring roots of the Real and Imaginary worlds of the mother–infant matrix (Kristeva 1989, 2000, Mieli 1993). Put another way, the feminine identification could be thought of as the holes or spaces in the symbolic net, imparting a palpable knowing that experience is never fully captured by the symbol—even the most articulate symbol. The feminine subject has less currency in the symbolic order of things, because at the very least, gender politics has contributed to there being less of the female experience articulated in language (something the second and third waves of feminism sought to counter). The feminine subject, therefore, often first desires words from the loved and desired other—words describing and recognizing her personal uniqueness—as a prelude to putting her (or one's) body (bodies) (actual body plus the libidinal psychic body) into play with that of the other.

Both threads and holes comprise a net. Neither is better; each is different. Both are needed. Lacan's concept of the masculine and feminine as symbolic positions that may or may not correspond to anatomy is clinically useful when working with the problematics of multiple oedipal configurations. Either oedipal position opens the possibility for the individual to claim desire while at the same time accepting the necessity of personal and social limits. Family and social values associated with establishing an ego ideal during the oedipal passage combine with the effects of secondary repression generally to reinforce one's symbolic identification as either a masculine or a feminine subject. But irrespective of oedipal position, the unconscious, desirous, and pleasure-seeking aspects of an infantile fluid sexuality incessantly strive, in their own ways, for satisfaction.

Perhaps in the final analysis, whatever form an oedipal organization may take, it represents a compromise formation (Chodorow 1994). It has a trajectory parallel to that of Klein's depressive position: it must be continually worked over a lifetime because there is never a definitive ending of the oedipal complex per se (Freud 1924, Loewald 1979). Just as preoedipal omnipotent wishes and magical identifications are never finally extinguished, neither is tabooed desire totally expunged.

Academic theoreticians have employed Lacanian concepts to deconstruct normative heterosexuality (e.g., Dean 2001, 2000, de Lauretis 1994, Silverman 1992),[11] but such theorizing is often not familiar to individuals who are suffering difficulties with their oedipal passage. Also, because of the uneven ground of the conscious/unconscious mind, what one knows consciously does not necessarily calm unconscious conflicts. What follows is a glimpse into the work of two individuals navigating the turbulence of these currents within the analytic encounter.

MS. Y: A TRIBAL DANCE OF SYMBOL, SEXUALITY, AND AGGRESSION

Ms. Y., a twenty-something-year-old of mixed race, entered psychotherapy, which later became analysis, as an angry, sloppy, but stylish adolescent with striking green hair and three studs in her ear. She dared the analyst to judge her relationship with a woman many years older. Angry that the analyst would not *label* her sexuality and relationship status, she was verbally intimidating in trying to provoke confirmation from me of what was "the right way." It was clear in the countertransference response that there were only wrong ways to choose. Although sexuality was the red flag she waved, this was only a small part of why Ms. Y. had come. A hostile, aggressive inner world led her to look for and provoke, through her own body language, sharp words and demands—the very cutting responses from others she feared the most. (As Bion [1959] might note, as soon as she would make a link she would attack it.)

Ms. Y.'s sessions increased from once a week to three times a week over the course of the first year and a half of treatment. (One increase came in response to a dream of hers and one in response to her pushing the limits of the frame.) Ms. Y. shifted from face-to-face work to using the couch when sessions reached three times a week. This shift in position brought about associations that lying on the couch was like being within the womb. The couch reminded her of the color of "dried blood" and she then began to express fears that I would "abort her from the treatment." More primitive

11. See Dean's *Beyond Sexuality* (2000), especially the chapter "Lacan Meets Queer Theory."

paranoid fears also emerged; she feared she "would be seduced into allowing [herself] to become vulnerable, only to be left stranded with [her] raw need unsatisfied and then [she] would feel humiliated." She would have almost a hallucinatory anticipation that I would kick her in the head as she lay on the couch after saying something she imagined I would disapprove of. And at times, I did feel the pulling of dark undertows drawing me toward being harsh and critical toward Ms. Y.; at the same time, I often felt alienated and saddened by the degree of sadism Ms. Y. seemingly expected as ordinary fare. And then in some moments there could be an almost excruciating tenderness. For purposes of my own containment, I often drew from Freud's (1920a, 1924, 1930) later views on affect's differentiation from the two roots of Eros (binding) and the death instinct (unbinding or defusing). Also helpful were Winnicott's (1965) actual words that at first in the infantile psyche "Love means just existing, breathing, and being alive, to be loved. Love means appetite. Here is no concern, only the need for satisfaction" (p. 14).

Ms. Y. brought alive for me the reality that while to become a human being is to become structured via a preexisting Symbolic order, it is crucial that during this process of becoming, a baby experience her self becoming alive in her body and mind in a particular and personal way (Winnicott 1945, 1949). For Winnicott, this aliveness is first grounded in an other's, usually a mOther's, being sufficiently attuned such that her symbolic interpretation of her baby's need helps attenuate the fact that the world—that preexisting symbolic order I have been talking about—was already present and was not created by the infant him-/herself (Winnicott 1958, 1963). In other words, a period of illusion is necessary. To create this illusion, the "mother must hold the situation in time" (Winnicott 1954a, p. 263) so that the space between infant need, the infant's call or demand, and the interpretive response by the mOther is neither too cavernous nor too intrusive, so as to be psychically catastrophic in Bion's (1962) terms. When the good-enough mother "holds the situation in time," the infant becomes able to work through to being able to "surrender to what is going on inside herself" and this leads to "feel of [being] real" the infant's inherent creative impulse versus setting up defensive reactivity to impingement (whether this impingement is actual or perceived) (Winnicott 1956, p. 304).

But of course, Ms. Y. was not an infant, and thus the provocatively sensual and aggressive verbal manner in which she strove to take possession of my office and mind was viscerally disturbing, irritatingly exciting at moments, and very often anxiety provoking in the early years of the work. Bion's (1962b) description of the contact barrier as an accumulated coherence of alpha (protosymbolic) elements that can be under attack and be dispersed into bizarre objects (particles containing elements of archaic superego and ego) seems an apt characterization of the kind of forces operating within the analytic discourse during these early years. Thus, I saw as the primary task during this phase of the work to symbolically contain the patient, along with psychically surviving myself so that a kind of analytic capital could be accumulated that might be spent interpretively later on. The interpretations of Ms. Y.'s aggression were, at this time, framed as her reaching for contact in a climate where the ever-present threat was that one member of the analytic couple could, and probably would, be psychically annihilated at any moment. (See Winnicott's [1958a] concept of "ruthless" love, p. 22.)

Experiences that at first are entirely sensory in the infant must eventually find substitute channels of expression. The instinctual body must become imaginatively elaborated. It is in the sounds of letters and words that language first links up with the body on its way to making meaning and metaphor (Lacan 1955, 1964, Sharpe 1940). Thus, the spontaneous metaphors of a person's speech carry not only repressed material already linguistically encoded, but the material language of infantile experience as well, which will insist its way into the discourse of the individual (Kristeva 1982, Lacan 1955). The metaphoric world of Ms. Y. careened between the hardness of that anticipated "kick" from me and the mushiness of things all going to "shit." (She said "shit" frequently.) It was necessary to live through a series of unsymbolized experiences (via projective and introjective identifications) with Ms. Y. before any infantile fantasies could be co-constructed or memories recovered and interpreted. It would take different kinds of time to truly help her differentiate from a tangle of Eros, sexuality, and destructiveness (Green 1999b, 2002).

When any individual's body-ego boundary is unstably drawn, language often functions in a concrete manner. In this sense language and speech are like action itself (Ogden 1994). Thus, for Ms. Y., it was frequently a matter of psychic life or death that she be the one in charge of the situation. This was especially so in relation to any authority figure like an analyst. It was hard work to keep in mind that the concreteness of her speech was because psychosomatic pain had not been sufficiently psychically transformed so as to become the ordinary suffering that a human subject can bear to endure (Bion 1958, 1962a, 1970). This was especially true when the emotional intensity of the sessions was very demanding, as when Ms. Y. would express the fear that I might kick her in the head with an emotional intensity powered by the primitive defense of evacuation.

Approximately nine months into the treatment, Ms. Y. ended her relationship with the much older woman. A several-month period of sexual acting out followed. For Ms. Y., action had to be used to fill an experience of emptiness or space, for she had no belief or enduring faith that suspending action and bearing the emptiness would bring forth any creative response or new understanding in herself. My interpreting her sexual acting out as a defense against the analysis soon brought this to an end. Her level of engagement in the work deepened now. Prior fears of receiving a call from me canceling a session were now replaced by the fear that someone else would call to tell her that I was dead. Ms. Y. moved between the subjective positions of wanting to curl up like an unborn fetus on the couch, to being suffused by an unconscious evocative sexuality. (Once, she caught herself in the ritual of removing her shoes prior to lying on the couch, and then beginning to remove her rings as if she were getting into bed. She commented upon that fact.) Unconscious evocative sexuality became a conscious fear of sexual intrusion—"How do I know you will stay in your chair behind me?" Her earlier, but more recently receded, provocative style began taking on a more definite form. This form became apparent in a pattern of creating tantalizing situations within the sessions—that is, indicating she really wanted to talk about something but then failing to, almost daring me "to make her" tell. What was evoked in me was a feeling that I did want to sadistically pull it out of her, a feeling I resisted through interpreting it when I felt the time was ripe for her to be able to hear.

One day while walking to the door at the end of a tantalizing session, Ms. Y. thrust a chestnut toward me, saying she had picked it up in the yard on the way into the building. She had wanted to give it to me and couldn't until now. I could feel her desperation, and, feeling ambushed, I automatically took it and regretted doing so. There were myriad countertransference reactions to make use of here, only part of which were brought into the next session. (I held the rest of the chestnut(s) for later.)

By this point in the analysis, interpretations had shifted more in the direction of Klein/Bion (envious attacks and omnipotent control) and Lacan (the jouissance/pleasure in limitless destructiveness), insofar as I began to spend some of the analysis's accumulated capital to interpret more directly her aggression and the sexualized tinge it carried. In unspoken thoughts about the chestnut, I mused that the gift was in one way negated by her giving me something that was already mine (since it was in my yard). It also felt envious, and felt, as well, as though her Eros was infused with aggression. Perhaps she was simply warding off my aggression or hers by trying to give me something. Musing to myself on the word: "chest"—female, "nut"—male, I wondered what did she want me to understand about being female or male? The darkest countertransference feelings surrounding this incident were feelings associated with an image of my being raped.

In the following session the spoken interpretation focused upon a desire misfired. It was clear she wanted to give me something, yet I felt coerced to take it. If it were really to be a gift, it seemed, I said to her that there must be room to say "no" as well as "yes." In forcing me to receive it through ambush, it was as though she was saying that she could not imagine that her love was anything but a toxic poison—that no one would really want or desire her. Ms. Y. at first felt spurned by these words. She wanted the giving action to speak for itself. Continuing to hold a place in-between—not rejecting/returning the gift—but speaking a wish to have had different conditions for receiving it, neither she nor I became obliterated. I said that it seemed so much easier for her to imagine kicking or be kicked by someone as opposed to kissing or being kissed by someone.

This is just one moment of many in sessions that required a "living through" as I was "searching for and trying to preserve the minimum conditions for symbolization" (Green 1999a, p. 303). I was also keeping in mind that it is the mOther's response to the infantile subject's gesture that contributes to its being real, which leads on to the infant's being able to make use of the symbol (Winnicott 1954). Only retrospectively could the analytic pair begin to symbolize what at first could only be enacted in an aggressively dependent and eroticized manner. Many of these mental and emotional states had never been sufficiently captured or linked together in symbols. Therefore it was a long and challenging process of sorting out a tangle of unmodulated affect and sexuality to find words that could transform what had seemed unbearable to the bearable, the bearable to the livable, the livable to the desirous.

Three sessions per week became four sessions per week during the fourth year of treatment as the work deepened further. Unbeknownst to me, one day Ms. Y. saw me emptying my wastebasket in the minutes before the session as she (Ms. Y.) was walking toward the building. In the manner in which she entered the consulting room, it was evident that it was going to be another hard session. She was agitated, angry, and attacking, and I was quickly flooded. Her spearing words pierced. I felt increasingly angry and struggled unsuccessfully to think and make an interpretation that might transform the tangled situation. I hated that her most passionate tie was to be in such combat. Feeling hateful, I fell into silence (Winnicott 1947). She continued her attack: "Oh, now you aren't going to say anything. You are going to give me the silent treatment aren't you? Are you going to just sit there? Can't you say anything?" I continued to be silent for a number of seconds before I could gather enough of myself together to say, with as much of an even tone of voice as could be mustered, "I can't say anything that would be useful right now, so being silent is the best I can do. When I can say something useful, I will."[12] To say that I felt inadequate would be an understatement. Now, Ms. Y. fell into silence too. The silence continued for some time. Somewhere in this shared silence I felt the mood shift. In my reveries this shift felt like Ms. Y.'s moving from a pit bull mode of relating toward a quieting—the image of a pond with ripples slowly disappearing. I spoke first: "Something seems to have moved." More quiet. Then Ms. Y. told me how she had seen me taking out the wastebasket. When she saw me in this action she had wondered to herself, "Does she have to empty me out with her wastebasket after each session?" She quickly put this thought out of her mind. Only now had the thought returned. She then began to speak of all the "awful feelings about her body," particularly about being female, a woman. She spoke of her erotic body and how she often feared and defended against having an orgasm because it felt like a shattering loss of control for her.

Later in the analysis, and on more than one occasion, Ms. Y. returned to this moment, saying that it had been a pivotal incident because she could feel how mad and hateful I felt, and yet held back and did not attack, and even struggled to think and somehow stay connected. "How was that possible?" she had asked herself. Being in a separate but shared silence, my not attacking back, the admission of my own limits, and trying to think but not being able to, had made it possible for just enough mental space to occur in Ms. Y.'s mind to remember the wastebasket incident, link it to her feelings about her body, especially her sexual body, and then risk speaking to the analyst of both her vulnerability and shame. This shared silence

12. At a later time, this position shifted to one of interpreting how she wanted something from the other—but only if she could control it—thus leading her to attack the other's mind—resulting in her getting nothing or making shit out of whatever she did receive because it had been coerced and not given freely. The demand she feared from the other, she herself issued.

became a generative space, a space somewhere between loss and intrusion—the space where the symbol can come alive.

Needless to say, many months of work led up to this moment of the discovery of me as an external object rather than a subjective object (Winnicott's notion) or imaginary other (Lacan's notion) of her internal world. Certainly this moment of discovery was found and lost many times.

Drives of all sorts only become moderated and differentiated through sufficient symbolic containment over a period of time. Without adequate symbolic containment, the infant's thrust toward life (what Winnicott called "ruthless love") becomes aggression as a destructive force, rather than aggression becoming woven with Eros to fuel the individual's own creative acts in encounters with an external world. When the external world is first discovered to exist, thereby putting a limit to fantasy, the external world may become used creatively (Winnicott 1969). When aggression as destruction is paired with Eros as the jouissance of infantile sexuality, and not sufficiently contained, however, sadism (masochism) can be the result (Lacan 1953).[13] Infantile erotized aggression, generated by a combination of factors, had only became accentuated in Ms. Y.'s adolescence with sexual maturation. In those moments of silence, before Ms. Y. spoke of her bodily shame, she had psychically stopped, surrendered to her inner experience, and within this experience connected to knowledge that there was a jouissance/pleasure in her unabashed, self-righteous, aggressive attack on others. And in that moment she began to question why, and how it is that some others are different and do not act in these ways.

Bion (1967) describes the dialectical movement between paranoid/schizoid and depressive positions—between the place where words are things to be used as shields or weapons and the place words have a capacity to hold, to create metaphor, and to evoke what is even beyond the symbol's capacity, as is the case with poetry. This was such a moment of dialectical movement, where even though I felt angry, frustrated, and paralyzed, in Ms. Y.'s mind, the analyst moved from the all familiar imagined persecutory Other, to someone separate and outside herself—someone who was not all powerful, someone in fact she might be curious about. From being only a part-object, the analyst also began to be experienced by Ms. Y. as a subject, at least some of the time. In that moment she experienced

13. While Freud and Lacan agree on the intimate relation between sadism and masochism, Freud put sadism as primary and Lacan put masochism, due to the infant's passive position in relation to the Other.

what Bion would consider a full emotional experience—where feeling and thought mutually informed the other.

Toward the end of the fourth year of the analysis, Ms. Y. had begun to look more like an attractive young woman rather than a defiant teenager. She altered her posture in the waiting room from being perched somewhat like a hawk, vigilantly watching for my appearance, to being more sprawled upon the couch, sometimes looking like a toddler in momma's lap, sometimes a seductive woman wishing to be noticed. Indeed, her hair style was attractively different on this particular day, and when I did not comment on it (I rarely comment on someone's physical appearance) she mentioned later in the session that she realized that in the past she wouldn't have wanted me to say anything about it. To say anything at all about it would have made us too separate, whereas now it brought up in her mind, "How attractive am I if she doesn't even notice?" She tells a dream of buying a dress that first seems lovely and then changes as it begins to look like a costume of Snow White. (MI says, perhaps she wonders and worries if the sexy young woman can be seen or will an older woman's envy need to spoil it? Can she really feel feminine without its seeming that she is wearing a costume?)

A few months pass. A time of silence in the session brings her to note that instead of just, in her words, "babbling all the time," she can now experience silence as a way to feel present with me in ways that speaking breaks up. And at the same time, words also work to connect. Toward the end of the session she says she has lost her lipstick. "Is it here in your office?" she wonders. Only recently, and with embarrassment, had she begun to wear lipstick, following a history of comments on how "stupid it [lipstick] is," in the words of her father, and how she "can't believe you [the analyst] wear lipstick." (The internalized father in her use of "stupid" foreclosed many areas—one of which was the arena of being a desirable woman.)

It is two sessions later and suddenly at the end of the session, she sits up and then plunges her hand into the crevice of the couch and pulls out her lipstick. We are both surprised by her sudden action and her discovery. After this shared moment of shock and surprise, she leaves, lipstick in hand.

The next session opens with her remembering this incident. I wonder aloud what she may have wanted to leave inside me. She is quiet for a moment. She then muses out loud, "Am I wanting to leave you a kiss now instead of a kick? Am I showing you how I can be a lipstick woman too now? Did I want to leave you a little dick? Or, was I leaving a used tampon behind—leaving yet again some toxic part of myself that I wanted to be rid of." We were both quiet for a moment. I say, "Now there are not only fears that you might give me toxic shock syndrome. Now it seems you are entertaining several different fantasies: of how you might like to be like me, or to be with me or to touch and/or be inside me like a baby, or what it would be like to touch me as if you are a man, not a woman."

In this interpretation I as analyst am intentionally marking the overlapping and layered psychic territory of infantile sexuality and the erotic stage of Oedipus that are heard in her words. I hold in my own mind that "the analyst is like the day's residue in a dream—something onto which desire is transferred . . ." (Lemaire 1977, p. 200). It is apparent in her musing, in her ability to surrender to her own experience, and in her capacity to think out loud with me that she has moved a significant distance from the tangle of unmodulated eroticized aggression she used to employ—where words were shrapnel, used to wound (a biting of the breast, so to speak). Words can now function for her as more useful vessels for expressing her unique subjective experience and for beginning to interrogate her own desire. Ms. Y. has moved some distance from life as a battlefield on which to survive toward a location where questions of sexual difference, gender role, sexual desire, and symbolic limits can find their way into words and begin to be talked about. The interpretation as made does not presume a knowing of what kind of woman she should be, or presume to shape her desire as to what sexed being should catch her sexual desire. Neither does this interpretation imply that she ought to resonate with an active or receptive moment of her sexual drive, but that she wants to experience herself as a sexual being. More work was needed before she would be able to walk comfortably onto the field of sexual desire and safely engage another in a loving sexual relationship—but this field was now on the analytic horizon.

It was not until the middle of the fifth year of her analysis that Ms. Y. met and became romantically involved with a woman of her own generation. Now, the issues of sexual object choice, her primary identification with a masculine position (in Lacan's terms and Freud's), and the elaboration of the meaning of her gender began to become more fully differentiated. At this point her "carnivorous need" of me, as she had put it, had been waning and even becoming ego-dystonic.

In the context of the constituted oedipal triad of Ms. Y., her girlfriend, and the analyst, Ms. Y.'s unconscious fantasy that the desire of the Other was always a demand to which she must submit began to become even more laid bare in the transference and articulated. A fantasy was slowly co-constructed of the intrusion of paternal sexuality (rather than father occupying his role of Symbolic Third) into the mother–infant couple. The fantasy elaborated mother's physical and emotional reserve, which, when linked with Ms. Y.'s own constitutional predisposition, fostered a sadomasochistic eroticism of the infant–mother couple and later confusion surrounding erogenous zones. (Reports of childhood: father had an intrusive gaze, along with occasional touches, calling attention to his two daughters' most minute bodily changes. Father was also verbally, and in his gestures, inappropriately exhibitionistic of parental sexuality in the presence of the children.)

Furthermore, in Ms. Y.'s family, father (true of mother also) did not establish symbolic limits to which he, too, was required to submit, but rather made many decrees from which he remained exempt. Thus father took the position of an omnipotent father rather than a symbolic father, himself subjected to the Law (Lacan 1953). From latency age Ms. Y. had resisted this faux symbolic order of things. Shouting matches often ended with father stomping out of the house and mother crying, saying to Ms. Y., "Why do you do this? You know how your father is. You can handle this better, don't start with him." Thus it appeared that Ms. Y.'s oedipal love was in part received, in part rejected by mother. Mother's passive position of not being able to protect herself or her children by calling father on his violation of marital and parental (symbolic) limits of authority, stacked the psychic deck toward identification with father and with the power of the word/signifier. To add to the confusion, father was the more emotionally and physically available parent, especially during the early years before the verbal precocity of Ms. Y. began to assert itself. Father's intrusiveness at the level of his gaze and his need for control of the entire household seem to have been factors in loosening Ms. Y.'s libidinal tie to him (in terms of sexual orientation), while leaving an intense ambivalent love in place. This framework of Ms. Y.'s family landscape offers a glimpse as to how it might be difficult for Ms. Y. to differentiate demand versus desire, to know her sexual object choice, to know where to psychically stand, oedipally speaking, and to know how to fill out the figure of a woman. These interlinked confusions took their time to be unknotted and reknotted into an oedipal compromise formation that was viable.

A primary signifier for Ms. Y., which reflected the condensation of the multiple psychic layers, was the word "back." The "b sound" frequently insisted itself into her speech; the charge was heard and felt. Negative meanings of the word were a part of her Imaginary world[14] dominated by a paranoid-schizoid position in which she had lived (primarily) early on in the analytic work (Ogden 1994). This word also pointed to a phantasmatic erotic horizon of anal eroticism (Freud 1905, 1924). Over time, and at strategic and potent moments, this word, *back*, became an object of imaginative symbolic play in the analysis (e.g., in the analyst's initial office building, the bathroom was in the "back" of the building, which the patient would have to walk past in order to enter my office). When I used these letters and words in my interpretations, Ms. Y. experienced it as receiving something that was returned as her own.

In Ms. Y.'s unconscious mind there was no exit, no way to "back" away from the Other's desire—therefore it was always a demand. And there was no way for her to "back" down from a demand she had made to the Other, so interpersonal aggression would escalate. And, of course, there was no space for the Other to refuse her, without there being a collapse of self/ego; there was a libidinal excitement attached to the "back" of it as well. In other words, her identity was very much "backed" up (both constituted and conflictually compacted) by these identifications.

Through unfolding time, interpretive word play on the word "back" and its sounds (in that intermediate space between) was one element facilitating a shift from her self-defeating/destructive subjective position (i.e., the shift from paranoid-schizoid to depressive position). She became excited during one session in the sixth year when she noted that by "allowing more penetration of your [the analyst's] words, I then can also see from inside my own response, forming to make a creative link. I guess that is a creative intercourse." (Implied in her wry tone: And not the anal intercourse of a controlling Other.)

Her love relationship, moving into its second year (sixth year of analysis), continued to weather its storms—Ms. Y.'s weather system being the struggle with limiting her omnipotent wishes. Weather conditions were significantly improving when in a session in the seventh year, she could reflect upon seeing in herself the wish that her girlfriend would hold or take responsibility for her so she wouldn't have to bear life's trials, tribulations, and disappointments. Ms. Y. could tolerate seeing the wish and also regretfully acknowledging its impossibility. "It's like what Peter Pan tried to do with Wendy—to turn his peer into his mother, and yet disavow it at

14. For Lacan, the depressive position is also included in the realm of the Imaginary.

the same time." (Embedded here but not spoken to in this moment was Ms. Y.'s identification with the masculine position.)

> MI: Then it is a question, isn't it? What time do you want to live in? The time of your own particular life or a timeless fantasy?

The last year and a half of her analysis, Ms. Y. began her mourning for the ending of her analysis, which was now visibly on the horizon. This mourning was intermixed with times of protesting and short regressions. Yet she was obviously (even to herself, despite protests) finding her way within a now four-year relationship. During these years she had successfully repositioned herself in her professional work as well.

Ms. Y. truly began to mourn what she had called her "exuberance." No longer seeing it as simply benign excitation, she could notice now when it (the excitement) "isn't all good." In other words, she could locate when and where a perverse jouissance/pleasure would come alive (Ogden 1997a). It had been so evident in her earlier self-righteous rages, but with her feelings of excitement it took longer to see how they could be infiltrated by a pleasure that ultimately had negative consequences for her as well as others. Typical of her discourse during this period, she said almost ruefully, "I think that when I swear now, I much more often say 'fuck' than 'shit.' Something has changed." "Ah, yes," I said. "Connection, even competition, isn't so deadly anymore."

The story of Ms. Y. began with a look at the foundational floor of the erotics inherent to the symbol. For Ms. Y. there were far too many holes in the symbolic net as it had been woven via its mediation by her parents. This preponderance of holes left too many places for her to fall into or be pushed into the traumatic Real (often dragging others along with her). Sadomasochistic avenues of jouissance/pleasure were too prominent. She began treatment as an adolescent-like young adult who aggressively and sexually provocatively thrashed about, injuring others and herself, while blaming the world for her tumultuous inner world and her lack of satisfaction. Hating her own female body, she defiantly and ragefully demanded a recognition from her parents of a lesbian relationship that even she secretly knew she did not want—but she did not know what she wanted.

The analysis of Ms. Y. ended with her having become unstuck from a position/identification within her primary signifying chain that had her "backed," by being in a position of the bad one, the shit, in which she remained confused or ambivalent as to her psychic position (feminine or masculine), choice of object, and her sex and gender. Freeing the word "back" from operating as a sign or symbolic equation equaling bad, such that "back" could become a signifier, meant that this signifier could be reorganized within her particular set of primary signifiers. (In other words, she could back out of being stuck in a shitty position.) Along her analytic path, her aggression (as destructiveness) in relation to her Eros (in terms of her sexuality and love of the Other as a subject versus as a part-object) was transformed. She could put brakes on a pleasure/jouissance that was beyond reasonable limits—death drive's jouissance. The desire that was singularly hers became organized. In other words, in Freud's two realms of love and work, Ms. Y. could finally seek and find her own measure of human satisfaction, no longer leaving a trail of destruction in her wake—either in the world of others or inside herself—by going over human limit(s).

MR. X.: PENIS VERSUS PHALLUS: A RECONCILIATION OF PSYCHOSEXUALITY, AGGRESSION, AND DESIRE

I turn now to the case of Mr. X., whose life illustrates a different difficulty in terms of assembling the various pieces of psychosexual identity, sexual difference, and object choice into an oedipal configuration that is nonnormative yet viable.

What immediately struck me in the first meeting with this man was how unbelievably handsome he was, and yet how asexual—almost disembodied—he felt. (Embodied here refers to how his psychosomatic presence impacted me as the analyst.) His presentation suggested something beyond the depression he came to consult about. His analytic psychotherapy lasted approximately two and a half years, two sessions per week.

The youngest of three children (ten years younger than his closest brother), Mr. X. felt closer to his mother, who seemed to rely on his listening ear. But this attachment was characterized by an intense ambivalence. His father had been emotionally contained and often absent from the home scene—so absent that Mr. X. said that if it were up to him, he would not even carry his father's name. This rejection spoke volumes with respect to Mr. X.'s unarticulated felt sense of what power there is in the Name of the Father and what it means to bear the name of one's father, or not, especially for the male subject.

When he entered therapy he was in a state of withdrawal from everything and everyone, including his girlfriend and their sexual life together.

He was near to failing out of the university. His world had become completely centered on his fantasies, fantasies he had told no one. These fantasies were about being either an actual android or a Mr. Spock-like character (someone without real emotion or desire) who was a friend of a vital and virile male character who was usually falling in love and was also involved in violent encounters, especially to rescue the beloved. These fantasies reflected not only his conflict concerning aggression and masculinity, but also his own wish to be sought as the object of desire, and the sense that not enough of himself was felt to be carried by the signifier. The violent themes of his fantasies aroused great anxiety in him because he considered himself to be a committed pacifist, like his mother. How could he ever comfortably be a man? Was he even a man really? How could he expect to be a sexual being who would be welcomed or loved by his girlfriend when he was the fantasizer of such violence?[15]

For Mr. X., words were not to be trusted, and he did not inhabit them fully. I hospitalized him briefly, to his surprise, when, in his words of depression, he spoke of suicide, his fears of his suicidal fantasies, and mentioned, within the same stream of words, that maybe he should be hospitalized. The hospitalization served as an interpretation in action. It shocked him into realizing the impact of his speech and at the same time put him in a situation where he had to encounter others who were much more disturbed and psychically dislocated than he. The hospitalization had the effect of making him confront his desire, or lack of it, in a different manner. The arrangement of his hospitalization, plus the manner in which he tested the frame by wanting to change appointments or by coming late, prompted the following in one session. "It seems," I said, "that you do not know what you need more, the paternal part to help you experience that words—your words and agreements—matter, and that you must stand in and by them; or the feminine part to bear witness to the life in your fantasies (which he was speaking for the first time), and to receive all of what is somehow unspeakably present in you." These words sought to address his parental transference—which the analyst would try to "make him" come to treatment—by speaking to the parental functions themselves and his need of them still.

By the second year of the treatment, Mr. X.'s fantasy world was transforming. Occasional songs, now less compulsive in nature, complemented

15. From a Lacanian perspective, Mr. X. would be seen as inhabiting the position of an hysteric.

his fantasies. Sometimes he heard only songs running through his mind. On occasion he awoke with a song running in his mind. These voices were not persecutory, as the suicidal ones had been in the past. They were voices of his desire, primarily—his desire and not his parents' or girlfriend's—a voice heretofore unable to be heard. At first he felt tormented by these songs: "Why? What was the point?" At first he ridiculed my curiosity and the questions provoked by them. But soon he opened to, and discovered, a kind of knowledge that he did not know he knew. In his fantasies the unconscious subject of desire (Lacan 1953) was not only speaking, now it was singing. Time went on.

Within this second year Mr. X. remarked that he not only had those alien fantasies now, but additionally he had ones in which, in his words, he was a "shapeshifter." His gender shifted, or he shifted from human to nonhuman species in these fantasies. Soon he was able to have the insight that all his fantasies, even from the beginning, concerned the theme of recognition, somehow. He began to talk of and wonder what he really wanted recognized. I spoke of his being pulled to change his shape for others so much so that he had become unable to recognize his desire. His songs had helped him locate the voice of desire, but he was also confused and wondering about its and his own shape. He valued his sensitivity and receptivity—but to be receptive is associated with being a woman, activity with being a man. Was he wondering how his primary receptivity could live in a man's body comfortably? I offered that perhaps he was not sure how he wanted to receive recognition from me since he was surely male, but he carried much of what seemed feminine. Mr. X. responded first with a full silence without looking at me—and then he quite deliberately met my gaze. (This interpretation falls in the category of "understandings." A more evocative interpretation might have been to punctuate and end the session by asking, "What shape do you want to bring here?")

Mr. X. began to actively check out his father, discovering to his surprise that his father shared some of his "alien" nature: both liked science fiction, and each had separately watched a particular television show. (This search and discovery mission vis-à-vis his father seemed to be an outcome of the prior interpretation.) A shared ritual was soon begun of watching this particular television show with his father.

Over time, a different kind of woman also began to appear in his fantasies, although by this point in time the fantasies were receding from the center of his psychic life. In these fantasies, Mr. X.'s Eros was not by proxy via another heroic character, nor did the woman really need rescuing. In fact, in some of his fantasies the female character was more of an action figure than he was. This newly emergent female character of his fantasies, he said, was modeled on a character of an older woman doctor in the television show he and his father viewed together. As he described this he turned to look at me with a shy, but decidedly seductive, smile. I dare say we both felt the jouissance of embodiment in that moment. We both laughed, no doubt as its expression. He went on. From this period forward, Mr. X.'s engagement with what he wanted from his girlfriend, what he wanted to give her, and what he wanted versus what his parents wanted for him, decidedly quickened. In one of many of life's paradoxes, as Mr. X. claimed his desire, he could more fully embrace a receptive/passive position as organized by a primary feminine identification.

In this treatment Mr. X. became what many would describe as more embodied, in that he moved into inhabiting his male body less ambivalently. Nonetheless, it could be said that at another level he remained in a primary feminine identification, in Lacan's (1972) terms. One indication of this was that his basic distrust of words remained. It was a palpable experience for him, as for anyone with a primary feminine identification, that however empowering words are, there always remains something beyond the words, which also needs to be acknowledged.

In resuming his sexual life with his partner, Mr. X. was more able to find greater safety and pleasure in the link between his sexuality and aggression—a link that had previously terrified him. Mr. X.'s assemblage of his male sex, his feminine identification, reshape, if you will, particular cultural definitions for his male gender, and his heterosexuality speaks to the fact that every oedipal solution need not add up to an equation of complementary terms. One's identification need not fix or prescribe an opposite object choice, as in male subject = masculine identification, and therefore female object choice. In Mr. X.'s case, we see a mixing of oedipal imperatives, and an increase in embodiment and jouissance as an outcome.

CLOSING DISCUSSION

Early emotional development is contingent upon how well the symbol is anchored in the Imaginary body. This anchoring provides the means whereby a coherent sense of self can become established in a working partnership with external reality (Winnicott 1945, 1965). Metaphorically speaking, throughout infancy, during the process of parental care, layers of acoustic letters, images, and later words accumulate upon and in the body—especially around the body openings. They become the psychic stuffing, so to speak, of our psychic body. Not unlike the Internet, some somatic sites get more attention than others, and body openings are where most exchanges between inside and outside occur. The emotional tones, as well as the meanings each parent gives to the infant's body, its products, and its functions as a female or male body, all influence how the patterns of these various symbolic elements will become internalized. What is internalized may be likened to something like an irrigation system carrying and directing the flow of bodily drives, or "surplus-jouissance." Hopefully, this psychic irrigation system works well enough, especially in actual interaction with others, because there is always some difficulty involved in maintaining one's narcissistic integrity while in discourse with another as the disturbing currents of bodily drives are ongoing. If one's psychic system doesn't work well enough, there can be psychic blockage—causing somatic symptoms, or spillage—and resulting in overwhelming affects, thoughts, and impulsive actions. It could be said that Ms. Y.'s psychic irrigation system was blocked in some areas and spilling over in others, while in the case of Mr. X. there was primarily blockage where all of his aggression could only exist in fantasy or be directed toward himself.

As to how this infant body-ego (Freud 1914, 1923, 1924) or this irrigation system is related to the adult erotic body, let me offer a supplemental metaphor to the psychic irrigation system. Imagine that when a baby is born she or he is in the shape of a pine or fir tree that is commonly used to make a Christmas tree. The parents, as members of our particular culture, have a limited selection of lights (much as each culture has a dominant language with a limited number of words or signifiers and meanings) that they may use to organize and raise their child—or, in this metaphor, to decorate the tree. (This shape—that of the Christmas tree—reflects a social reality that Christianity is the dominant religious institution in the United States.) When a sufficient number of lights have been attached to the tree, we would be able recognize this particular tree, when the lights were illuminated, as distinct from all others by the particularity of the pattern of lights. Think of this unique pattern of lights as only another metaphor for that psychic irrigation system we spoke of earlier. The lights framing the tree are akin to a baby's having formed a working body-ego within the matrix of parental care. The electrical current running through the wire and its pattern of lights correspond to how a body-ego functions as an irrigation system moving the energy/jouissance of the drives throughout the psychic body—a body that functions as an interactive template laid over the organic body. Whenever the baby, toddler, or child becomes excited, these lights would perhaps blink or get brighter. But if there have been problems in the initial stringing of the lights—that is to say, the parents' interpretation and responses to infant need were somehow inadequate—there may be too few strings of lights, leaving significant holes in the overall lighted gestalt of the tree. Or if the wires carry too much current of adult aggression and/or sexuality, some of the lights may be strained to the point of burning out. (Circumstances such as these foster Green's [1998] "destructive work of the negative" where early primitive psychic defenses that have destructive effects upon relations with others remain primary ways to regulate the self.) In an actual child, unlike on a tree, there would be more strings of lights encircling the body openings—the places of most exchange between inside and outside. During the oedipal years, the Imaginary body-ego (original pattern of the set of lights) becomes consciously woven into language and verbal thinking, while the imagistic and protosymbolic elements of the body-ego are repressed and become part of an unconscious landscape.

Lacan posits that letters of the signifier/words spoken by mother/father to the infant function as the constituent material used in the making of his/her founding identification. In other words, the infant subject's body-ego includes language—in the form of the sounds of the letters delivered via the parental voice, with its tone, inflection, and so forth—that has a set of palpable effects upon the Imaginary body. These effects are then transferred into/onto the biological body via transmission by the Imaginary or body-ego's being constructed. This, then, is the beginning point of the building of a symbolic chain that will encircle the place of the subject as she/he strives to articulate her-/himself. He/she begins with a series of letters, usually the name, as in Megan or Tom, and expands over time by adding more and more symbolic elements. In later development (oedipal passage) the ego is articulated in language via words/signifiers that generate meanings, but it is the infantile situation that sets up the conditions for repetitions involving desire and drive satisfaction. This early original identification with an unconscious fantasy, promising a wholeness/one/all/unity, adds a layer of verbal rationalization when the subject moves through the oedipal and postoedipal passages.

To continue along in linear time concerning erotic enlivening of the body, when the child enters puberty the sexual maturing of her or his physical body brings another reorganizing dimension to the body-ego or psychic body. Usually there is something special reserved for decorating the top of a holiday tree, and it is often put in place last. When this final ornament is put in its place, there is a retroactive reorganization of how the Christmas tree is visually perceived—all the lights now seem to direct attention to the top of the tree. When an adolescent sexually matures, it could be said that another amperage of jouissance comes into play. The current of genital adult sexuality infuses the wires and lights, adding a new quality of intensity or brightness. This added electrical amperage or intensity, combined with the added special decoration at the tree top (i.e., mature genitalia), then retroactively reconfigures the tree/body under a new placard: "adult sexuality." Thus it could be said that the same tree, with the very same lights, becomes yet something more. Therefore, if the infantile body-ego consists of too few lights or they are not stable somehow, psychic distortion, dysfunction, and various symptoms will inevitably ensue when his/her maturing body turns on the adolescent's libidinal current. That something along these lines occurred with Ms. Y. seemed quite evident. (Such symptoms can also occur prior to adolescence when a child is subjected to the intrusion of adult sexuality.) For Mr. X., his physical maturation via increased testosterone levels complicated the expression of his sexuality in the context of a strong conscious pacifist identification. The stage for a battle was then set out in his fantasy life.

Ms. Y.'s mapping of sexuality was in some ways more complicated than Mr. X.'s. Her sexual desire more strongly encircled the female, rather than the typically expected male sex, as her preferred sexual object. One psychoanalytic view of female homosexuality has been that it is a regressive return (fixation) to the preoedipal maternal body (e.g., Friedman and Downey 1998, Kristeva 1989, Quinodoz 1989). When desire for an other is in fact collapsed into identification with sameness rather than an encounter with Otherness, sexual desire is surely eclipsed. This perspective, then, does not account for any sustained female homosexuality. An alternate psychoanalytic formulation is one representing female homosexuality as one woman's desiring an other female, but from the psychic position of a man (Freud 1905,1920b). This formulation retains and establishes the quota of difference or Otherness needed to fuel and sustain sexual desire, but is less than satisfactory or complete enough to include those women for whom a masculine identification (in Lacan's or Freud's terms) seems not operative. A more recent formulation has been to reframe and take the invisibility out of female desire by calling the negative oedipal complex the "primary maternal oedipal situation" (Elise 2002), or to offer alternative dynamic formulations (Aron 1995, Burch 1993, de Lauretis 1994, McDougall 1995). Female homosexuality may also be fueled by a desire for the jouissance of the Other. See Lacan's (1972) graph on sexuation in Seminar XX as the additional component of the subject in a feminine position (Patsalides 1992).

Sexual desire is by definition only inflamed and sustained by a discovered Otherness in the desired one (via projection of one's own piece of the Real causing desire—the "object a"), a critical legacy of the oedipal passage. In lesbian desire, Otherness is not anatomically concretized in terms of genital complementarity as it is or appears to be in heterosexual relationships. But neither is anatomical difference itself enough to sustain the psychic difference needed to fuel sexual desire over time. For men or women who desire and love women, if the psychic reality of that relationship is primarily situated in a preoedipal world (body of mOther), the result will be an inevitable diminishing, if not cessation, of sexual desire over time. This diminishing occurs because there is a return to too much sameness in psychic position, too little differentiation, and not enough real Otherness to oxygenate desire's flame—a flame dependent upon a space, a gap—existing between two subjects. Thus until Ms. Y. became able to reliably recognize and encounter another individual as an Other subject with her own desires, her romantic relationships (with men or women) were brief and for the most part disappointing affairs.

In terms of the very notion of Otherness, when Lacan (1972) said there is no sexual relation it was his way of saying that as far as Plato's mythical beings who were cut in half and left longing and searching for the missing half were concerned, there will never be another half that can make any of us a One. We are each inscribed by the symbol in a unique way. A male and female may fit together in terms of biological reproduction, but any popular book on sex will confirm that male and female sexuality and its aims do not fit, so to speak. The point here is that there may be two people who can create another through reproduction, but there is never another person, however much longed for, who can make of us a One. Apart from the most general symbolic inscriptions that are internalized by individuals within the parameters of each culture, the unique specificity of how each individual's body and mind (including sexuality) is refracted through the

Symbolic is such that there exists an unbridgeable singularity and difference from one person to every other person (only bridged by the collusion of fantasy).

When the unconscious pulses to make a tear in one's own ego fiction, it is often experienced as a gap or hole in the illusion of wholeness that the ego carries for us. Yet because there is a need for an illusion of wholeness for daily functioning, the gap in being usually disappears quickly, and the voice of the unconscious goes silent again. The fading of the self as a subject in a mutual sexual moment is or can be, at one level, a very welcome relief from the everyday demands of staying in one's own psychic skin, bravely bearing the traumas of separations, and suffering the division the symbol makes in the human being.

It could be said that Martin Buber (1958) spoke of an I and thou—not a me and you—because the me and you are in the realm of necessary illusions of wholeness (primary repression), where the other is a subjective-object of fantasy (like mother once was), in which we use them psychically to seal over the separations and divisions in our being. In contrast, I and Thou are in the realm of one subject to another subject. Here, as Lacan (1964) put it well, one loves another for what s/he doesn't have but that which we project to make the person desired in the first place, and s/he accepts, sometimes lovingly so, to stand in that position (of being the object a as cause of desire). But beyond this, I would say that one desires and loves the chosen other as a subject for how he/she has etched him-/herself around the particularity of his/her losses, lack, and a death not yet.

Lacanian theory can[16] function to remind, and/or orient, the analyst to the fact that any two subjects (each being Other to the other)—of the opposite or same sex—may co-create, if not procreate, in a psychic and sexual encounter. The categories of psychosexual identification, sexual difference, sexual object choice, sexual aims, gender definitions and roles (which are cultural-historical productions of the interplay of two structural positions vis-à-vis symbolization) are each different threads. These threads must be knotted together and psychically woven or linked within the symbolic net of current society—even if this link is to take a position at or beyond the net's margins as outlaw. The marginal link to society's sym-

16. Lacanian theory can also be used to reinforce traditional patriarchical categories as well.

bolic net is the sense that the subject's oedipal knotting may not be normative, but nonetheless there remains a relation to the symbolic netting as a necessary coordinating structure. In these postmodern times, if the analyst can keep in mind that sexual difference, object choice, sexual aim, gender, and psychosexual identification are different threads, knotted within a linking function, the struggling analysand can have both a secure symbolic framework to work within and the psychic flexibility to work out the multidimensionality of her/his own identity and sexuality.[17]

In the final analysis, each analyst or psychoanalytic practitioner strives to facilitate the positive play of the erotics of the symbol upon the human body and mind. If the analytic encounter works well enough, there is both an adequate symbolic gathering and transformation of psychic conflict and pain, as well as the facilitation of the generative space of desire, that enables the possibility to realize enough Real (drive) satisfaction—all of which is played out within a fruitful encounter with the limits of symbolization. This dialectic between possibility and limits is perhaps no better illustrated than in the oedipal knotting that is necessary to enable the uniqueness of any subject/person's desire to emerge and be claimed in her/his own unique way. The living stories of Ms. Y. and Mr. X. illustrate potential variations among workable oedipal compromise formations. In the end, the dialectic between the psychic stability that symbolization can provide, and the possibilities and the hollow of desire that the symbol leaves in its wake, defines the space in which the erotics of the symbol must indeed live.

POSTSCRIPT

The next time I saw Mr. X. was approximately seven years later (he was now 30). He called for an apppointment because he had had a return of depressive symptoms. When he arrived for his appointment he was dressed in the manner of Keanu Reeves of the film *The Matrix*, and he told me he had just recently bought a black BMW Z3 as a present to himself when his "ship came in." He went on to explain that during the past seven years he and his closest friend had established a computer software company that they

17. See also Green's *Chains of Eros* (2000) for another formulation of sexuality as an erotic chain composed of a series of different formations.

had recently sold for several million dollars. Until these last few months, the focus of his life had been work. His relationship had ended a few years earlier, in part due to his commitment to making the company work. His current postpartum depression was not unexpected—even to him. He asked if we could meet weekly for a few months so that he might explore what he wanted to do next in terms of his life. I agreed. A couple of months later Mr. X. did not show for his regular appointment and had not called to cancel. Shortly thereafter I received a phone call from his father, who said that his son had been killed in an automobile accident. At his parents' request, and with deep sadness, I attended his memorial service.

5

When a Body Stutters: The Girl with Two Names

> ***A baby is an instinctual being living all the time on the brink of unthinkable anxiety.***
>
> **(Winnicott 1962a)**

When she telephoned for an initial appointment, she stuttered throughout her message, especially when speaking her name.

"I haven't been able to feel any sexual feelings. It is like my body is dead since summer when I was in Europe and felt threatened into having sex with a guy I was traveling with. I didn't even like him that much. I just don't want anyone to touch me. It doesn't feel like my body anymore. I can't even remember what my body did feel like. I don't know what I want in my life anymore."

These are the words of Tracy, a 19-year-old woman who felt cut off from her sexual desire, her body, and her own life as she had imagined it becoming. Only a frantic pace of journal writing and painting had enabled her to keep herself "glued together" during the last few months of a year abroad—and she was no longer sure she could keep it going as fall semester began.

The degree and nature of the anxiety and bodily dissonance suffered by Tracy raised provocative questions: When is one's body one's own? Does one's body ever just belong to one's self? What is the relationship between one's body as ego/psychic envelope and one's actual biological body? And what of one's sexual body? In this chapter I wish to explore these questions in two parts. In Part 1, I offer a theoretical discussion of several issues related to the body-ego and the psyche-soma: (1) how the symbol is a basic "building material" in structuring the human infant, (2) the significance of the place of necessary illusion in the mother–infant couple for the infant's making of an ego-body, and (3) the links between the body-ego of the once infant and the psyche-soma of the present-day sexual adult. In Part 2, I offer a description of the psychotherapy with Tracy for whom all three of these issues were in play.

PART 1

The Symbolic Third in the Making of a Body-Ego

From the moment a pregnancy is known, a third enters the prenatal scene through a woman's imaginings of her yet-to-be-born infant, as some "one" who will be an Other to herself. These unspoken fantasies are crucial elements in weaving a baby's safe, or not so safe, psychic net. The threads a mOther[1] uses to weave such a psychic net are not random—they are culturally and familially determined. Each culture has its own consensual expectations of how the world is to be ordered. Included in this set of expectations are cultural/symbolic codes for maternal care, as well as other social codes of behaviors that each mOther is in relation to (Muller 1996). All of these elements that precede the baby, but may be used in the weaving of the psychic net that will hold and delimit him, can be collectively referred to as the Symbolic Third (see Chapter 3, this volume).

A particularly impactful facet of this Symbolic Third concerns mOther's degree of integrative thinking and feeling capacities, that is, to what extent she is able to allow, to give form to, and to express experience, and to what extent is she able to recognize and respect the psychic boundaries of another person. These qualities of "thirdness" set the parameters for the affective and symbolic containment available to the infant within the mother–infant relationship (Bion 1962b). This symbolic containment, in turn, calibrates the degrees of psychic separation that are possible for that baby. While mOther must be able and available to function as a container for that baby, at the same time it is imperative that she psychically recognize her baby as "not-me" to herself, through how she speaks to, touches, and cares for her infant. Thus, simultaneously, mOther is the first object relation, but also the first Other—the first representative of the Symbolic net into which the infant is born and within which he/she must make an identity.

---

1. Reminder: mOther represents the mother as object and the mother as representative of the big Other of symbolization.

The Symbolic Third is that inextricable web of preexisting symbols—images, language, and cultural codes—into which each baby must place him-/herself with the help of others in and beyond the family. The psychic structure, introduced by symbols, structures the human being's experience as being wholly apart from pure instinctual satisfaction like the rest of the animal kingdom. The combination of mOther's active attention to and interpretation of the baby's needs, and the baby's receptivity, necessarily make for an ordinary primal seduction of the baby into the symbolic network, as Lacan (1953) or Laplanche (1995) might say. Or, as Winnicott (1960, 1962a) might say, there is a seduction by the mOther of bringing the baby into the peculiar aliveness of the human condition that is inextricably entangled within a Symbolic network.

We can chart an infant's progression with respect to his/her taking up a position within the Symbolic as follows: In a matter of weeks after birth, a semiotic code, a kind of working third, will already have become established between mOther and baby in their day-to-day interactions (Muller 1996). This semiotic code refers to the setting of a certain rhythm, cadence, and set of expectations in an interaction as to what will follow what. When mOther violates this semiotic rule, the baby will react to its violation. Baby will first repeat his/her signal, then escalate again if mOther does not respond. Finally, the baby will begin to psychically fall apart in a regressive and/or aggressive manner if there is no answer from the mOther. This semiotic thirdness is not conscious in the usual sense; it is not the stuff of the mental space required for thinking, which comes later. It is, instead, the beginning of the baby's encountering the thirdness of the symbol and the trail of jouissance[2] it leaves as an excess in the body (Lacan 1960, 1964), and her/his beginning to relate her-/himself to these. This excess trail of energy contributes nothing to the homeostasis of the infant body as an organism per se, yet nonetheless it is a part of what the human infant must come to terms with in this life called the human condition.

The baby's encounter with thirdness begins something like this: Inevitably there will be a space—a partial miss, as it were—between a baby's call and a mOther's interpretive response, because mOther's own mind is split in two, into conscious and unconscious responses. For example, the baby wants to explore the world by looking around, but mOther, because

2. Symbolization does not entirely capture (nor will it ever capture) the whole of a human being's experience. That which is uncaptured by language, and therefore left over as energy remaining in the body, is called *jouissance* by Lacan.

of her own conscious/unconscious division, interprets the call as meaning something else. Or, the baby needs to feed, but there is an unconscious communication from mOther that the breast is, for her, first a sexual object, even as she is offering it consciously as a source of nourishment and comfort to her baby. Thus, mOther's responses to her baby's cries will always remain in part enigmatic to the infant (Laplanche 1995).[3]

Nonetheless, the mOther is urgently needed as a subject by the infant because the quality of the misses—between the infant's signal and mOther's interpretation—has crucial effects upon the baby's construction of what Freud (1914, 1923) refers to as a body-ego, Kleinians, a psychic skin (Anzieu 1985, Bick 1968), or Lacan, the Imaginary ego (1951, 1953b). The effect of the quality of the miss is felt in terms of how the baby pulls his or her bodily experiences together via identification with the mOther. The mOther's recognition is key in this process. If the baby is not recognized as a person coming into being in his/her own right and held in the mind of mOther as a separate person whose signals she is trying to understand, the baby will be unable to form a viable psyche-soma separate from mOther's. The infant will remain symbiotically encapsulated within mOther's psyche because mOther will simply provide the baby with what she wants to give rather than attempting to interpret infant need. When this is the case, entry into the Symbolic order of things is foreclosed (Lacan 1955–1956).

On the other hand, if mOther's emotional containment and recognition are profoundly unavailable (for whatever reasons), the quality of the miss between what the baby needs and mOther's interpretation can approach the catastrophic (Bion 1962b, 1967). For instance, a self-alienating armorlike ego-body may be constructed by the infant to protect against too much intrusion or neglect (Ogden 1989, Tustin 1990). This kind of psychic envelope may have tears or holes that exist as knots of excess jouissance. This would mean that what is not sufficiently processed by language, and therefore is left over as energy remaining in the body, would be experienced as nameless/wordless trauma. In such a case, the child's physical body might later in life manifest psychosomatic symptoms related to this disturbance in the making of the initial body-ego, or the infant's mind might develop precociously and come to exist as a thing apart rather than as part of an integrated psyche-soma (Bion 1957, Lacan 1955–1956,

---

3. Laplanche specifically focuses upon the sexual dimension of the excess existing beyond the signifier in his concept of the enigmatic signifier. Lacan does not circumscribe this excess to the erotic.

Winnicott 1945, 1949). (See Chapter 3, this volume, for examples of mOther–infant couplings speaking to these kinds of problems.)

In the baby's making of this first body-ego/psychic envelope, there is, of course, an ongoing dialectic between experiences coming from his/her own internal bodily sensations, and sensory experiences generated in response to something coming directly from the outside world. For Winnicott, an increasing space between the baby and mOther occurs incrementally, whereby the infant knits his/her own psyche-soma together as a unit within which to live (Winnicott 1945, 1962a). For Lacan (1953), the knitting together of the body-ego/psyche-soma occurs through an organizing fantasy shaped by the mOther's desire, which the infant uses. In other words, the infant identifies with some aspect attributed to him/her by mOther's fantasy that brings an order. The infant's identification with this outside feature(s) desired by the mOther (Lacan 1951) is comparable to Bion's notion of how the mind can organize via "selecting a fact" around which a psychic structure can be built (Bion 1962b, p. 72). Identification with the object is at the bottom of every person's relation to the object. (If a death drive can be posited, perhaps it proceeds from the human infant's willingness to lend him-/herself to actually being psychically annihilated by becoming the object of mOther's desire and enjoyment.) In this respect it can be said that every baby's body-ego/psychic envelope becomes constituted by first becoming an object for the mOther (Lacan 1953b, 1954)—before ever becoming a lived body of a subject who is in touch with his/her embodied needs and desires.

It should be noted that a mOther's symbolic interpretation does not, indeed cannot, ever entirely capture (nor will symbolization ever capture) the whole of a developing infant being's experience. That which is uncaptured by language, and therefore left over as energy, remains as "jouissance." Inherent, then, in this critical task of constructing a body-ego/psychic envelope is the infant's work of organizing these trails of energy/jouissance in his or her body left in the wake of mOther's symbolic interpretation of the infant's needs and wishes.[4] The infant's collecting of his/her own islands of sensory experience into a boundaried entity involves constructing a fantasy that serves, in part, to regulate the ongoing sensory experiences within his/her infant body. (It could be said also that

4. An excess jouissance in the body that manifests as somatic symptoms marks places where the psychic envelope has not been adequately constructed, in that sensory experience has not been symbolically processed or transformed adequately.

once the Imaginary ego forms there is a retroactive attribution of anxiety about falling to pieces—and not a developmental gathering as is being described.) Imagine trails of jouissance as the leftovers of the symbol (that which is uncaptured by language) accumulate on the body, especially around body openings (because these are the locations where most frequent exchanges occur between the body and the outside world). The differing biological instincts associated with these body openings are refracted into drives through mOther's symbolic interpretation of what the baby needs. A crucial implication of this refraction is that even under good-enough circumstances, the body-ego/psychic envelope constructed by the infant never exactly matches the instinctual or the biological body. This discontinuity is ordinarily obscured in "normal" development. However, in acute or chronically traumatic circumstances, any part of the infant body, or any bodily function, can take on the psychic role of an alien part or a persecutory process—a psychic reality that is not uncommon in more disturbed individuals.

A working body-ego/psychic envelope, not unlike regular skin, should provide an adequate boundary between inside and outside, while also remaining supple and semipermeable. Holes or tears in a developing body-ego/psychic envelope can occur when infantile traumas are simply too great to bear (Grotstein 1991). Alternatively, a hard and brittle "second psychic skin" (Bick 1967, p. 185) may be constructed by the infant as a protective buffer against repetitive trauma (i.e., too much jouissance). Such a psychic skin has a rigid and impenetrable character, so although it offers some psychic protection, it severely limits what internal experience can be expressed and what external experience of the world can be taken in (Grotstein 1991, Mitrani 1992, Tustin 1990). (When Tracy first came to treatment she appeared as if she were wearing body armor. However, in short order, there appeared something else as well—we would run into discontinuities or holes in her psychic envelope, which became evident relatively quickly as knots of acute anxiety.)

Given the ongoing dialectic within the baby—between experiences arising from internal stimuli and those experiences generated as a response to external stimuli—the formation of a body-ego/psychic envelope could be said to occur somewhere between the theories of Winnicott (1962a, 1967) and Lacan (1951, 1953b). Winnicott emphasizes the mOther's crucial recognition of aspects of the baby's true self that facilitates the infant's gathering together of his/her body-ego or psychic envelope with a sense of authenticity; Lacan emphasizes the body ego as an alienating identification with something outside the baby's self. It is a double recognition that the infant requires—emotional attunement and containment (Winnicottian), yes, but also a recognition, given through a pattern of appropriate, though not perfect, parenting responses, that facilitates the infant's becoming able to link into the Symbolic web of the culture into which he or she has been born (Lacanian).

Oedipal Passage: Moving toward Inhabiting a Sexual Body

According to Lacan (1953), the child's early body-ego/psychic envelope is subject to a retroactive reorganization in language as the child passes through the oedipal years. What this means is that one's initial sense of a coherent and ongoing body and self (primarily represented in imagery and fantasy) will become reorganized by identifications linked by, and through, language and speech during the years from 4 to 6. This Symbolic sense of one's self is comprised of the many identifications that reflect taking a named and gendered place within the Symbolic order of the family and of the wider society. For instance, I am the oldest child in my family. I am a girl who in becoming 6 must now enter first grade. When the imaginary body-ego becomes reorganized by and through language, an initial template concerning future love relationships as well as a map of desire and arousal begins to be etched. These will later become activated with the blossoming of adolescent sexuality. Our first Imaginary body-ego organization, along with its associated fantasies, falls under a veil of repression. Under this veil of repression will live the passionate desires that have been solely focused on our parents. But after the veil falls, at a conscious level, there begins a lifetime journey of seeking substitute passionate attachments as sources of satisfaction.

The sexual body only finally matures and takes its place in the human theater of Eros during adolescence or later. In this postoedipal period, the adolescent's conscious awareness of being male or female, his/her unconscious masculine or feminine identification, and the young person's appropriation or rejection of society's gender expectations, must somehow become reconciled within her/his mature sexual body if satisfying intimate relationships are to become possible. I say reconciled here because I am making use of Lacan's (1972a, b) revisioning of oedipal identification as psychic positions within language, that is, that a male may take up a feminine identification in Lacan's terms, be situated comfortably in his male body, but have difficulty with social expectations of how as a man he should be or act. (See Chapter 4, this volume, for an elaboration of Lacan's revision of Oedipus.)

Lacan's recasting of the oedipal passage increases the number of possible oedipal compromise formations (Chodorow 1994) and possible conflicts concerning how the infantile body-ego/psychic envelope, psychosexual identification, object choice, sexual behavior, and gendered role expectations are all woven into the fabric of a viable adult identity. As such, it is actually easier to think about individuals in whom the unconscious oedipal identification is not congruent with their sexed body, but is instead complementary. All these entangled issues were the very nexus of the difficulty for Tracy, the young woman who had been referred to me by a colleague who realized that short-term psychotherapy would be inadequate.

It is not much of a stretch to say that it is the fate of everybody to live life among at least four simultaneous experiences of her or his own body: (1) a singular physical/biological body (birthed in the Real) that one lives within until his/her singular death, (2) a shared body-ego/psychic envelope, first etched in the Imaginary, shaped by the symbolic recognition of the mOther, (3) a sexual body, organized and put into play through the matrix of both oedipal and postoedipal identifications (Benjamin 1991) where the Real, Imaginary, and Symbolic are knotted together, and (4) a female or male body (the Real of sexual difference) that must navigate the currents of meanings tied to sociocultural gender expectations (also knotted in the Real, Imaginary, and Symbolic). The consequences of living a life within these four interrelated contingencies, of course, vary greatly for each person.

Let us return to Tracy's initial complaint:

"I haven't been able to feel any sexual feelings. It is like my body is dead since summer. I just don't want anyone to touch me. It doesn't feel like my body anymore . . . I don't know what I want in my life anymore."

When Tracy first entered treatment, she experienced multiple disturbances at the level of her basic body-ego/psychic envelope, her physical body, her sexual body, and her gender identification. Tracy suffered from what I would call "deficits of recognition" from preoedipal (or early oedipal period, according to Lacan and Klein), oedipal, and postoedipal periods of her life. A brittleness reflecting an armored psychic skin characterized Tracy's psyche-soma when she first entered treatment. This presentation dominated the early period of our work together. Only after a hard-won foundation of trust had been established between us could the more primitive and deeply disturbing experiences of punctures or discontinuities in her psychic skin become acknowledged and spoken of within the treatment. So, despite her initial presentation of loss of sexual desire and confusion about what she wanted from her life, Tracy's body-ego (which radiated simultaneously intense "stay away" anxiety and the demand for close contact) required attention before these other concerns could be addressed.

Oftentimes in the clinical literature, clinical issues such as the ones I am describing occur only in the context of three or more sessions-per-week analyses. But there are times when, due to a combination of factors such as age, ripeness for change, and the nature of the analytic dyad itself, that reconstructive work can be possible within a twice-a-week analytic frame.

PART 2: THE PSYCHOTHERAPY WITH TRACY

Thirdness, the Frame, Attunement = the Possibility of Containment

At her first appointment Tracy failed to turn on the signal light to notify me of her presence in the waiting room. I waited, but then I had the sense she might be there. Rather than waiting for her to discover her mistake or possibly to leave, I decided to go look for her. I did not know if this was an intuitive response to her subjectivity or an expression of my own eager anticipation of the possibility of a new patient who had been referred by a valued and respected colleague. Toward the end of our first session, however, I interpreted that perhaps her forgetting to turn on the light switch expressed her wish for me to understand that she needed to be found and seen—but perhaps not exactly in the usual way. She smiled and I was left wondering how or if this "finding" would occur.

Referred to me by a senior colleague whom Tracy had seen briefly, Tracy reported this dream in the first session: She is crossing a river. She has been given some numbers and letters to take to another therapist to whom she has been told she must transfer.[5] She doesn't want to transfer to a new therapist. She then wakes up. So it was that I began a treatment with someone who seemed to not really want to be there, but who brought messages in letters and numbers to be deciphered nonetheless.

---

5. Why it was a jumble of letters became clearer later. Numbers can be associated with a mark where there is a traumatic accumulation of unsymbolized experience that is calling for further symbolization.

Tracy was born prematurely. Her first two months were spent in an incubator. In Tracy's first year of life her mother had a depressive breakdown and was hospitalized for several months, following upon Tracy's father's leaving the family. During mother's hospitalization, Tracy was cared for by her maternal grandmother. As a child, and even as an adult, she experienced a high degree of sensitivity and reactivity on her skin. She did not like being touched and she radiated a feeling of "prickliness," like the sensation of trying to hug a porcupine.

Frame issues needed to be addressed immediately in order to secure even the possibility of a viable treatment. Trips of mine, occurring shortly after our work began, served to repeat her traumatic beginnings. Also, a split soon began to develop in Tracy between me and a parental figure outside the therapy. Although it later became clear how such a split reflected her inner world, at this time it intersected my already amplified concerns about wanting to be a "good-enough therapist" because of how, and from whom, the referral had come. I recommended that we increase our sessions to twice a week. Increasing sessions required Tracy to make her first direct financial request of her biological father. He agreed to help support her therapeutic work, and his financial support continued until she obtained a steady job after college graduation.

Once, in the early months of the treatment, she called over a weekend break and left a message, asking in a rather demanding manner for a double session that coming Monday—"I have too much to say," she said. I responded by asking her to come to her regular appointment time, and if need be, a second session could possibly be scheduled that day. In actuality it became apparent that she didn't really need a second session; she seemed to need to know that there could be a flexible response. Perhaps the infant in her was calling to begin to determine my presence or absence, and whether I would keep her on a rigid feeding schedule?

Second-Skin Armor

For several months she came to her session each time with a list of topics that she rigidly went through—effectively keeping me silent and still. She became angry, rejecting, and denigrating if I spoke in an effort to penetrate her wall of words, but she was also vigilantly aware of whenever my attention wavered in the slightest (Mitrani 1992, Ogden 1994). Lacan's (1953b) emphasis upon how one's ego must be continually reconstituted via discourse with anOther was helpful in understanding how tenuous her ego must be that she had to place me in such a rigid or still position within her Imaginary (inner object) world. No doubt this contributed to the fact that for at least two years she would suddenly fall into moments of panic, thinking I would throw her out of treatment because she was "too much," such anxieties often occurring after she had called leaving a message between sessions. This fear of ejection alternated with expressed doubts as to whether I could really help her at all anyway. During this same period I experienced moments of pervasive anxiety, depersonalization, and acute rushes of terror. I only hoped that if I could contain these feelings long enough, the mental space to think about them would open up. Nonetheless, these difficult and disturbing experiences led me to dread our appointments at times in the first years of our work. I also sometimes wondered if I would be able to help her.

The Sounds of Words: Anchoring the Body

It is in this context of acute emotional and bodily states that I am reminded of the work of Ella Sharpe (1940) of the Middle School.[6] Metaphor, she said, evolves alongside control of the body's orifices, such that experiences that are at first entirely embodied in the infant find substitute channels—first in fantasy, then in language and speech. It is in the sounds of the words—their phonemes, letters, and the tone of voice—that language first links up with the body. The letters of one's name as sounds (and elaborated in infantile fantasy) operate to embody the person/subject in her/his name (Concina 2002).[7] Language must therefore be anchored first in the body, before it can make its way to symbolic meaning through the capacity to make metaphor. Metaphor in turn can do two things: (1) create something entirely new in language, and (2) evoke that which is beyond what words can capture of human experience. This grounding of speech in the

6. Lacan elaborated this territory later. He makes the point that there are various aspects of language—the materiality of language and letters of the body residing in the Imaginary world of our inner objects. Metaphor and the possibility of creating new meaning reside in the Symbolic dimensions of language in speech.

7. In like manner, the writing and rewriting of a word that has the effect of reworking meanings does so, in part, by the sound plus the sound triggering a phantasmatic element wrapped around it—in this way both sound and the imaginary elaboration are closer to what we think of as being real or Real than simply a polyvalence of meaning.

Imaginary body was how I attempted to anchor myself while listening to Tracy's speech, which I knew carried not only repressed material but also her disturbing infantile experience.

I decided not to set any limit during the six years I saw her on the number of calls she might make to my answering machine. It was my intent in doing so that my voice would always be available to her for psychic wrapping—as a relational object to be used. But while I did not limit the number of calls, or her requests for me to return calls, I did limit the actual time of any conversations that occurred in order simultaneously to hold the symbolic function of providing limits and to support a secure frame.[8] Sometimes I set this limit verbally, sometimes not, depending upon the relational matrix of the moment. The nature, rhythm, and frequency of her telephone calls followed the ebb and flow of the treatment. These telephone calls were not explicitly discussed as such until much later in the treatment, when attention to them would not be experienced as an annihilating attack.

Transferential Landscapes

The first transference dream appeared four months into the treatment. She ran into me at an ice cream store (I am a cold breast?). I am warm and touch her arm as we greet each other in the store; she likes it, but it feels too sensual. The person behind the counter waits on me first and does not seem to recognize her—even when reminded that she and Tracy had known each other in the past. Tracy also does not know what flavor ice cream she wants. In working with this dream, it seemed to suggest both oedipal and preoedipal worlds, marking her infantile longings, but also saying something about intrusive adult sexuality, and about how very difficult it was for her to identify with any position from which she might desire.

A very significant association to this dream was that of a strong visceral memory from latency age—of mother coming to tuck her into bed, smelling of sex and hugging her too tightly and too long. This seepage of

8. Insofar as limits are maintained by the analyst/therapist, within a good-enough holding experience, the necessary conditions are being established for the voice to later function as a partial object to support the desire of the analysand.

adult sexuality was accentuated, I found out later, at Tracy's age 12, when her biological father, who had been called Mr. G. by mother, reappeared on the family scene wanting to see Tracy. This appearance, combined with her adoptive father's handsomeness, was coincident with (and seemed to provoke the emergence of) verbal conflict between her and her adoptive father. At least in part, these conflicts appeared to be needed, to keep at bay her transgressive oedipal wishes toward her adoptive father (and father's toward her). As if to further intensify Tracy's oedipal position, Tracy's mother's second marriage began to disassemble at this same time, placing Tracy in a triangulated position with respect to the two parents.

The Imaginary Body-Ego Reorganized by and through Language

It was not until the second year of treatment that Tracy discovered, through a conversation with her mother, that when the mother had remarried (when Tracy was between 2 and 3 years old), not only had her last name been changed to that of the adoptive father but her first name had been changed as well. In effect, then, her body-ego was initially organized around a different name, a different set of letters, a different set of sounds, if you will, that later became overlaid by a name attached to entirely different letters, sounds, and meanings.[9] In thinking back to Tracy's first transference dream in which she did not know her desire, I wondered to what degree an acoustic dissonance living within her body contributed to her difficulties.

During the first year of our work (her last year of college) a "parental couple" became established in her mind between one of her college professors and me. I essentially became the abandoning, intrusive, uncomprehending mother, while a world-renowned professor (who mentored her through the process of developing a narrative analysis of the series of drawings she had collected from her traumatic trip to Asia) became the idealized father. The creative narration she completed became a numinous text of images and words that we would return to throughout the treatment as holding and linking many aspects of herself.

---

9. The letter is for Lacan (1953, 1972a) an element of the Real—it means nothing in itself, but provides the material base of language.

Without Adequate Symbolic Meaning, the Body Talks

Near the end of the second year of our work, two coincident occurrences—(1) a dream, and (2) the patient's development of skin rashes—directed my attention to the dialectical tension between her psychic skin and her physical skin as an actual body surface. Somatic symptoms can reside in different bodies, so to speak. At the infantile or psychic envelope level, somatic complaints indicate insufficient gathering of the psyche-soma through the organizing medium of symbolization: image and fantasy.[10] As a result, there is too much jouissance or anxiety living in the actual body, which has not been corralled by the symbol/signifier. At the oedipal level, somatic complaints are linked directly to symbolized fantasies and/or ideas that *have been symbolized and repressed* but make themselves known through their return by a somatic symptom. In this case the somatic symptom will follow the path of the symbol/signifier—that is, a limb paralysis will correspond to the words, not to the reality of how the body's nerves are known to function biologically. (For example, a person has a disturbing aggressive fantasy of hitting—thus he/she dis-arms him-/herself.) Thus, throughout her treatment, I viewed Tracy's intermittent somatic symptoms through two filters: one, that of her actual body and initial psychic envelope as they bespoke infantile trauma; the other, that of her personality structure as hysterical.[11]

To return to the content of the dream fragment, it was as follows: Tracy and I are in a room; I am holding some red underpants and a slip for her. The dream ended before she was able to retrieve her red underpants and slip as images of adult sensual sexuality. This incomplete ending seemed to speak to the fact that work at the level of her infantile psyche-soma was needed first before such a claim could be actualized.

The following memory emerged that contained elements of her multiple losses—beginning with her premature expulsion from the womb. As a budding adolescent she was in a parked car arguing with dad. In his anger he reached across the passenger seat, opened the door, and pushed her

---

10. See the discussion of Lecours's levels of symbolization, Chapter 6, this volume.

11. The hysterical structure is one in which the repressed sexual libido often shows up in somatic symptoms. Lacan added the interesting element to understanding neurotic structures by saying that the hysteric's personality is organized by the question, "Am I a man or a woman?" In other words, how am I to desire—to be the lover or the beloved? (The obsessive's question is, "Am I dead or alive?" That is, can I feel desire without being killed?)

out of the car upon arriving at the destination. As he did so, she said that she psychically dissociated from her body. In describing this incident, she revealed to me, with considerable embarrassment, that at times she did not really experience her body as being fully linked together in one continuous skin. While the oedipal tension was immediately evident and available in her description of this conflictual event, reverberations of this incident back to her premature expulsion from the womb were slower to make sounds we could hear and understand.

A subsequent dream a few months later revealed the nexus of her oedipal and preoedipal difficulties. In the dream she is waiting for therapy and I say to wait a few minutes. She is talking to a guy although she hadn't really wanted to. In contrast, I am sitting on a bench and talking to a younger man in a relaxed manner—almost flirtatiously. She "becomes mad" because I am not paying attention to her. We then go into session. She has brought with her a "paper bag filled with scraps of paper." A "single letter is written on each piece of paper." She dumps the letters on the floor between us. She then asks me to help her spell her name with the letters.

In exploring this dream, it is said that only I, as the Other, may openly have desire, seek, and find some satisfaction. Her desire is "benched," so to speak. I interpret that in wanting me to help her spell out her name, she is seeking a stable, named position from which she can claim her own desire. I ask what name we are spelling in the dream, her baby name or the 3-year-old's. She stuttered her 3-year-old name—Tr—Trac—Tracy. This is a good example of the retroactive reorganizing effect of language. Despite her having a different name from birth to age 3, her Symbolic identity or oedipal identification is organized around and attached to the name of Tracy. When she speaks the letters of this name, however, the letters fall apart. She needs help at a more primitive psychic level so the letters can hold together adequately enough and not leave somatic symptoms as an excess.

In my own thoughts, but not shared with Tracy, I considered the paper bag and the letters inside as referring to her actual infant body. Once the scraps of letters were dumped into the potential space between us, these letters referred to the fact that the psychic body-ego is hooked to a subject's identity as carried by her/his name. It appeared that she was bringing her infantile fragments to the "talking cure" for a reknitting. In the context of her developmental history, her prematurity, along with the inconsistency of mother's actual presence, plus the change in primary caretaker, had all served to rupture the mother–infant matrix from which a developing body-ego/ psychic skin evolves. There had been a psychological catastrophe (Bion

1967) of huge proportions. At another level, there was also the disturbance of the string of letters in her first name having disappeared from her family discourse at age 3, to be replaced by another name and set of letters. This change made for a kind of dissonant music in her body and an only tentative linkage to her name—as heard in her stuttering.

Regression to Infantile Rupture and Depression

The dream just discussed was followed by a slow descent to a state of deep despair, in which over a period of months she seemed to reenact a return to the time of her birth and of being in the incubator. As I experienced her descent, my own anxiety increased. Would I be able to hold the primitive agonies she was about to experience? One day she called and found me at home.[12] Her emptiness and fear were palpable. It was difficult for her to speak and for me to interpret and assess what her call meant. At one point, when she must have realized I was assessing her suicidality (more to contain my anxiety, as it turned out), she plaintively said, "No, that isn't it. It just feels like—I don't know, something like, do I have the will to live or not. . . . I don't know. " I realized then that it was more about her needing a reliable wrapping presence from me than anything I might say, and that it was likely that it was my voice itself that mattered—less so the words. So I spoke in a quiet tone to how the current situation may be similar to her beginnings, that my too many questions perhaps felt like painful pokes no matter how helpful I might be trying to be. She quieted.

This somatic reaction occurred other times as well. Places on her body would sometimes react in session as if I had pierced her with my words. At first she merely reacted by moving or wincing and could not speak. Then I would stop and ask what had just happened. Since these piercing words were not linked to any meaning that she was aware of as disturbing to her, it seemed that it was the sound of letters or phonemes or the tone of my voice itself. As we began to put these sounds and tones into play between us, we engaged in a game of search and discovery as to which ones had palpable effects. We were actively reinscribing—diffusing and changing their impact—in the banter in the in-between area between us. We constructed a narrative, relating these experiences to where and how she may

12. This case spanned into the early 1990s, when I included my home telephone number as part of the message on my office answering machine. This is no longer so.

have felt assaulted at birth, punctured in the incubator, and so on, and how she might have experienced a depressed and then an absent mother. In a sense these experiences were a known part of her psychic reality, but until now they had been unable to be thought or expressed (Bollas 1987). And yet it can also be said that these relived experiences were being newly created within the lived moments of transference. Where the timeless presence of a particular but formless psychic pain existed, an understanding was co-constructed in the analysis so that she might begin to form a past she could then be able to forget (Green 2000, Kristeva 1996).

The palpable and tragic significance of the early rupture of this mother–infant couple was poignantly expressed in a comment made by her mother in a visit during this period. In response to a question Tracy posed as to how her mother had perceived her level of anxiety as a child, her mother replied, "Oh, you have been anxious as long as I have known you." Tracy and her mother began to become able to speak about the realities of how the early disruptions in their relationship during Tracy's infancy had truly caused severe difficulty for each of them individually, and in their relationship to one another. As this happened, the rage Tracy had often exuded toward mother (and others who psychically occupied a maternal position) began to dissipate, and other feelings became possible.

Some months later we experienced a disjointed session where Tracy's perception of what was inside her versus what was inside me was in a state of painful confusion and disconnection. In the midst of that session, she suddenly looked at my hand as I gestured and said, "Stop. See how the skin ends at the end of your fingers?" Holding out her own hand to demonstrate, tracing the end of her finger, she added, "I hate that." She continued saying how she hated to be forced to see, and thereby to experience, an excruciating separateness from me. It was shortly after this that we switched from face-to-face work to using the couch. (Earlier in the treatment she had commented to me that she could not imagine using the couch because not to see me would be to feel like I wasn't there.) Watching my hands gesture, she became acutely and painfully aware of our separate skins and boundaries; she wanted us to be in one skin. I would surmise from how I carried her in my mind during this time that, at moments, we were as if inhabiting one psychic skin.

A fantasy she carried during this same period was a wish to take me underground with her and "just be there awhile," saying she felt she had never really had someone with her in quite the way she felt me with her now. I heard in this statement her longing to return to the maternal womb—

to perhaps catch up on those two months she had missed. As a premature infant she had really not been ready for this human life. I did not speak this as an interpretation because it was my view that to do so would have made words into an annihilating assault upon her.

Later I did say to her, however, that perhaps sexual intimacy had always felt so dangerous for her in part because she was at risk for falling into one of the holes in her skin—and that she would cease to exist somehow. This was resonant to her. She experienced her earlier sexual encounters as times when she consciously felt anxious and would often need to dissociate. We understood that her place in these encounters sprang more from an unconscious wish to fuse with the Other—to start over, if you will. Sexual desire as an experience of true psychic separation and recognition of difference had yet to be fully born.

Words as Transitional Phenomena

Tracy is the only person I have worked with who unconsciously picked up certain words or phrases of mine and used them as transitional objects (Winnicott 1953) in a consistent way over time. Seemingly out of nowhere, she would begin using a word or dropping in a phrase that I knew to be my own. This would go on for a period of time and then, without any fanfare, it would disappear from her speech. A little while later a new word would pop into her discourse. This behavior lasted over a period of six to eight months and then stopped altogether.

Her movement from needing the consistent presence of an Other to beginning to be able to use the particularities that are singularly my own (Winnicott 1969a) became more clearly evident when she talked about a confusing experience she was having in one session. She said that she felt alienated by my external persona of blond blue-eyedness and tailored clothes—she would never dress in the same way. And yet, she felt my emotional presence and was aware of my reliability over time. "How can people so different also be so connected?" she asked.

Sexuality and the Oedipal Nexus

It was three and a half years into treatment when she began to notice my sexuality and femininity with curiosity, not only as an intrusion of my subjectivity arousing anxiety and/or envy. She felt a lack of confidence in her own femininity, and wanted help. She tried dating for the first time again. The red underwear I had been psychically holding since the earlier dream could now begin to be taken back. Her complex family configuration—having two fathers, and a mother who was significantly absent during her infancy, only to be so sexually present later as to crowd out Tracy's own emergent sexuality—all came to the transferential foreground. Erotic transferences slowly emerged bit by bit.

"It sounds crazy," she said one day, "but I get confused sometimes about whether I am a woman or a man, and even whether you are a man or a woman." For example, she imagined that she could be a rival of my husband, whom she had spoken to a number of times when she had telephoned me at my home. Perhaps it could be said that this rivalry came from her taking up more of a masculine position in language—a desire to feel her body in action—as if she were in a competition with him for an active erotic connection with me as an object of desire. Another time she dreamed of us laughing together and talking. In this dream she told me that she had sexual feelings toward me—but now as a woman for a woman—and was uncertain what it meant. In the dream I had said, "Talk about it." I said the same thing in the session. Her use of me as an oedipal third—needing me to recognize her sexuality in its active and receptive modes and her shifting gender identifications—was demanding. Lacan's delineation of masculine and feminine positions vis-à-vis the position of being lover/beloved helped to provide a containing frame in this regard (see Chapter 4, this volume).

In the countertransference, I felt pushed and pulled by her during this time. When she inhabited a feminine position, it seemed that she wanted to hear my words of love and desire about how she was special; when in a more masculine psychic position, she wished to possess me and told me a fantasy of making a physical display of claiming me in the presence of others. I drew on Lacan to try and put words to these two different positions of experiencing desire versus concretizing it in gender roles. In an aggressive but loving way, it seemed that she found needed psychic bits in me that she creatively used (Winnicott 1969a).

In the midst of this oedipal nexus, she noted our generational difference and wondered if it were really possible for her to have the potency of her youthful sexuality without inciting my envious retaliation. This awareness in the transference led her to realize the lack of guidance she had received about sexuality or femininity at home. Seemingly she had been left to piece together her own ideas concerning sexuality from her interpretation of a pervasive sexual atmosphere in the home—and from the hidden pornography she had discovered.

As if following a psychoanalytic text, Tracy initiated a series of conversations with both fathers during this period of work. She discovered that her father's affair with another woman is what had come between her parents before and after her birth. After this revelation, she decided to address her biological father by his first name so as to put her adoptive father, whose last name she carried, more clearly into the paternal position (a position that he had actively sought). She came to see how both fathers had been psychically absent (for different reasons) and unable to take the role of the oedipal father, to confirm her separate identity from mother by receiving her love and desire.

Over time, Tracy changed her hairstyle several times, experimented with different kinds of clothes, and began to wear some make-up as she experimented with different forms of a feminine persona. How to feel herself a woman with a sexuality that was neither intrusively present nor entirely absent: that was her central question. One element in what was to be her incremental embodiment, within a body that she could feel to be more and more her own, was her taking up of yoga. After this rather extended period of work in the treatment, Tracy met a young man with whom she stayed involved until she relocated out of state. Given how the treatment had unfolded, it did not seem unexpected that this young man had been in psychotherapy himself; he appeared to have a more developed feminine identification than many men whom she had met.

Termination

Our psychoanalytic psychotherapy ended at approximately year six. At this point Tracy was able to claim desire, separate from me, and risk pursuing something she had generated for herself. This identifiable object emerged from her experience of having two different jobs and a year of graduate school behind her. She realized what she most wanted to do was architecture. She applied to a school in another location and was accepted.

At the point of termination, Tracy still stuttered her name on occasion, but less frequently, because she had moved more fully into the letters of her name by having taken up a recognized position within the structure of her family of two fathers and in her society. It could also be said that the artistic aspect of the work she pursued evidenced how much she valued life in those spaces between the letters (i.e., the places where the symbol does not reach). She and her mother continued their rapprochement with each other. Each father, through her effortful internal and interpersonal work, had a more separate and different place in her life and mind. During our termination phase Tracy reviewed her journals and drawings from earlier periods of our work. One day she pulled something together for herself when she said: "I have an internal solidity now, a place to rest inside. I have a place to counter the negative critical part of myself that for the longest time was the loudest voice inside me."

At our last session she spoke in a way that reflected a diminished sensory "prickliness" and a more supple psychic skin when she asked if she could hug me goodbye. I said, "Yes." For several years after this termination, I received a periodic postcard telling me of her further psychic and external travels as I remained in my office, in my body, in Berkeley.

Closing Discussion

Despite the fact that Winnicott and Lacan offer quite different ways to conceive of how the infant's body-ego is constructed and its place in human subjectivity, both perspectives facilitated the psychotherapy with Tracy, a young woman who experienced her body as an enigma. The notion that the body-ego or psychic skin can have tears or holes resulting from traumatic ruptures during the infantile period of necessary illusion was very true for Tracy. The Lacanian notion that one's body-ego must be continually reconstituted within an ongoing discourse with an Other—either in reality or in one's own mind—was also very germane. Tracy's pervasively intense free-floating anxiety was the residue of an early infancy wherein she had been subjected to a traumatic degree of impingement by her premature expulsion from the womb and invasive incubator experiences, as well as a later infancy that included the trauma of emotional neglect caused by mOther's depression and hospitalization during her first year of life (Anzieu 1985, 1990, Bick 1968, Tustin 1990, Winnicott 1945). Such historical circumstances fostered the creation of a psychic reality for Tracy wherein the position assigned to any Other in a discourse had to be quite rigid, lest Tracy lose her consistent sense of self or body-ego. Tracy experienced the discontinuity of her body-ego as acute moments of anxiety. When this discontinuity was combined with her actual somatic sensitivities, these interacted to produce intermittent somatic symptoms. Her "prickliness" and periodic skin rashes could be read as writings on her body's surface—as primitive attempts to make a boundary that could limit the traumatic degree of excess jouissance she was subject to. Tracy's experience of her body had never been safe; she had not been able to establish a body-ego that could function as a reliably safe place to live within (Winnicott 1949, 1962a).

Lacan's description of the body-ego as an alienating identification was very much alive in Tracy's stuttered speech. The silent question of her life had always been: Under what name was her own desire to take up residence? Tracy's body-ego included a quality of armoredness, which existed simultaneously with tears or gaps at its surface. These, when combined with an uncertain feminine identification, made the presence of sexual desire anxiety-provoking and, at times, even fragmenting. Thus, sexual desire, which by definition lives and moves in the space between one person's psychic skin and that of another, was for Tracy either fraught with anxiety or devitalized and split off. Her sensuous body and sexuality had never felt integrated, and in fact, she said that her body had never felt like it was truly her own. If there was a measure of change in her day-to-day capacity to allow the vulnerability of emotional risk taking and sexual intimacy, this change occurred because, as Winnicott said, Tracy and I "lived an experience" together (Winnicott 1960, p. 43). This lived experience enabled her to revisit the infantile task of re-collecting fragments of infantile experience and, through reconstructing an infantile narrative, further claim her body as her own (Kristeva 1996, Winnicott 1945).

Postscript

As evidence that the unconscious field is indeed without time and space, I received a phone message from Tracy a few weeks after presenting a version of our work at a conference. In her message, Tracy said she had attempted to send me a card the year before. The card had been returned because I had moved my office. She said she had been thinking about me more in the last few months and suddenly realized she could try calling and ask for my new address. She called. I returned her call and we had a conversation in which she filled me in on her life since I had received her last postcard from some number of years before. When it became clear that her thoughts of me and our work had been especially present lately, beyond serving as something of an internal reference point, I told her that perhaps this was not so surprising since she, and our work together, had also been very much on my mind too because I had been working on a paper about our work. She then asked if she could read my paper. I hesitated but agreed, upon the condition that we have a conversation afterward. I was concerned, I said, that the manner in which I spoke of certain periods of our work might be emotionally provocative and confusing to her. After Tracy had read the paper we did have another telephone conversation. She did voice a range of reactions: She had been "very touched and a bit overwhelmed too," especially reading about my feelings of distress, and remembering, and to a degree, reliving, while reading the paper, that "prickliness and severe anxiety." It had "really felt like a reknitting" of herself in the treatment, she said, and she drew on this during her graduate school years. "Even now," she continued, "I see it as a foundation in myself I can, and do, refer back to." It was gratifying to her to know that *I also* had learned from our work. She resonated with the idea of her psychic skin as armor and when she looked back on that time now, she remembered that armor as "one of the many filters she had to go through in order to actually experience anything." The power of the signifier was also noteworthy in Tracy's comment that her male advisor in grad school was also named Marty. Being able to say and hear this name day to day had always meant something positive to her that she had never entirely understood.

6

Art-Making in Adult Psychoanalysis: When Graphic Language Becomes an Analytic Third Bringing Body to Speech

> ***Language is situated between the cry and silence.***
> **(Green 1999a)**
>
> ***Dread is only memory in the future tense.***
> **(Margaret Little 1990)**

INTRODUCTION

Listening in the "talking cure" is many things: listening to the music, in a manner of speaking—registering the parapraxes, lapses, or sudden stumblings in the analysand's discourse; experiencing the visceral impact of speech, but also the shared silences. All are common elements of the psychoanalytic discourse shared by both members of the analytic dyad (Dor 1999, Fink 1997, Leclaire 1998, Nasio 1998). Spontaneous images and/or reveries drift through the analyst's mind, refracting the discourse through a prism (Bion 1970, Boyer 1978, 1989, Ogden 1989, 1994, 1997, 1997b). These refractions are culled by the analyst for use in the analysis. Such refractions may appear instantaneously, or may be like an object emerging slowly in a darkened room. Sometimes there can be an evocative interpretation, spontaneously describing an image, which captures something, in and between the analysand's words—as surprising to the analyst as it is to the analysand (Bollas 1992, Nasio 1998). In these instances, images or protofantasies (somatic traces as precursors to fantasy) lead to words and then speech.[1]

1. A brief impressionistic pastel drawing by the analyst/clinician, done immediately following the analytic session, can be yet another way of reaching toward form when the residue of the clinical hour escapes, or is simply not yet available to, verbal processing (see Chapter 7, this volume).

In this chapter my intent is to offer a context for the use of "art-making" in adult (versus child) psychoanalysis. Art-making has the potential to express primitive protofantasies of the body, offering potential meaning through its form and color. It can, simultaneously, offer access to more integrated verbal understandings of previously known, or even unthought known, experience. Thus art-making can actually provide a bridge among multiple elements of symbolization comprising the psychoanalytic discourse.

Art produced by any analysand will in some measure always be a co-creation of both members of the analytic dyad, in a manner similar to the way in which certain dreams come to be co-created during an analysis (Apollon 1998, Ogden 1996). It is the meeting in the unconscious field between the analysand and the analyst that shapes the likelihood that art-making may, or may never, become an analytic third in the treatment (Green 1985a, Ogden 1994).

The context for art-making in adult psychoanalysis is situated in the lively interplay between symbolic representation and affect. Conflicting ideas exist as to the relative status of representation and affect in the analytic discourse, as well as to their relation to the unconscious itself. André Green (1999a, b) thinks of affect as a quasi-signifier, insofar as affect has different functions depending upon other contextual elements. Lacan (1953–1954g) and Harari (2001), on the other hand, characterize affect as an effect of language itself and thus as existential.

Despite many shades of difference as to the nature and function of representation and affect, there is a good deal of convergence around the idea that, of the affects, anxiety is the most fundamental to be dealt with in any psychoanalytic treatment. On this, Freud, Klein, Winnicott, Green, Lacan all agree. In the most general way, it could be said that the degree of an individual's primitive or catastrophic anxiety is directly related to the magnitude of intrusion by the Other. This Other can be described as the Other of the Symbolic network itself (Lacan), and the other as the primordial object of infancy (Klein/Winnicott). The intrusion can be Real or perceived. Catastrophic intrusion by the Other also includes intrusion via neglect or absence. As noted by Bion (1962b), it is the absent breast that is the bad breast. Infantile experience involving such intrusions make for a corruption of the very foundation of symbolic speech, and will make treatment significantly more difficult (given that analytic work is a "talking cure") for both members of the analytic dyad.

IMAGE AND LANGUAGE IN THE TALKING CURE

How the analyst conceives of the relationship between image and language, and the nature and significance of each, greatly affects his/her analytic interventions. Freud, Klein, Lacan, Winnicott, Green, and Lecours, whose work I draw upon here, have all contributed to a rich discourse about the place and function of the image versus the word(s) in the "talking cure."

For some in psychoanalysis (e.g., the Kleinians—Bott-Spillius 2001, Hinshelwood 1994, Isaacs 1948) the ego and the image, in the form of the ego's protofantasies, are present at birth. For others, the ego is seen as having to be psychically constructed by the infant. From this perspective, imagery/fantasy develops only after a body-ego or psyche-soma has been adequately constructed. This construction requires a viable meeting and relationship between the infant and the external world of the Other. In this meeting/relationship, the mOther represents both the object world of relationships and the Other as the symbolic network (Freud 1914, 1923, Lacan 1953, Winnicott, 1971).

It is noteworthy that Freud (1915) viewed imagery as a form of representation in its own right. He saw it as different from language, but certainly as psychically potent if not therapeutically useful. For example, in his case of the Wolfman, the Wolfman spontaneously drew his dream during the analysis and this drawing was a significant contribution to the analytic understanding achieved (Freud 1918). The salient difference between image and language in terms of its clinical implication is perhaps best articulated by Freud's (1915) metaphorical differentiation of a Thing presentation from a Word presentation, and the relationship between them. The Thing presentation,[2] he said, "consists in the cathexis, if not of the direct memory-image, of the thing, or at least remoter memory traces derived from these" (p. 201). The Thing presentation thus is a perceptual signifier, meaning that it is closer to immediate experience and remains open to being affected by external and sensory stimuli. In contrast, the Word presentation is a linguistic signifier. The linguistic signifier is one step removed from the Thing presentation and from sensory experience. Word presentations function within a closed system of other separate and differ-

2. Thing presentation follows the path of philosophy of Kant's "thing in itself."

ent Word presentations—therefore the Word presentation is not subject to a continuing influence by the sensory world.[3]

Of particular importance for art-making in adult psychoanalysis is that a pairing of a Word presentation with a Thing presentation in the (preconscious) mind is required before conscious awareness of an idea or verbal processes can be accessed. For example, whenever one encounters either a bizarre or a beautiful object in the Real external world, the mind first references the unconscious realm of Thing presentations to establish whether that object, or something like that object, has ever been psychically registered and represented as a Thing presentation. If there is a Thing registration, the mind then references the existing linguistic network searching for a Word presentation as its paired link. Once the Thing presentation is linked with a Word presentation, verbal processing then becomes possible. For example, the question might arise, "Why is this beautiful sculpture perched on a bus stop bench?" It is only at this point in the encounter that one can begin to process the experience of this encounter with the bizarre or aesthetically beautiful object. For the most part, all of human experience is symbolically mediated. The absence of such (verbally mediated) processing would mean that one would essentially disappear as a reflective subject—even if only for a moment—through merging into an experience of complete "at one-ness" with the object, only to emerge as a reflective person a few nanoseconds later. To be at one with the object is to be immersed in the Real as such—whether that be an excruciating or sublime aesthetic ecstasy.

A different psychic sequence occurs when one experiences an unexpected encounter with a Thing presentation that arises internally. The Thing presentation, being closer to sensory experience, invades one's conscious (ego) mind with intense affect (often negative) and somatic accompaniments (symptoms), but without adequate Word presentations with which to be linked and paired. Without the linkages between Thing and Word presentations, verbal understanding is missing. It is such traumatic circumstances as these that can, and often do, bring the individual to seek psychoanalytic treatment.

The British sector of psychoanalysis has elaborated the theory and technique of symbolization in the context of Thing presentations (or the role of unconscious fantasy), consistent with its interest in the preoedipal

3. See Kaja Silverman's *World Spectators* (2000) for a thoughtful presentation of the libidinal signifier, its link to the visual, and the evocation of beauty.

period and emphasis on primitive mental states (e,g,, Bion 1962b, 1967, Joseph 1981, Segal 1994). The French sector (e.g., Green 1999; Kristeva 1984, Lacan 1974, Leclaire 1998, Nasio 1992) has elaborated the theory of symbolization more on the side of Word presentations (linguistic signifiers) in the analytic discourse, emphasizing Freud's turn toward the importance of language and speech in "the talking cure." (Both of these psychoanalytic perspectives often hold overly rigid boundaries concerning the relevance or possible contributions of one another's perspectives.) The tension between the Symbolic (Word presentations or verbal signifiers) and Imaginary (Thing presentations and images/fantasy) is what is most often highlighted in discussions of difference between Kleinian and Lacanian psychoanalysis. However, it is Lacan's later emphasis on the dialectic between the Symbolic (system of symbols/signifiers whose meaning is generated only in relation to other signifiers) and the Real (that which is beyond the reach of the signifier to represent) that I find most salient to the discussion of the place of art-making in psychoanalysis.

THE PLACE OF THE REAL IN UNCONSCIOUS FANTASY

In the later Lacan (1964), it is stressed that an element of the Real, that of unsymbolized experience, remains embedded within unconscious phantasy. As such, it is as much in the dialectic between the Symbolic and the Real, as in the dialectic between the Imaginary[4] and the Symbolic, that the clinical implications concerning the use of analytic construction and that of art-making take place. In the dialectic between the Symbolic and the Imaginary, words are *found* and returned to *repressed* experiences as labels of a sort; in the dialectic between the Symbolic and the Real, words are created and given to experience that has never been symbolized. Where interpretation is for the Kleinians (Symbolic/Imaginary dialectic), constructions (Symbolic/Real) are for the Lacanians (Freud 1937a). From the Lacanian vantage point, those kernels of Real infantile satisfaction that are at the heart of fantasy can never be fully symbolized—only nibbled at, like "Pac-man." Art-making and the analyst's verbal constructions can function as pac-men at a different level.

4. The Imaginary is the register in which meaning is elaborated via its intersection with the Symbolic.

It is a Lacanian tenet that the kernels of the Real (bits of sensory experience) hold unconscious truths for each subject in terms of her or his desire. There are also times when the Real presents, not as kernels, but insistently as a larger troublesome knotting of traumatic experience (knots of too much jouissance) in need of further symbolization (Lacan 1953d, 1955, 1964). Via either pathway—the pathway of desire or of knotted trauma—the Real must be claimed somehow by the individual and woven into her/his life's narrative. This needs to be a weave that contains not only symbolic threads, but the Real (yet tolerable) gaps/spaces that remain between the threads of the symbolic net (of language). Thus, as an analysis proceeds, the work includes a dual focus. It includes the interpretation of repressed material, which consists of Thing presentations paired with Word presentations (at the intersection between the Imaginary and the Symbolic). But it also includes analytic constructions, which consist of psychic traces of the drive, paired with Thing presentations, paired with Word presentations (at the intersection of the Real, the Symbolic, and the Imaginary). Art-making may bear on all such processes. Art-making, when contained by the analytic dyad, can be a part of a "cutting into the Real" by the analysand in the effort to move toward constructing linguistic links—links that will yield new verbal meanings, but will also leave inhabitable spaces in which play and desire may Imaginatively live.

Each individual has a uniquely etched template of the Real (sensory elements of satisfaction and trauma) that is acquired via the infant–mother relationship, and elaborated by fantasy. The Kleinian notion that primitive anxiety repetitively brings the subject back to the same place would, in Lacanian parlance, refer to the traumatic "knots of the Real." But the nontraumatic aspects of remnants/kernels of Real satisfaction, embedded in unconscious fantasy, also remain as insistent partial objects (e.g., a quality of voice, a look, a gesture or movement, etc.). And these are what evoke desire in the human being. The rationale for interpretation, then, varies accordingly between these two analytic perspectives. In the Kleinian perspective, the focus of therapeutic intervention would be singularly on the residua of trauma and the attendant anxieties generated by these residua. In the Lacanian perspective, the focus of therapeutic intervention would include both aspects of the Real—residua of both trauma and satisfaction. As such, a Lacanian analysis will, at points, respond to the singularity inherent to this particular individual in the context of his/her nodes of enlivening desire—rather than focusing only on trauma.

The infant's movement of instinctual needs is refracted through the Symbolic frame of mOther's care, to be returned to the infant's body as psychic tracings and as kernels of Real satisfactory or traumatic experience. Some of these kernels of Real satisfaction will later be the roots of what causes desire for another (through the projective attribution of these early traces of satisfaction). Yet other kernels, or what might be called snarls of the Real, are trauma. These snarls remain in the body as insistent knots calling for further symbolization.

A further difference between Kleinian and Lacanian perspectives is particularly instructive with respect to art-making in psychoanalysis. Unconscious phantasies for Lacan are tied to an aspect of the Real (drive satisfaction) in contrast to phantasy for Klein. Therefore, unconscious phantasies for Lacan are less appropriately accessed via interpretation, and more via an analytic co-construction—woven by the analytic couple through their evolving discourse.

Considering the dialectic between the Symbolic and the Real rather than the Symbolic and the Imaginary, discontinuities in the analysand's speech (i.e., verbal lapses, parapraxes, blockages, signs of the body) are evocative signposts of something beyond what is the territory of the unconscious of secondary repression. The unrepressed unconscious would be the territory of Freud's primal repression where infantile experience is first registered as psychic traces, or perhaps images, but not linguistically represented. Art-making often enters an analysis here—first as an intrusion of the Real, insofar as the analysand her-/himself does not know "the cause" for the art-making, or why s/he needed to bring the artwork into the session. This bringing of the artwork into the session is a Real intrusion for the analyst also, who does not know what it means in the moment, or what it portends for the analysis. The use, as a starting point, of the interpretation that artwork is a "resistance" can be an effective way for the analyst to evacuate her/his own anxiety with respect to this intrusion.

ART-MAKING WITHIN THE PROCESS OF SYMBOLIZATION

At the risk of creating a bit of chaos for you, the reader, I will be making a bit of my own art by interweaving ideas from both Kleinian and Lacanian perspectives as I approach and discuss the clinical situation of Ms. A., who unexpectedly arrived for her session one day with a piece of art—a collage. In doing so I will be framing Lacan's Symbolic function in developmental terms that actually do not exist in his thinking (and that he might very well experience as a Kleinian/persecutory version of his work). Likewise, I will note where there seem to me to be unnecessary foreclosures of Lacan's contribution to psychoanalysis by the Kleinian school (and who might experience this as an envious attack).

From a Lacanian or structural perspective, the three registers of experience—the Symbolic, the Real, and the Imaginary—preexist the birth of the infant, so in this sense, there is nothing developmental about the Symbolic itself. In day-to-day life, however, we observe the infant develop a symbolic identity in stages over a period of time with the help of mOther and others (see Chapter 3, this volume). The work of Serge Lecours (Lecours and Bouchard 1997) provides a bridge over which the developing infant passes from the sensory to the symbolic. Lecours's elaboration of how sensory elements become mentalized or symbolized brings a synthesis to the elements of image, affect, and speech and language thus far at play in this discussion, and helps frame how art-making may be able to function within the matrix of adult analysis. Lecours's framework elucidates Bion's (1957, 1962b, 1967) theory of thinking with respect to how sensory elements become mentalized or symbolized, while drawing on Lacan's contribution as well. This four-level framework is a useful schema for keeping in mind that it is through the infant's orientation to mOther, as both the primordial object and that of the Other as a symbolic network, that symbolization awakens and moves.

According to Lecours, the first level of psychic elaboration involves expression entirely through the soma and motor activity. At this first and most primitive level of psychic transformation, affect cannot yet be psychically contained. Disruptive implosions/explosions of what Bion (1962b) would call "beta elements," physical movement evacuations, and/or somatic symptoms are the order of things (McDougall 1989). The visceral trail of what the symbol cannot carry is left in the body. This trail of jouissance, along with the pressure of the infant's bodily drives, only becomes regulated through the infant's becoming able to construct a body-ego/psychic envelope. Until that time, beginning at this most primitive level of psychic elaboration, the necessity for containment by an Other who is a fully functional symbolic subject cannot be overstated. Were one to think of an example of art-making in analysis that would correspond to this Level 1 of psychic elaboration, it would be something akin to simple scribblings on a paper. What would stand out in the picture would be the quality of movement of the lines, the quality of the marks on the paper, and not much else. Daniel Stern's (1985) notion of vitality of affects as related to an emergent sense of self would seem to manifest in this kind of art-making.

Lecours's second level of psychic elaboration is in the form of imagery or pictographs. In terms of an art-making metaphor, at this second level of symbolization, it would be as though one were looking at a scribble drawing as if it were a Rorschach, and seeing the shape of, let us say, a cat. In this instance the suggestive form of a line would become Bion's (1962b), "selected fact" (p. 72) around which a mind could organize. This second level is equivalent to Freud's (1895, 1900) primary processes of dreams and fantasies, where some would say that a primitive form of affect containment and thinking becomes possible—in pictograms (Bion 1962b, 1992).

It can be assumed that at this point, the infant's body-ego has come into being through having been at least minimally regulated by the mOther. Despite the fact that a body-ego/psychic envelope is now operative to some degree, symbolization is not yet sufficient to provide the space for internal reflection because the mind is operating only in the realm of Freud's (1915) "Thing" presentations. (The body-ego at this point is Lacan's (1953b) "moi" of the mirror stage or Winnicott's me/not-me boundary.) In this respect, then, the position of an "I" in the Symbolic network cannot yet be assumed, because this would require that identity be constituted by links made among Word presentations or Lacan's linguistic signifiers, which is not yet happening.

An adult verbalizing at this second level of symbolization would speak in a two-dimensional manner, as if words were Things. Here speech would be used primarily to evacuate negative mental states from inside to outside.[5] Here the analyst may feel that the words of the analysand are "bizarre objects" (Bion 1970) that attack her/his capacity to think on the person's behalf. Thus Words are functioning as signs or symbolic equations (Segal 1957, 1994), and not as true symbols in either a Kleinian or Lacanian sense. But, as Freud (1918) said about the Wolfman, there is a primitive kind of thinking going on at this level. Thus, even though thinking is primitive, there is still a dim kind of thirdness present in the analysand that the analyst assumes will respond to interpretation, not at the level of words, but at the level of affective links and somatic traces between the infantile emergent self and the almost perceived primary object/mOther.

---

5. See Tom Ogden's *Subjects of Analysis* (1994) for a rich clinical discussion of the modes of speech salient to each of the Kleinian positions.

Art-making can be particularly useful in this psychic territory. The psychoanalytic art-therapy literature has repeatedly demonstrated this to be true in the treatment of severely disturbed patients (e.g., Kramer 1979, Lowenfeld 1941, Naumburg 1950, etc.). Art-making can play a significant part in accessing, expressing, and ultimately helping to reorganize traumatic experience into verbal narratives. Contemporary memory and brain research (e.g., Schore 2001a, 1994, Solms and Solms 2001) has affirmed what Freud (1900) underlined in his early work—that the visual character of dreams is particularly helpful in accessing childhood and traumatic material. Traumatic experience is not initially encoded in language associated with the left hemisphere, but rather imprinted in somatic and imagistic traces located primarily in the right hemisphere. It follows, then, that art-making, which also draws from the right hemisphere, would be a useful point of entry on the way to verbal discourse.[6]

At Lecours's third level of symbolization, images and fantasies can now be fully symbolized in words—that is, a Thing presentation can now be linked with a Word presentation. Therefore, greater modulation of emotional expression and an increased capacity to think are both possible. Following the art-making metaphor, the cat we see in the scribble drawing could now have a story to go with it, and that story could now be repressed. This repression would, of course, be breached by the return of the repressed in discontinuous speech acts and/or other kinds of symptoms. These breaches would provide the material for the analyst to decipher memories and/or interpret repressed fantasies of the person whose story it is.

Finally, at the fourth and most sophisticated level of symbolization, a combination of words and imagery/fantasy can be used to describe and impart one's most private and unique personal experiences to another. At this level there is the most emotional expressiveness and the greatest complexity of thinking. The capacity for performative speech (Lacan 1952–1953), as well as the ability to observe one's unconscious slips or actions "as if" it were an "other" within, becomes possible. For instance, the cat emerging from the scribble drawing and the story attached to it will reveal aspects of the storyteller's inner world. The question could be posed to the storyteller, or the storyteller could pose the question to her-/himself: Why

6. It matters not in regard to brain processing whether one takes Freud's (1895, 1917) view that trauma is always a retroactive effect (deferred action or après coup) or whether trauma occurs in present time.

was a striped cat seen in the scribbly lines and not a tiger, whose story might be more aggressive?

Having completed a summary of Lecours's theory of symbolization, let us take a step further in terms of particular types of speech and how speech can make use of art-making in the talking cure.

Performative speech is a crucial concept in Lacan's framing of analysis. It is of a different nature than descriptive reporting or a verbal compliance, because it is speech arising from the letters of the body itself (i.e., kernels of the Real as cause of desire) and not solely from the mind. These basic elements or "letters of the body" are the musical, visual, vocal, and kinesthetic semiotic traces inscribed in the infantile Imaginary body. The basic speech elements leading to performative speech may arise through an analysand's touching upon the Real kernels wrapped fantasmatically via her/his art-making. Performative speech is a creative act in analysis. New potential spaces for living are created and more subjectivity may be claimed through an act of performative speech. This stands in contrast to an analyst's explanatory interpretation. In Lacan's (1953–1954g) words, "It isn't a question of recognizing something which would be entirely given, ready to be co-opted. In naming it, the subject creates, brings forth, a new presence in the world" (p. 229).

ART-MAKING WITHIN THE ANALYTIC DISCOURSE

Sometimes spontaneous art-making in an analysis is the analysand's only means to access layers of infantile mental and emotional life. It is the infant's processing of mother's body, speech, and desire that carries the seeds of how each individual will symbolize his or her experience, color that experience affectively, and configure a phantasm that supports (clothes) desire. Despite the fact that this all occurs in the nonverbal realm of experience, it does not actually occur outside the realm of language but only outside the arena of speech. For the patient who spontaneously draws or paints in an analysis, he or she may be moving forward toward reformulating something of the mother–infant world, and may be on the way to repairing and/or revitalizing for her-/himself the symbolic function of speech in its myriad dimensions. As will be presented in the case of Ms. A., there are those whose suffering and psychic pain fill many analytic sessions with what amounts to the sound of a voice, because his/her words are unable to fully function as symbols to adequately convey the uniqueness of his/her life suffering.

Art-making by an analysand can be used to facilitate symbolic transformation—from the most primitive to its most sublime forms. A Jungian or Kleinian analyst (Schaverien 1999) would no doubt explore the art images themselves—and this indeed occurred at times with the later art pieces Ms. A. brought to the analysis but this was not the most vital or customary way of approaching the artwork in this treatment. I will be primarily presenting the artwork from the stance that the phenomenology or interpretation of images per se in the drawings is less important than the discourse they facilitate.

ART-MAKING AND THE ANALYTIC DISCOURSE OF MS. A.

Ms. A. described a poster on her living room wall: horses were in dramatic movement—heads turned with manes flying. She loved this painting because she could identify with both the kinesthetic nature and sensitivity of horses. What she had not seen, but finally did see, during our work is that she had split the painting with her gaze. Yes, the horses were in intense movement of galloping freedom; however, what she had not recognized until the second year of analysis was that the horses were fenced in—thrashing against confining walls, straining to break out. This split in her gaze, between the alive movement and the painful constriction of walls, summarized her split between the jouissance of infantile sexuality, infantile trauma, and her anxious inhabitation of an ambivalently held feminine identity.

INITIAL PRESENTATION

Ms. A.'s presenting conflict concerned childbearing; she was at that time 38 years old and her biological clock was ticking loudly. She came to me through my words—she had read the book I had written related to this topic.[7] I assumed because of this that she had placed me in the position in which a transference had already been established (a someone/subject who supposedly knows what she wants, etc. [Lacan 1953]). Time revealed that it was as

7. *Reconceiving Women: Separating Motherhood from Female Identity* (1993) was the outcome of an in-depth interview study of 100 women. It is a descriptive presentation and a theoretical analysis of three pathways leading to adult female identities that do not include motherhood.

much about what she read between the letters of my words as it was the words themselves that constellated in her the wish to seek treatment with me. Over time I came to know that while my writing did address several of her conscious concerns, it also evoked something beyond or in excess of my words that may have been more at the unconscious heart of the matter.

Her childbearing conflict was abruptly replaced when, within two weeks, her boyfriend of two and a half years announced unexpectedly that he wanted to end their relationship. The break-up catapulted her into an emotional crisis. Treatment immediately increased to two sessions per week. Her actual analysis began at eleven months into treatment, when sessions increased to three per week. (Her dreams indicated she wanted to see me more and I made this interpretation.) Once Ms. A. started using the couch she immediately plunged into an affair stimulated by transferential fears of becoming enmeshed and being subjected to my desires or demands. The nature of the transferential fear/desire/demand surfaced in haunting memories of her mother's jealousy and humiliation of her when she developed her first "crush" in grade school, as her mother discovered her making out on the couch at age 14.

FAMILY HISTORY

The question of from what parental desire of her mother and father was Ms. A. born became important in her work. Her parents had married knowing each other only a few months, due to circumstances regarding their work in a foreign country. Mother never worked after the birth of the first child; father's continuing work was such that the family moved every two to three years. Ms. A. was born nine years into a marriage to a mother who was the youngest of nine children herself. Mother, at a young age, lost a beloved father. Ms. A.'s mother was the more available parent, and yet this availability came with a severe requirement—the demand to be the same, and to cut off all passions—especially negative emotion—and to negate any wishes to be recognized or seen in her uniqueness. Mother's disapproving look could cut like a "dagger," and she could disappear into silence for days if crossed. Yet mother expressed interest in her and indeed had "inhaled" her every day after school.

Mother died at 60 from a massive stroke. One way this was understood by the analysand and me over time was that it was a result of all the unfelt feelings and unthought thoughts that mother could not have by choosing to stay with her husband. Finally her circuits just blew. This interpretation was a significant motivation for Ms. A. to stay in treatment even when things felt hopeless and unbearable—she did not want to suffer the same fate as her mother.

Father was described (and manifested in the transference/countertransference) as a constricted man who had angry outbursts in response to any challenge to his authority. He withdrew when emotionally overwhelmed. She described his anger as being like a "sledge hammer." Abandoned by his own father at an early age, he was the object of emotional abuse by a stepfather who wanted only his own sons. Psychic deadness would be the most apt description of his presence in the family, while he clearly was more alive at his work.

The patient had three siblings, a brother born when the patient was almost 3, another brother born when Ms. A. was 9, and a sister when she was 10. Shortly after her first brother was born, the family, living overseas, relocated, rupturing a primary attachment of Ms. A. to a nanny. Another rupture of a similar attachment to another nanny occurred again when Ms. A. was 7.

Very bright and gifted, Ms. A. had excelled at almost everything she had taken up. She had mistakenly thought her parents would be pleased with her pursuit of art, since in childhood they had given her art materials. But art was deemed too impractical. Her parents threatened to cut off financial support if she persisted in pursuing the arts in college. She resigned herself to fulfilling an unfulfilled desire held by both parents—becoming a lawyer.

INTRODUCTION OF ART-MAKING

Within the first three months of treatment Ms. A. brought dreams of incest, murder, and of a little boy's body being dismembered simply by a nun's piercing gaze. Oedipally speaking, Ms. A. appeared to be in the position of chronic dissatisfaction—or of an hysteric (Dor 1999, Lacan 1955, Nasio 1998).[8] On a more primitive level of identification, these dreams and my countertransference experience of intrusive violent images said to

8. Lacan framed the hysteric's dilemma in terms of an organizing question: Am I a man or a woman? The obsessive's question concerns: Am I dead or alive?

me that a disturbance at more primitive psychic layers was attempting to speak (Boyer 1978, McDougall 1989, Ogden 1989).

In the third month of treatment, Ms. A. spontaneously brought into a session a collage she had made a few months before, composed of cutout magazine photographs. She brought it, she said, because she had had a dream of the two of us sitting on a couch looking at this collage. Although the appearance of her own drawings did not come until some months later, the dream of the collage was the first moment of art-making entering the treatment. In positioning me in the dream as sitting beside her, she was, I thought, showing her wish for the Other to be in her eye/I's position in order to be seen. My response was simply to ask her to speak about the collage now lying on the floor between us. I offered no interpretations but only descriptive comments of the photos I saw, for example, "I see a boat," so as to invite her speech.

In thinking about this offering of the collage, I understood her need to bring it to her session as a need to bring forward parts of herself that had somehow remained wordless, even to herself, but that were very important. For reasons unclear to me at that time, it was evident that Ms. A. had learned to protect parts of her experience by splitting these parts off into sequestered areas of silence, while continuing, at another level, to report her daily school events to mother.

Speech for Ms. A. had long been corrupted by the time she came to speak to me. Her speech served as camouflage. I felt bombarded and walled out at the same time. Her words were like a machine gun: they came hard and fast—erecting barriers of all sorts and sizes between herself and others. There was no space left for the Other to make a reply, and often when I did reply, it was received as criticism equivalent to that spoken by an archaic superego. In the first year she nearly, and suddenly, broke off treatment because of a misunderstanding concerning my cancellation policy. She became terrified that my words did not mean anything reliable. She needed help desperately, and yet her machine gun speech left little opening. In this respect, her spontaneous drawings, collages, sculptures, and paintings became a primary means in the analytic encounter of refounding her speech and apprehending the primitive anxiety she constantly warded off by a rush of words.

I will be focusing on the art of Ms. A. when we were a little over two years into the work and she began to talk about adding a fourth session—which we did at approximately the two-and-a-half-year point.

CLINICAL MATERIAL

The clinical material that follows is focused on one of two traumatic periods appearing in the analysis, approximately two and a half years apart. In a series of clinical moments over several sessions, a process unfolded. In the year before, Ms. A. had moved from the medium of collage to doing many drawings with charcoal or colored felt-tip pens. These drawings could only be described as scribble drawings in which the main impact was to make me, the viewer, aware of the quality of movement—sometimes stressful, chaotic, violent, and sometimes even lyrical. Some drawings were different kinds of lines, while others also contained reinforced colored shapes (outline of shape gone over and over with intensity), with absolutely no color going outside the lines, yet giving off the quality of the colors fighting or straining against fences. The movement of the interior colors seemed to press against the reinforced outlines. I cannot count how many of these drawings I looked at with her—but there were many. We would both look at the drawing in silence for awhile and then I just listened to her describe how she made the lines, selected the colors, and so on. In terms of Lecours's schema of symbolization, these drawings corresponded primarily to Level 1, where somatic movement alone carries the subject's experience. On a few occasions one of these scribbles would move Ms. A. into a level of symbolization characteristic of Lecours's Level 2. For example, in looking at the scribble together Ms. A. would find a form or figure (i.e., bird or face) in the scribble she hadn't noticed before and then would perhaps begin to elaborate a fantasy.

In this particular session she brought a pencil still life she had been drawing for art class that she had recently begun. One definition of the Real is its insistence upon returning to the same place—the trauma of the Real calling for more symbolization (Lacan 1952–1953, 1953, 1964). For Ms. A., the trauma of an impending separation in the treatment constellated such a return. I had realized I was going to be away for three weeks occurring approximately at the two and a half year mark, which echoed the time frame of many of the family moves and the birth of her brother. (My trip had been planned several years before Ms. A. began treatment, so it could not have been the result of an unconscious communication concerning the significance of this number or time frame.) This would be my longest absence to date. Synchronistically her emerging desire to add a fourth session entered her discourse in this session right after a weekend break.

As had become usual, she put the drawing on the floor in an intermediate space where it was not in front of her or me, but located such that she could see the drawing from the couch as I could see it from my chair. It was a mixing bowl with a utensil handle sticking out. The fact that the bowl appeared feminine and the spoon masculine was noted by her as she lay them down. After she described the drawing, this conversation ensued:

Ms. A.: I had a difficult weekend.
MI: Perhaps a mix of the upcoming three week break and how it marks somewhere between two and three?
Ms. A.: I have been thinking of wanting more in the last week—of coming four times.
MI: Perhaps it would be useful to think and talk of my upcoming absence before the "more."
Ms. A.: I am doing a lot of drawing kinesthetically these days again . . . (meaning in addition to her art class assignments—which suggested she was experiencing a regression).

Session a Week Later

By this stage of our work her artwork had begun to be a partial way of emotionally containing herself at times when at home alone and experiencing difficulty.

Ms. A.: [silence] . . . I don't know why I'm crying, it just hit me when I lay down.
MI: Relief? (Drawing upon the reservoir of affect felt to be present, I did not make use of her signifiers here, even though masochism came to mind from her use of "hit."
Ms. A.: Yeah, there is something about walking around holding it together that is a strain.
MI: If you let yourself go, where do you go? (I am thinking, if her ego shatters, then what?)
Ms. A.: I don't know, blank—it is like dreaming but can't quite hold it—I have no idea why I'm upset, but driving over here there was a shock from realizing that I am not how I thought I was—I don't know, I don't know what I want anymore . . . (She talks

here of how her car has always been a self-object and now the car is falling apart.) I feel alone and hopeless—like there is a hole in my life.

MI: Perhaps it is the shock of the whole, who you are is more and less of what you thought, and you are wondering how much of your hole can be filled?

Ms. A.: (long silence) I've been making this drawing for a week and it feels like "my baby." It's very precious—it is a class assignment to draw three selected objects of different heights and in atmospheric perspective—I'm thinking about it (the drawing) all the time. (The drawing, which has been placed in its usual position, is of a teapot, smiling Buddha, Tibetan bells. The teapot was breastlike in shape, a happy-looking Buddha, two bells with a cord connecting them.) This drawing has been taking up all my energy for the last two weeks—my fear about drawing (meaning she "shouldn't" have access to such creativity that is not ultimately productive) has been balanced by the love of it. Right now it is the most important thing in my life; it is like when I was a kid and was really attached to my ragdoll. . . . It feels like everything has gotten turned upside down and inside out. I feel like I have been dropped from a helicopter in a foreign country.

MI: Your discovery in the analysis is like something foreign, but also known.

Ms. A.: I know all this wouldn't be happening if I didn't trust you to a certain extent, but sometimes it feels like I am turning into another person—and this is a huge shock, but somehow it is also a relief—after all, I'm not 20 anymore.

MI: No, you aren't, and you feel the time lost. (The intention here is to recognize and punctuate the end of her session with the full subjectivity of her statement. Implied in her words is that it is very unlikely she will ever have a child to replace the ragdoll. It is another kind of baby she must birth.)

Session Two Weeks Later

Increasingly over the months her artwork had also become a means to her bringing primitive states of being into some form that she could then bring into her sessions to speak about. It seemed to be her way of bringing aspects that had lived only in silence or in her body exclusively. On this day she brought two drawings. She had them in hand but did not lay them down right away. One drawing was of a charcoal-burnt tree and a black moon and a primitive self-portrait where the left eye looks painful; the second drawing was a scribble in which it looked like a bird was trying to come out of the chaos of movement.

Once she took her position upon the couch, she just cried for a number of minutes.

MI: I'm right here (I say softly).

Ms. A.: I stayed home sick today. I couldn't sleep last night. It was like I felt nothing. It was weird. The weekend was awful, lonely and horrible.

MI: Say more. (She goes on awhile here about how life is empty, etc.)

Ms. A.: I've been looking at apartments again. It's depressing what is available. There is a suicide case at work . . . I've been needing to cry and just couldn't.

MI: Couldn't until you were here. (Cries again in confirmation it seems, and then is quiet for awhile. She then shows me the two drawings.

Session after Three Days

This time she brought in a drawing. She put the drawing on the floor between us. It was a pencil drawing of soft, breastlike shapes with spikes all round the edges poking in toward the soft shapes. She opened the session:

Ms. A.: I had wanted to put in a small creature in the center, but when I got to a certain point in the drawing I just knew I should stop. I started drawing last night when I thought I could not tolerate the fear I was experiencing. Last night when I was drawing it was like when I could let myself feel something—it would be as if I was going through one of the piercing ones and then it would go away somehow. Strange, when I was crying last night, even though it was terrible in a way, it was not so scary because it feels like it is me and you against them—the piercing ones. Afterwards I sat in front of the TV. I wasn't really even watching it but I needed the sound of the voices.

MI: Uhm, I hear you. (I am thinking of the double use of the voice here—as psychic wrapping and as an *objet a*, cause of desire. In a later stage of treatment, the analyst's voice would be taken up by the analysand as an object to transport her to Real kernels of satisfaction around which her fantasies could be aroused and could support her desire—a desire that in time is directed by the analyst beyond the consulting room.

Next Session after Weekend Break

Ms. A.: I had a weird night last night. I had stomach pain real bad and yet I couldn't drink anything, but I didn't throw up or have a bowel movement or anything. I slept fitfully, but it never developed into anything more than just a terrible pain. It felt in a way I was like an animal who had to lie in one spot, very still, and just not move for a long time. . . . (She then pulled out two drawings. One was a simple bamboo shape; the other drawing was almost a scribble, but with a bit more definition. It was fragmented and disturbing. My private associations: One drawing looked like a phallus. The other drawing was very chaotic and violent looking. I wondered if her somatic symptoms were perhaps resonant of infantile experiences of being psychically murdered after the birth of her brother. I also recalled that mother, throughout Ms. A.'s childhood, looked to her for emotional sustenance and containment in the manner of a spouse, and that on more than one occasion mother had had a jealous rage regarding Ms. A.'s boyfriends and/or lovers.) The pain in my belly; it was a colicky pain, a kind of pain like a baby might have—and then I was very starving, but I was also afraid to eat. . . . It makes no sense, but I feel like I weigh half of what I used to and I haven't lost that much weight. It's like I'm insubstantial—I'm less. It feels sort of like leaving a heavy backpack behind, but it is also strange. I feel small and childish.

MI: Perhaps it is less that, than that your body is registering the psychic changes you are weighing.

Over the Next Few Months

Ms. A.: I feel that I am at the very bottom of the well of despair, of what have been unbearable feelings before. I am still scared but not entirely hopeless now, because I don't feel entirely alone, and I haven't had that experience before. (During one session she said she had been thinking about Berlin. She had brought to session photos of the Berlin Wall a few months before and yet hadn't known why. She now realized that the whole image of this city is like the island of her life. Part of the city had been walled off from people who might want to escape into it. She has been protecting her half-dead parts and walled herself off from where she really would want to live.) It's like parts of me have been in a cocoon . . . so it's just like in 1989 when the Berlin Wall came down, I have had a constant fear of creating unstable conditions in myself—it could be dangerous. And I now see what it is—these last months I have been living those dangerous unstable conditions. (It is now that she will notice her split gaze—the horses in the poster she loves are not free, but fenced in.)

In the month before I was to leave for those three weeks, she discovered an apartment she "loves," after having looked for almost a year. This was not just an apartment she could "make work"—as she had made many things work in her life through a distorted lens of fantasy. To Ms. A. it felt amazing that she could actually have a space she would "really want to live in." Is it really okay for her to have a room of her own? Her discovery of the apartment was both exciting and a comfort to her as my departure drew near.

There will be more grief to bear for the time lost in her life. "Not being alone now I feel perhaps I can survive these feelings rather than just wanting to die. Wanting to die isn't there now." I know, however, that she is putting aside what cannot be borne precisely because soon I will be leaving—and at one level she knows I will return, at another level she does not know this.

Through the unfolding artwork and discourse that accompanied it, Ms. A. approached a confrontation with her fear of breakdown (Winnicott 1974) and in fact did reexperience a small breakdown of sorts (or desubjectivization of Lacan). My hypothesis was that an early breakdown in her toddler's body-ego had left a vortex of anxiety that threatened to pull her into oblivion. In ordinary discourse with another, the oscillation between her palpable body and her psychic integrity was felt to be too precarious, and as a result, she often felt the need to fortify her ego wall by using an impenetrable speech pattern. In the analysis, she had regressed through a series of identifications, leading her to a place where she, like the walled city of Berlin, came apart. And as her body-ego began to fragment, multiple somatic symptoms and primitive mental states had to be lived through. One of her somatic symptoms was of being flooded with excess arousal that she evacuated primarily either by intense exercise or by masturbation. This experience of too much jouissance was described by her as a wish to "jump out of" her skin. Masturbation was for her a reliable way to reconstitute a positive infantile environment. Her hypersexuality had served her at two levels: masturbation as self-soothing touch to help repair or keep her psychic integrity; and a compulsive sexual drive as a reliable experience of intrapersonal aliveness and as a means to interpersonally connect and secure an attachment. A split in her ego had been needed to psychically survive, but this had meant that she inhabited a day-to-day world filled with psychic deadness or threatening anxiety rather than spontaneous aliveness (Ogden 1997, Winnicott 1949).

After this ego-shattering experience, Ms. A. began dreaming of the psychic pain and terror behind her walls and she began to speak of that which had existed only as unformulated experience. The analysis entered a tender period in which her dependence was palpable. Ms. A. described in detail one day during this period a winter solstice ritual she had created and then had enacted for herself. I said almost nothing in this particular session. In this session I functioned simply as a witness to her life as she was specifically marking a space with her art, her words, her fantasy, and her ritualized action, for the presence of her desire. A new art of the subject was beginning. This instance of performative speech, I believe, could not have been possible until she had revisited and begun to reconstruct elements of her body-ego envelope. In these moments of speakable desire, moments that must occur again and again in speech, she laid claim to, and assumed more of, her particular and singular destiny as a human subject. Much like the time of winter's solstice when the darkness gives way to light, Ms. A.'s destructive work of the negative (Green 1998) could turn a corner. Now let us also turn a corner and discuss in more detail the role of the art-making for Ms. A.

THE ROLE OF ART-MAKING IN MS. A.'S DISCOURSE

The collages, drawings, sculptures, and paintings Ms. A. brought to her analysis were not simply, or only, a repetition of an imaginary internal world concerning the demands of the Other. (Recall her daily reports after school to her mother—whose own aliveness was eroded by a commitment to a deadening marriage.) This particular repetition also revealed the insistence of the Real in her unique psyche-soma. One aspect of this insistence was to bring forward sequestered and unsymbolized snarls of the Real (or Winnicott's unthinkable anxieties) calling for further symbolization, which over time, through her own speech, would enlarge her own subjective experience. On various occasions Ms. A. had said she often "didn't feel quite human," later saying, "I can see that the feelings I am afraid of have had everything to do with the fact that I wasn't there enough to be able to bear and understand them. And I am always surprised how it [the capacity for bearing and learning from experience] can become more, even when I think I might be done with it."

Ms. A. sought to enter a process of being recognized, heard, represented, reflected upon, and elaborated in the analytic discourse so that certain snarls of the traumatic Real within her psychic body-ego could be reduced and a claiming of her own desire could begin to become a part of her life's narrative. Art-making was central to her process. For Ms. A. it was necessary to construct a fantasy that could facilitate the reshaping of an ego, an ego that could allow for traumatic disruptive somatic experiences as well as include previously disavowed identifications. Critical to this analytic process was my listening to Ms. A. speak and draw/paint/sculpt herself into being through a series of identifications, without stopping or sticking her to any one of them in particular. There were many transferential moments of severe anxiety related to the idea that I might fix her to one or more of these identifications and make her "do it my way"—much as her mother and father had done. Where the infantile body-ego has incurred significant damage, and disassembles too easily in discourse with another, the work of de-centering interpretations must be superseded by considerable affective attunement and support for the flow of the patient's speech. The voice, the gaze, and the close palpable presence of the analyst are often used during this period as partial objects (in a Kleinian sense) in the patient's reconstructive work on the ego envelope.

The analysis with Ms. A. seemed to indicate that mixed states of representation and affect (Green 1999a,b) can indeed be unconscious and that infantile somatic memory and affective traces may seek form and signification through art-making activities. Freud (1915) once described "unconscious affects as potential beginning(s) which are prevented from developing" (p. 178). Ms. A. appeared to return to such "potential beginnings" via her art-making, leading her into a period of psychic chaos and partial psychosomatic breakdown.

Green (1999a,b) observes that affect can serve variable psychic functions depending upon its context, as elaborated above. Affect in Ms. A.'s artwork did function in the various ways described by Green. Her art was a motive force for more than one action or idea in the sense that what motivated her bringing in the first collage was both her primitive somatic anxiety and her desire for recognition. Secondly, there was relief, even pleasure, accompanying her drive to move, to discharge her anxiety and aggression in the movement of drawing and in the images. Finally, there was a fear of judgment and abandonment wrapped up in her relationship with me as a transferential Other, that some of her art-work would reveal her basic badness or unworthiness to be loved. The intense range of affect evident in Ms. A.'s art-making was an element that led to the necessity to make a symbolic construction to wrap around it, so to speak, so that she could live.

THE ANALYTIC CONSTRUCTION: THE REAL OF SEXUAL DIFFERENCE IN RELATION TO IMAGINARY AND SYMBOLIC ELABORATIONS OF GENDER

Ms. A.'s art-making began with the most primitive of scribblings and moved to artwork that could be elaborated in her discourse. Her art-making was only one element, but certainly a substantial element, contributing to symbolization, symbolic speech, greater differentiation of her affect, and modification of her inner world of object relations. An analytic construction concerning misrecognition served to weave together for Ms. A. disparate affective traces, somatic symptoms/experiences, and confusing thoughts and conscious fantasies.

Insofar as a dream may also be a fantasy, Ms. A.'s first dream (our joint side-by-side observation of her collage) was her call to the Other, to recognize her differently, accept her into analysis, and provide an analytic space for her to show her cognitive confusions and highly charged unformulated experiences. The first collage Ms. A. brought in appeared to me to express psychic splits versus a psychic dimensionality, and yet it also revealed her unique and personal aesthetic (Meltzer 1988). Having made this collage a few months before beginning the treatment, without knowing what "looking" would bring, Ms. A. and the collage were a twosome seeking a Third in whom to engender a symbolic look of recognition. I would say that her first collage was a lure (Lacan 1964) to arrest my gaze so that I, once in the position of the symbolic Other, could then really "look" at her drawings and listen to her. It is significant to denote the difference between a "gaze" that can be associated with capturing and fixing the subject in a particular psychic position, versus a "look" that can be located in the field of desire that has the potential to reanimate in someone what in fact has been frozen within him/her by a primordial Other's gaze (Silverman 1996). I could thereby assist Ms. A. to recognize and name something else in her own subjectivity that would ultimately enable her to imagine, to speak, and then to enact her life differently. Concerning the field of vision itself, I saw Ms. A.'s early scribble drawings as less a screen/pose (which, by definition, has the aim of approximating an ideal image to be seen by the Other) and more as art presentations of diffuse somatic states. These diffuse somatic states presented her body in pieces—an experience characteristic of, and that precedes, the "threshold of the visible world" where the body-ego is constructed.

Ms. A.'s psychic deconstruction manifested in a feeling of her being dismembered into pieces, and, for a time, being held and contained (as opposed to frozen) by my gaze, my voice, and my symbolic capacity to hold a space open until she might re-member herself somewhat differently. Part of her re-membering of the body-ego was a reinterpretation or reinscription of disruptive infantile experiences that were lodged in her primarily as somatic symptoms and/or as kinesthetic knots of the Real (i.e., felt as intense anxiety states, compulsive exercise, and sexuality). Ms. A.'s process of doing artwork served to generate what Bion (1962b) would call alpha (symbolic) elements that could then be used by her unconscious mind in the making of dreams and to repair a faulty contact barrier. Later in the evolving analytic discourse, these alpha elements and those signifiers from her dreams could facilitate a reconstruction of her personal myth (Lacan 1953, Muller 2000).

Ms. A. had lived for many years with a persistent and intrusive fantasy. This fantasy was that there had been a "gender confusion at my birth" that required a surgical assignment of her gender to that of female. An accompanying persistent idea she knew for a fact not to be true was that she was really the "outcome of artificial insemination, and not of my father's seed." Insistent in both fantasies were her feelings of "not belonging." This quality of estrangement did not match up with her conscious knowledge of her gender, her paternity, or how much her mother had said she was a wanted child.

During the course of her analysis, in a phase of the work that followed the period of breakdown just described, her own personal myth was rewoven. This narrative weaving would be called a construction rather than an interpretation because its elements were constructed within the analysis as opposed to emerging from a repressive barrier as a whole previously formed. Her personal myth put together various signifying elements that emerged from her two intrusive fantasies, her artwork, repetitive somatic symptoms (wandering pains, a feeling her skin would burst), certain memory fragments of childhood play, two actual photographs of herself as a small child bearing mother's writings on the back of them referring to her as "a darling boy," and finally her dreams (i.e., dis-member, penis).[9]

At the second two-and-a-half-year point (fifth year) a transference reenactment became the culminating trigger for this co-construction. This repetition began when I abruptly announced to her I needed to make a schedule change—starting the next week. We would have to find another appointment time for one of our four weekly sessions. Such abruptness was not really characteristic of my approach to change, but there it was, I had done it. She exploded into a rage. She felt betrayed by my "dropping" her, "not holding my place," "not seeing me." This rupture echoed, at a different level, a very early rupture concerning a misunderstanding about my cancellation policy that had nearly ended the treatment before. By this time in the analysis, I, had been moved by her from being in the position

9. One dream that contributed to this construction appeared very early in the work. In this dream a nun's castrating gaze upon a young boy dismembers him, leaving him with one arm. The second and later dream concerned Ms. A.'s going to a friend's house to babysit. Upon her arrival the mother shows her one child (aged 2 or 3) in one room and then takes Ms. A. into the parental bedroom to show her the second child, an infant. On the parental bed is a 4-week-or-less-old infant. But the infant has a huge, and greatly out of proportion, penis. The baby is "masturbating furiously," Ms. A. says. The more she looks at the infant, the more the infant begins to look like an alien, except for the huge human male penis. The energy of the sexuality is of such intensity that Ms. A. feels a sense of unbearable shame and she quickly turns and leaves the room.

of the one who supposedly knows to the one who is now desired. Lacan (1964) describes this process nicely as the analyst becoming "a semblance" of the object that causes desire who is mistaken as being the object that the analysand "actually" desires. (See object a and the kernel of the Real, Chapter 4, this volume.) At this time an analysand, like Ms. A., thinks that it is me she loves/desires and feels not loved/desired back. (Through further work in the analysis she will reach the realization that the object of desire per se is not the goal, but rather it is to be related to the object a of one's psychic making that she/he moves one toward and into the world of others.)

Only over multiple sessions was it slowly determined that she had in fact heard me say that a session would have to be cut, rather than a session time needed to be changed. Her days of rage were then followed by a terror of loss and retaliation. She feared a psychic disintegration if I were "to throw me out of analysis." But at the apex of her building anxiety, she was able to abort her catastrophic fantasies by calling me in between sessions. We spoke briefly, just long enough to convey that the analysis was not threatened by the intensity of her feelings. Over the next several sessions we were then finally able to unpack and rework this rupture.

The analytic construction that then began to congeal was of Ms. A. first being held in mOther's loving gaze as a boy, not as a girl (an almost maternal phallus?). Did mOther initially hold her in mind, containing her in the Bionian sense, as a beloved son, only later to suddenly tear away this recognition and containment upon the arrival of a Real boy, her brother—much as she had experienced my announcing my need for a schedule change as a violent dropping of her? The catastrophic loss of Ms. A.'s first nanny via the family's relocation, followed by losing mother's exclusive attention after the birth of her brother when she was 2½, had registered in Ms. A. as psychic catastrophe—perhaps even as a murder of a part of herself.

This constructed personal myth served Ms. A. at both Imaginary and Symbolic levels of identification. Keeping in mind Lacan's notion of the mirror stage and Winnicott's notion of the necessity of personalizing the psyche-soma, the question arose: Had Ms. A.'s initial body-ego formation evolved through an identification with the feature of activity or pure physical aliveness, which was marked and recognized by mOther as male? (Freud 1905, Winnicott 1971)? Her fantasy of being psychically held in the desire of the maternal gaze as a boy, only later to meet demands (presented by mother and father) to reorganize her identification within another set of gendered identified features, offered a frame in which to hold and inscribe Ms. A.'s disturbing states of mind and body. This frame was not an interpretation of already linguistically symbolized material that had been repressed, but rather a construction drawing upon the linguistic and nonlinguistic signifiers, such as protosymbolic somatic traces, mixed affective states, and images in her artwork, that required further symbolic transformation to become linked together in words.

Viewed solely from an oedipal level of identification, this construction functioned as a castration fantasy that served to retroactively reorganize the Imaginary and Real collage of preverbal experiences. As an adult Ms. A. had had great difficulty tolerating, much less accepting, a receptive position—to be beloved. Father's inability, or perhaps unwillingness, to function as an oedipal father, to recognize and confirm her femininity, is captured in a memory of mother making Ms. A. model new clothes for her father who could barely look up from his newspaper or television program.

Ms. A.'s reconstructed personal myth created more psychic room so that previously split-off or warded-off masculine identifications, which had seemed to undermine her tentatively held feminine identification, could find their residence. This residence was established at the margins of traditional gender definitions and gender roles. Through her unfolding free associative discourse, suppressed and repressed features of Ms. A.'s mother (horsewoman and adventurous, prior to marriage) and maternal grandmother (college-educated and financially independent) offered a scaffolding for a more complex rendering of the meaning of the feminine. Another significant contributor to this new room of her own was the figure of Sarah Bernhardt, whose posters had adorned her adolescent room. This colorful and sensual actress was known for her male as well as female stage roles. When Ms. A. emerged from her psychic labyrinth of several years of interpersonal isolation, the man with whom she became romantically involved was an artist, offering her yet another kind of psychic room of her own.

In order for Ms. A. to take up such a reconceived oedipal position—first within herself, and then later in her external life—the work of art-making and psychic breakdown described was a necessary precursor. For Ms. A., any experience of lack or loss had in her past very quickly become the threat of falling into a hole of annihilation. Such a threat was to be avoided at all costs. Lacan's notion of feminine identification, marking the place of the "lack" where the Symbol meets its limit and where desire lives, is a truth only realized by someone such as Ms. A., when the constant threat of falling into a catastrophic hole can be partially transformed into a gap of separation and/or loss that can be borne (Kristeva 2001).

CLOSURE: ART-MAKING IS TO ANALYTIC FACT IS TO ANALYTIC THIRD

For this analysand, art-making was a crucial vehicle in her analysis. The art-making functioned at different times in her analysis as an autistic object, a self-object, a transitional object, and an object of sublimation. The content of the imagery in Ms. A.'s art-making was intentionally not taken up in this chapter because the discourse the art-making facilitated in the analysis was more important than the images per se. When art is received as a spontaneous element of the discourse itself, the analyst/therapist does not need specific art training to be able to receive and make use of art-making within a psychoanalytic treatment. Depending upon the intersubjective circumstances in the analysis, the art of the subject may be accepted and understood as an "analytic fact" within the individual's discourse that may have the potential to become an "analytic third" facilitating the work of the analysis. Julia Kristeva's (1996) summary of the analyst's work in the area of Freud's Thing and Word presentations, applies also to the analysis when art-making becomes such an integral element:

> We transform the patient's flesh, which we have shared with our own [in terms of one Imaginary body with another], into Word-presentations. By placing, repeating, and punctuating these word-presentations, however, we give words the consistency of reified symbols and link them to Thing-presentations. Thus the analyst uses sensorial fixations [of the nuclei of primal unconscious] as starting points for sensory play and then for words, but words that are word-pleasures, word-things, and word-fetishes. We could describe the analyst's naming process as the art of making the flesh of signs into transitional objects. [p. 247)

The matrix of the analytic relationship has then the potential to act as a transducer with any art an analysand may bring, taking the marks of pure bodily movement and/or specific images, and/or quite developed visual scenes, and transforming them into the discourse of analysis—its sounds, signifiers, and felt silences.

7

Art-Making in Psychoanalytic Supervision: Drawing Links to Language and Speech[1]

In contemporary psychoanalytic training and practice there is a gap, which I intend to reframe in this chapter as a "potential space" (as Winnicott [1971] would have it). This gap—something artists would call a negative space—exists in the context of the British school of psychoanalysis's (substantially influential in the United States) thinking concerning early psychic development and severe psychopathology and its treatment (Bott-Spillius 1990, Meltzer 1978). In this psychoanalytic tradition, in which exploration of infantile mental states is central, there is the peculiar absence of dialogue concerning the use of art techniques as a potential (or potentially vital) avenue into this preverbal and primitive realm of human experience. (The work of Marion Milner [1957, 1993] and Winnicott's [1958] "squiggle game" stand as notable exceptions.) Significant attention is paid by the learning and practicing therapist/analyst to accessing his/her own transient nonverbal emotional and bodily experiences and fleeting thoughts/images/reveries as significant information sources for perceiving, understanding, and working with the client's shifting mental states. However, there is an apparent lacuna when it comes to the translation of such experiences into the transitional space afforded by visual/artistic media.

To understand this lacuna, we must understand the ongoing debate (and tension) within the psychoanalytic community regarding the role of

1. A shorter version of this chapter was published in 1999 as "Visions of Transference and Counter-Transference: The Use of Drawings in the Clinical Supervision of Psychoanalytic Practitioners," *American Journal of Art Therapy* 37:74–83.

imagery/fantasy versus that of language and speech in analytic treatment (see Chapter 6, this volume). Parallel to and intersecting this debate has been the consideration of affect and its relative status in the unconscious as contrasted with the role of representation in the unconscious. The issue of affect is one that bears significantly upon the potential role art-making might come to have in psychoanalytic training.

DIFFERING PSYCHOANALYTIC VIEWS ON AFFECT IN RELATION TO REPRESENTATION

Freud (1917, 1923, 1940) appeared to vacillate in his thinking as to whether affect could be thought of as only a conscious phenomenon, or could be considered to be both conscious and unconscious. In "The Unconscious" (1915), Freud said, "all that corresponds . . . to unconscious affects is a potential beginning which is prevented from developing" (p. 178). He thought at that point that the unconscious only contained representations. But later in "The Ego and the Id" (1923), he seemed also to include affect in the unconscious, in the context of an oscillation between the instinctual states of Eros and the death drive. Later still, in "An Outline of Psychoanalysis" (1940), he wrote that the unconscious (in what, by this time, had become the structural model) does not ever become conscious, but that it can attract mental processes that result in something being able to become conscious. For example, a Thing presentation (unconscious) may attract a Word presentation (conscious) in a particular context such that a person becomes aware of a memory, idea, or fantasy that had not been in mind in the preceding moment.

In Matthis's (2000) reading of Freud's "An Outline of Psychoanalysis" (1940), affect is defined as the psychical aspect of somatic processes. This conceptualization keeps the psyche embodied (in both conscious and unconscious), and precludes the kind of mind–body split that can result when affect is seen only as discharge, and the symbolic as representation.

In contrast to Freud, affect is seen by Lacan (1952–1953, Harari 2001) as directly related to the human being's castration by language. Anxiety is part of the human condition, and through the act of speaking various affects are of course generated. Taking up the position that only representations are unconscious, and pairing that with the fact that the object of analysis is analysis of the unconscious, Lacan (1953) positions the analyst as one who attends to, but does not focus upon, affect per se. In a similar manner, for Lacan (1953), the image as a form of representation, while compelling, fascinating, and possibly obscuring the fundamental lack at the heart of the human condition, should not be the focus of the treatment. Furthermore, since the image is more associated with the realm of the ego or Imaginary-world of fusional relationships, the focus for Lacan (1953) is to bring the subject to a position of being capable of performative speech.

André Green's (1999, 1999a) reading of Freud on affect offers a clinical position and foundation for using drawing within psychoanalytic supervision as a potent means of weaving of affect, images (signs), and words (signifiers). Affect, to Green, does not have a uniform psychic function, but depends upon the context in which it is embedded (see Chapter 6, this volume). Green's (1999) rendering of Freud also includes the possibility that mixed states of affects and representations can and do exist in the unconscious.

Always maintaining the frame of drive theory, Green (1999a) situates affect as a moving entity: it is of the body. According to Green, instinctual movement begins with the anticipation of the infant's (subject's) body meeting mOther's (another subject's) body. In this way, he/she launches the daunting postbirth task of constructing a psychic envelope/body-ego (which s/he does through psychically transforming his/her own sensory experience). Green focuses upon that which is between instinctual discharge and the experience of pleasure or unpleasure—the intermediate factor of the perception of motor action. It is these perceptions of motor action that Green identifies as leaving psychic traces, which are in turn involved in the elaboration of affect—and of symbolization. These traces of "object-presentations" are left by the individual's infantile experiences of Real drive satisfaction (and of the traumatic Real) with mOther. Clinically speaking, these traces, or intermediate factors, are experienced by the analyst in the context of his/her reactions to such elements as the rhythm, pressure, silence, and so forth of a patient's discourse, versus the verbal content per se.

Green's ideas as just described are focused upon mOther as object, but mOther as the locus of the Symbolic network is not excluded from his conceptualization, only intentionally backgrounded. Green's reading of Freud suggests that every future representative of the drive (e.g., a Thing or Word presentation) will also mobilize these traces of "object-presentations" left by the individual's infantile experiences of Real drive satisfaction (and of the traumatic Real) with mOther.

PRIMITIVE MENTAL STATES, THE ANALYTIC DYAD, AND THE ROLE OF THE THERAPIST'S DRAWINGS IN SUPERVISION

The infant's experience of the meeting with mOther creates an excitation that is not summarily discharged, but instead forms an "affective coloration" in the baby's developing attachment to mOther and the mind that is forming. The ordinary paradox is that under "good-enough" mOthering circumstances, this affective coloration supports a gradual and unintrusive differentiation of the infant from mOther, while simultaneously establishing the elemental psychic foundation for making and sustaining links between the infant's emerging psyche-soma and the world surrounding him (Freud 1895, Green 1999, Winnicott 1949).

What happens when the meeting of the infant body with the maternal body and the mOther is not only not "good enough," but goes seriously awry? Simply put, a disjunctive infant–mOther meeting (for whatever reasons this may be) produces varying degrees of psychic catastrophe (Bion 1962a,b). Instinctual experiences do not become adequately symbolically transformed (i.e., the traumatic knots of the Real remain in the body), and, in Winnicott's (1971) terms, the infant remains stuck in the realm of relating to the mOther as a subjective-object, and thus the mOther cannot be discovered as an external subject who can be used. (See Chapter 5, this volume: Tracy's mother was hospitalized shortly after Tracy's birth, leading to such difficulties.)

A seriously awry meeting of infant and mother constellates in the infant what Green (1998) has called the "destructive work of the negative" (e.g., foreclosure, negation, splitting, etc.). For example, there may be a constant attack within the mind of the infant upon making any links between his or her instinctual/drive activity and the object (mother and subsequent others) itself or worse—psychosis. Thus the infant's journey to becoming a subject who is linked to, and held within, a Symbolic net, and able to follow the movement of her or his own desire, becomes absolutely derailed.

The individual living within an infantile history that has constituted the "destructive work of the negative" would by necessity have to address her/his "destructive work" in the analysis, before full symbolic speech, a range of differentiated feelings, the fluidity of play or desire, and the capacity to mourn could become accessible. Art-making within analyses of such individuals can be a means for initiating and furthering transformational processes, moving from the soma to the psyche in both affective and symbolic dimensions (see Chapter 6, this volume). This is possible regardless of whether one theorizes affect as having a signifying and dynamic status of its own (Green or Matthis) or as being a by-product of the symbolic function itself (Lacan).

Analytic therapists/analysts attempting to work with such individuals are subjected to disturbing psychic forces that are a direct result of the "destructive work of the negative" that Green speaks of. This often occurs via nonverbal communications and through speech that carries less meaningful content, and more of an intensely disturbing and negative impact on the mind and body (e.g., creating confusional and emotionally intense mental states) of the clinician. This is destabilizing for the clinician and can be demoralizing for the treatment, even for the experienced clinician.[2]

André Green's (1999a) rendering of Freud includes the possibility that mixed states of affects and representations do exist in the unconscious—an idea that is consistent with how I have found art-making entering analytic treatment and functioning within it. In general, Green's reading of Freud on affect offers a clinically useful position, I believe, in terms of how art-making can play a role in two realms of psychoanalysis not usually thought of: (1) adult psychoanalysis or psychoanalytic psychotherapy, and (2) in the clinical training of psychoanalytic practitioners.

Images drawn by a therapist/analyst depicting his/her experience of the psychotherapy session have the potential to capture and render complex lived experiences occurring within the treatment. Often, the images capture what has not made it into the therapist's conscious verbal understanding of the case, and as such, could not be verbally presented to the supervisor, but only enacted in a parallel process manner. In supervision, a training therapist's drawings have the potential to render a graphic expression of both the known and unknown affects reflected in the immediate object relations of the current transferential matrix. By looking at and talking together about the drawings, the therapist and supervisor can slowly weave a verbal net of understanding between them so that a part of what is contained in the graphic image will be able to be brought back to the clinical work. In addition, the therapist's brief drawings of his/her session also serve the unverbalized purpose of putting emotionally difficult material at a useful psychological distance. Having more psychological distance

2. Imagine, then, the subjective experience of a graduate trainee in a psychoanalytic internship attempting to work with the psychic disturbance of such persons.

reduces the therapist's performance anxieties about his/her clinical work with a difficult patient, and thus the process of supervision is facilitated.

With the above thoughts in mind, I introduced an art technique into my clinical supervision with a doctoral-level psychology intern. This technique was introduced, however, only after our having established a good working alliance in our clinical supervision over a period of months. Would he be willing to try a technique that might facilitate his learning? He agreed.

ART TECHNIQUE: DRAWING THE SESSION

The intern was given a sketch pad of 18" by 24" paper along with a box of 12 oil pastels to keep in his office. With these materials he was asked to make a brief drawing immediately following his session with each client. It was recommended that he approach this task with nothing in his mind other than what it had felt like to be in the room with each patient in that particular session. "Letting your experience of the session direct you to a color might be one way to begin," I suggested. Since the drawing was done between sessions, ten minutes was the time limit he could spend on any one drawing. This procedure was completed with ten clients over a period of approximately nine months.

Each drawing of a psychotherapy session was then brought to clinical supervision along with session notes. In some cases I had listened previously to an audiotape of the session to be discussed. When he came to supervision the drawing would be placed on the floor between us. I would ask him to talk about what he was thinking while doing the drawing and whether he had a specific image in his mind before he began the drawing. We would then go on to his session notes. After going over the session notes, we would again direct our joint attention to the drawing. This time, however, when looking at the drawing I would say, "Look at the drawing as if it has been done by someone else and see what this drawing might tell you about a relationship between these two people. Let the drawing speak to you on its own terms." At this point both he and I would free associate to the drawing as a whole and to its various elements. We would look at such elements as the use of color, the size and placement of the drawing on the page, the quality of form, the interaction of the forms, line quality, and use of space. We would then speculate as to what these elements and their relationships to each other might inform us as regards emergent transference or countertransference dynamics.

Initially the therapist's drawings were stiff and self-conscious. This awkwardness was related to his fantasies about what I, as his supervisor, would see in the drawings that he did not know he was revealing. Within a short time, however, his anxiety abated and was replaced instead by curiosity and excitement because the value of this adjunctive art technique to our supervision process had already become very evident. The substantive contribution of the drawings is best demonstrated by presenting two case summaries from our work together. In order that the reader get as close to the case material as possible, I have included both levels of representation by the therapist—his actual verbal descriptions of the clients as well as his drawings. Each case thus includes the intern's own words (denoted by regular font), his drawings, and my contextual and supervisory remarks (in italics).

Case 1: Steve

First Therapy Session

This first case was one that terminated prematurely, but offered significant learning for the intern.

Steve, a 20-year-old freshman, was seen on intake a day following his release from University Hospital. He had been carried to the Emergency Room by a group of friends after having passed out during a drinking binge at a fraternity party.

Steve is an extremely handsome young man, polished and cosmopolitan. During the intake session, he spoke eloquently of his embarrassment and confusion at having wound up in the Emergency Room. He said he was generally able to hold his liquor, and concluded that he must be under some kind of unusual stress in drinking such a quantity of liquor and being so vulnerable to its effects. He commented that he had considered entering exploratory psychotherapy numerous times, and that this seemed like an appropriate moment. Steve was unable to state any particular goals for therapy, aside from improving his general level of self-awareness. He did state that he was growing weary of the promiscuous nature of his sexual relations with women, and hoped that one day he would be able to maintain a commitment to one person. The student therapist was impressed by this college freshman's dazzling array of social and verbal skills, as well as his apparent curiosity.

Supervision

The drawing of this first session was described by the therapist as an attempt to draw himself as a radar bowl ready to receive the client (Fig. 7–1). The client was drawn as a dazzling diamond. The therapist's review of the session was given in such pressured speech that I felt, in a parallel way, the therapist's sense of inadequacy with his client—there seemed to be no room to offer my supervisory comments and it was difficult to know what the therapist was in fact wanting, or needing, from me. This emotional experience guided our second look at the drawing. I noted that the radar bowl was not very grounded and that the client, while colorful, had no base or foundation at all—but was merely floating in space. The seemingly suave surface presentation of Steve perhaps was covering for something else.

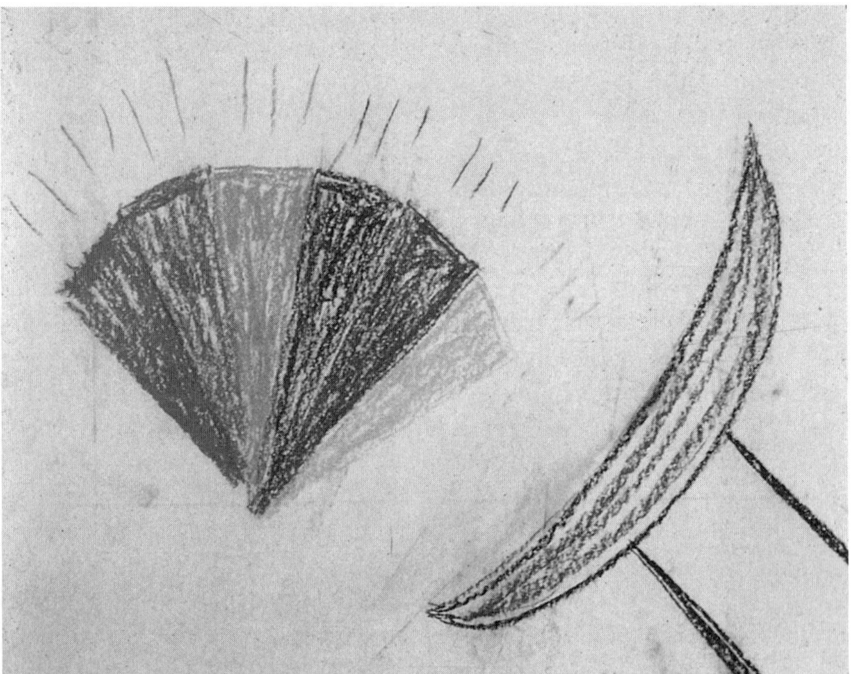

Fig. 7–1.

Therapy Session

In the second session Steve continued to put more energy into being impressive than into being authentic. His flamboyant veneer thickened while other strong feelings were kept at bay. The therapist had begun to resonate with some of Steve's deeper feelings, but continued to present himself as solid, structured, and emotionally low-key to the client and to his supervisor.

Supervision

For the first time in this series, a barely perceptible layer of white coats Steve's figure outside the veneer of yellow (Fig. 7–2). The veneer had indeed thickened from the first drawing. The continuing and increasing use of white in the therapist's depiction of Steve became a focus in the supervisor's attempt to elucidate Steve's character. Following his initial appearance in Fig. 7–1, with its bold, bright colors reminiscent of the "NBC peacock," Steve begins to fade into white. The therapist's own boundary of brown is also thickened—indicating his own defensiveness in the face of the client's challenges. The therapist has uncon-

Fig. 7–2.

sciously duplicated the red and blue colors of the client inside his own thickened defensive boundary; it is here we see the therapist's empathic resonance that at a conscious level he is not aware of. The supervisor titled this drawing "Dueling Defenses" and suggested to the therapist to shift from analytic thinking toward being in more of an intuitive, receptive stance.

Therapy Session

In the third session, conversation was rambling, inconsequential, sardonic at best. The client seemed to have forgotten about the incident that brought him into therapy, and made attempts to turn the spotlight on the therapist by asking about his personal background, his education, his career goals, and so on. As in his promiscuous sexual relations, Steve had shot his wad, so it seemed, in the first couple of sessions, and now found himself with nothing left to say. He tried to give form to his own presentation by borrowing the therapist's identity, shown in his drawing (by the repetition of the kidney-shaped chair).

Fig. 7–3.

Supervision

The figure of the client (right) shows a kidney-shaped chair (the actual shape of the office chair) with no legs to support it. The chair is empty, with what the intern had described as wilted balloons protruding (they also looked like used condoms, the intern said in supervision)—intended by the therapist to capture the remnants of the client's defenses. (Fig. 7–3) In contrast, the therapist's chair has legs and is filled with color. We note that the therapist has changed from the right side of the page to the left. His process notes reveal a kind of "as if" quality to Steve's presentation in the clinical hour.

With a second look at this drawing, it appeared that the borrowing of the therapist's form was perhaps an unconscious attempt to usurp the intern's position of authority, while consciously the client had been somewhat devaluing toward the therapist. Here was an opportunity to speak to the concept of complementary countertransference and its uses by pointing out that this is the reverse of the first drawing (Racker 1968). The client, rendered as an empty form, evokes inadequacy; the therapist, rendered as a filled-in form, has more substance and his form is more grounded. This is a reversal from the first drawing (Fig. 7–1), where the therapist had appeared more ungrounded and inadequate than the client. Thus Steve seems to vacillate between an overinflation of himself, seen in (Fig. 7–1), with the other being devalued, or, as in this drawing, seeing the other as full and himself as empty and devalued. In complementary countertransference the therapist is in effect occupying the psychic residence of the object. The change in the therapist's location in the drawing (from right-hand side of the page to left-hand side of the page) may be a graphic indication of his attempt to follow the supervisor's counsel and shift into a more intuitive mode. In human drawings the left side of a drawing is associated more with the unconscious mind, or right hemisphere.

Therapy Session

In the fourth session, casually titled "A Shot in the Dark," the frustrated therapist tried to provoke an emotionally related response in his client by insisting that some articulated goals were needed if therapy were to continue. (Fig. 7–4). Steve, by this time, was almost invisible behind the white smoke screen, as in the drawing. When discussing the events surrounding his "favorite" grandmother's funeral, Steve commented that he had dreaded her impending death for many months, but he was surprisingly unbothered when she actually passed away. Steve spoke further, with some curiosity, about the limited range of his emotional responses. He was aware that he barely responded to many events that stirred strong feelings in those around him. The client and therapist agreed that this concern about his emotional numbness was a suitable reason to continue therapy.

Supervision

Again, in this drawing the therapist is pictured on the left in the bottom corner (Fig. 7–4). The therapist described, and drew himself, as a cannon shooting into space in efforts to set some therapeutic direction. The client is lost in a white mist with barely a hint of green on the right side of the page. He has no real form to contain him. In a parallel process, as supervisor, I found myself needing to contain my own anger regarding what I saw as an "acting in" on the part of the therapist in reaction to a narcissistic injury suffered at the hands of the client's devaluation.

In our second look, the therapist was able to see how his feelings of wounded narcissism had gotten the better of him. Although a direction for treatment had been agreed upon, both supervisor and intern now wondered if at another level

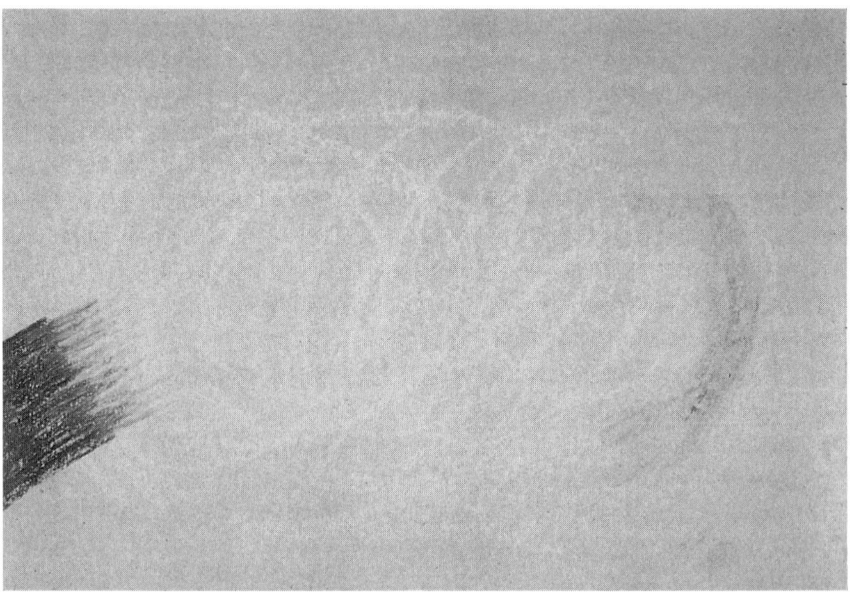

Fig. 7–4.

the repetition of bad object experience would be such that the client might be blown out of therapy. While the supervisor agreed that the therapeutic agenda seemed appropriate, the therapy should follow the client's lead. The degree of agitated movement in the strokes of color brought to mind how much anxiety must be behind Steve's suave façade. The green mixed in the white held the possibility that envy (i.e., green with envy), the other side of overidealization would soon surface. And in fact envy and overt aggression did appear later.

Therapy Session

By the fifth session, the therapist had effectively changed his approach to working with Steve. He focused far more on feelings, using himself as a model, but also helping Steve to identify the feelings associated with the events and persons he described. Steve began to emerge as a human form out of the white haze, and the therapist himself became more opaque in the drawing. This is the first time that both therapist and client were depicted in human instead of abstract form.

Fig. 7–5.

Supervision

In this drawing (Fig. 7–5) the therapist has returned to the right side of the page. The colors coming out of the figure were meant by the intern to convey how the therapist was helping the client attach names to emotions associated with events. The supervisor said that feelings for Steve were experienced more as concrete "things" rather than being integrated as emotions he experienced. It would be within relational context, which was what the therapist was hoping to create, that these "thinglike feelings" would become humanized and integrated. The therapist felt that his rendering of the human form for the first time expressed his greater sense of therapeutic alliance with Steve. He did not notice until the second look at the drawing that neither figure had feet or hands. The therapist would like to feel a large step had been made toward more human contact, but the lack of hands on the figures to reach for another indicated problems remained. Also, as in Fig. 7–3, the human form representing the client is empty; the question arises again regarding the degree of pathological narcissism in the client. On a second look it is also noted that neither figure is looking at the other, but instead is looking outward to an unidentified third—the viewer, the supervisor? Perhaps the therapist was looking toward the supervisor for approval more than toward the client.

Therapy Session

Steve appeared to be interacting in a more genuine manner when he came for his next session, and in the process of discussion revealed an extensive history of serious fist fights. He and his older brother fought so violently that his mother occasionally threw water on them to stop the fights, or simply fled from the house in tears. He had been suspended from prep school for fighting, and was now being reprimanded by his fraternity for getting into brawls with the town kids who tried to crash the fraternity parties. He described these fits of anger as coming over him without warning, like an alien force, and then disappearing as quickly, leaving him feeling confused and guilty. Steve became embarrassed that he had finally revealed this side of himself in therapy.

Supervision

In this drawing (Fig. 7–6) we see Steve's angry red, which had been held in check during earlier sessions, come to the forefront and be exposed to the therapist. The red covers the area where a mouth would be, as if to show, in an uncon-

Fig. 7–6.

scious, graphic way, how being unable to speak his feelings he must act them out. The therapist is reduced here to a small confused-looking head in the right lower corner of the page. The red band splits the picture in two. The emotional and confusing intensity of this session is clearly evident.

In the second look at the drawing, the supervisor points out how the red band looks like an arm and fist (which the therapist had not intended to draw), about to come down on the therapist's head. The concept of concordant countertransference was introduced here by way of saying that the therapist's experience of disorganization (seen clearly in his drawing of himself) in the session is a disavowed and split-off part of Steve's self (Bion 1959, 1962b, Ogden, 1989, 1996). Unlike the "Shot in the Dark" session (Fig. 7–4), here the therapist is able to contain the feelings without retaliating. The supervisor drew on Steve's history of fighting to help the therapist understand Steve's need to seek out an external person (to take the role of a hated other) to provoke a fight with, so that the rage inside him would not disorganize his mind and his capacity to function. This supervision hour was fruitful in linking the therapist's action in the clinical hour to notions of a "holding environment," "containment," and how to more viscerally understand what it means to make use of one's self as a clinical tool (Bion 1962, Boyer 1978, Ogden 1994, Winnicott 1958).

Therapy Session

Owing to the approach of exam week, the therapy was going to be at best broken off for the summer and possibly ended completely. The therapist felt that a deepening of the therapeutic alliance had occurred in this session. Steve was invited to continue treatment when he returned to school in the fall. He did not return to treatment in the fall.

Supervision

The therapist saw the figures in his drawing of this final session (Fig. 7–7) as appearing to be related, but reticent to make contact. He saw Steve's figure as looking injured or martyred, but saw himself as more stable in his footing and hovering near his hapless client. The somber interior colors and the purple shield across the therapist's body reveal his own discomfort and disappointment about this ill-timed and artificial termination.

In the second look at the drawing, the therapist's (figure on the right) reaching toward the client perhaps appears to have an unintended unconsciously rendered aggressive quality, insofar as the therapist's arm, as drawn, is reminis-

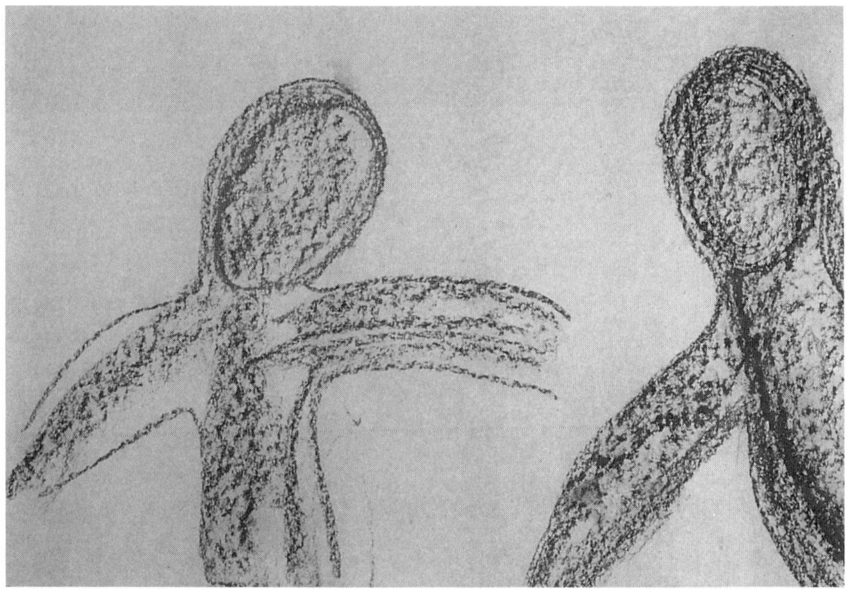

Fig. 7–7.

cent of the client's arm. The therapist's arm also suggests a phallus that portends that conflicted sexuality may have been a part of the clinical picture to be revealed, had the treatment continued. The fact that the therapist's figure hovers at the edge of the page also spoke to his unconscious ambivalence about working with this client. The darker colors hidden in the back of Steve's diamond figure in Drawing 1 (Fig. 7–1) are now fully present here. This drawing in particular offers a window into clinical material that had not yet been expressed verbally by the client or thought about by the therapist. Because the client did not return to treatment, however, this hypothesis could not be confirmed.

Case 2: Dave

First Therapy Session

Dave, a 24-year-old graduate student in international affairs, came to the Counseling Center upset about a sudden drop in his GPA. He ostensibly wanted some guidance about approaching professors to change his grades. In the course of discussing the events that led up to his particularly poor showing during final exams, he revealed the fact that he had just terminated a tumultuous two-year relationship with a male lover. Dave had moved out of the apartment they shared early in the semester, but the spurned lover had continued to hound him at his new address. Their struggle came to a crescendo just prior to exam week, when the lover broke down the door to Dave's apartment and physically assaulted him. The police were eventually called in to break up the fight. Dave was able to discuss these events in an upbeat, matter-of-fact manner. His bemused affect in no way reflected the fear, outrage, worry, or sense of loss one might have assumed to be associated with events such as he described. He only commented blithely that he would have to try to go back to having sex with women now instead, though he admitted that he was often impotent with both men and women.

Supervision

In the drawing of this first session, the therapist depicted himself as "an ear—open, receptive—but distant." Dave is portrayed as "spotty and diffuse, or perhaps in a state of cool chaos" (Fig. 7–8). In our second look at the drawing, the unconscious sexual and aggressive aspects of the therapist's listening "ear," along

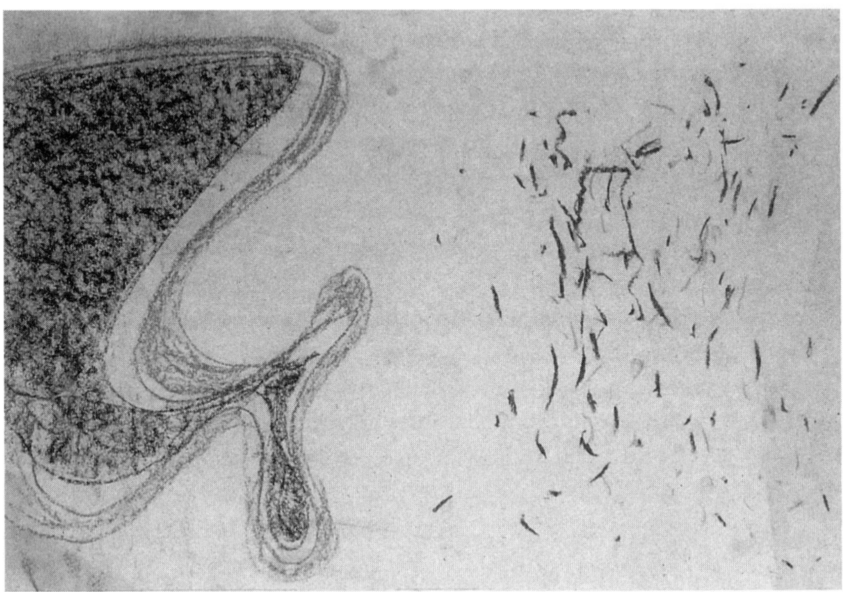

Fig. 7–8.

with the complete lack of boundaries in the intern's representation of the client, alert us to expect a borderline character structure along with an erotic transference.

Therapy Session

Between the first and second sessions, Dave met with the dean of his graduate program who assured him that he had a solid academic record and was in no danger of being dropped from the program. It may well be that Dave's academic status was never in peril, but that this concern was his "ticket" into therapy. He confessed that he was worried about what his mother's response would be to his poor set of grades. A simple reflection of this concern by the therapist unlocked a closet full of skeletons.

Dave's mother was an alcoholic. Though her drinking upset him, he spoke devotedly about their "special" relationship. He spoke of the intimate communication they had always shared, and of her often-repeated confession that he was her favorite child. He recounted with particular tenderness the way he would melt into her arms at the ages of 3 and 4 when his father would terrorize the household during his drunken rampages. His father had been alcoholic as well, but had been killed ten years earlier. He had fallen out of an open door of a moving train while trying to snap a photograph of the Alps. Dave had an older brother who was a heroin addict, and a sister who had sustained permanent brain damage when she fell off a sliding board at the age of 3. In this family, Dave had been cast in the role of the "healthy" one.

In succeeding weeks, Dave continued to reveal his personal history in almost promiscuous detail. He discussed every event, no matter how personal, embarrassing, or frightening, in the same amused but essentially affectless tone. It became abundantly clear that Dave had little or no awareness of the effect he had on other people. Not surprisingly, his impressions of others were murky at best. He was able to make only rudimentary distinctions between the individuals who crossed his path, and these distinctions were often made in sexual terms.

Supervision

The therapist described himself in this drawing as lines like arrows trying to contain the hot material, represented by the fire-like red, that had been revealed

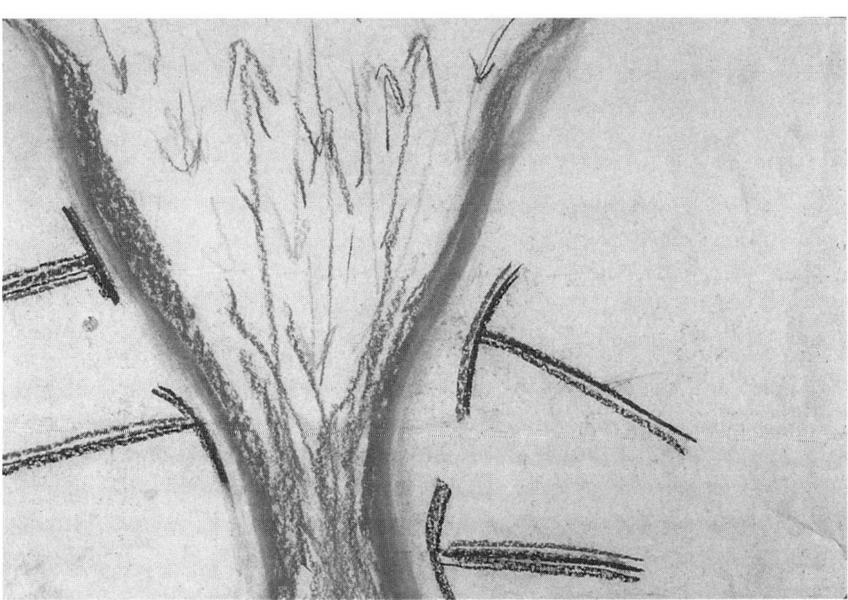

Fig. 7–9.

in the session. (Fig. 7–9). Again there were no boundaries to the client's form. Here the drawing seemed to make evident a raging chaos living under the cool but dispersed exterior seen the week before. In our second look at the drawing, the therapist noted how he had used rational understanding to try to contain the volatile forces he experienced in session. He had felt only partially successful. This drawing provided the opportunity to speak again to concordant countertransferences and how the therapist was himself experiencing quite overwhelming emotions that his client was consciously disavowing. The therapist was encouraged to "hang in there"—make the effort to contain the affect and not act quickly to evacuate it through premature interpretations.

Therapy Session

Dave's relationship skills were so poor that it was difficult to maintain a working alliance, and even his reasons for remaining in therapy were obscure. After his concern about his academic standing subsided, he said he wanted to keep coming just because he liked having someone to talk to. It became evident over a period of weeks that as Dave became more involved in therapy, his behavior became more seductive and his attachment more eroticized. The therapist's ambivalence about working with this sort of client became most graphic in the drawing from a later session.

Supervision

In this drawing (Fig. 7–10) the therapist described himself (right side of page) reaching toward the client to make contact. At this point in the therapy he felt he had become more empathically connected to the client—described as the weaker and more deflated figure on the left side of the drawing. What was not evident to the therapist until the second look was the fact that his arm reaching for contact had an aggressive quality, almost as if he were hitting Dave. Also unintended was the obvious phallic nature of the therapist's reaching arm. Up to this point in time, neither the seductive behavior of the client nor the therapist's response to it had been verbalized by the therapist in supervision. The phallic aspect of the therapist's drawing made a safe entrée into beginning to talk about two charged issues: (1) how eroticized vs. erotic transference differ (Ogden 1997a, Searles 1979), and (2) what are the countertransference difficulties associated with dealing with an eroticized or erotic transference.

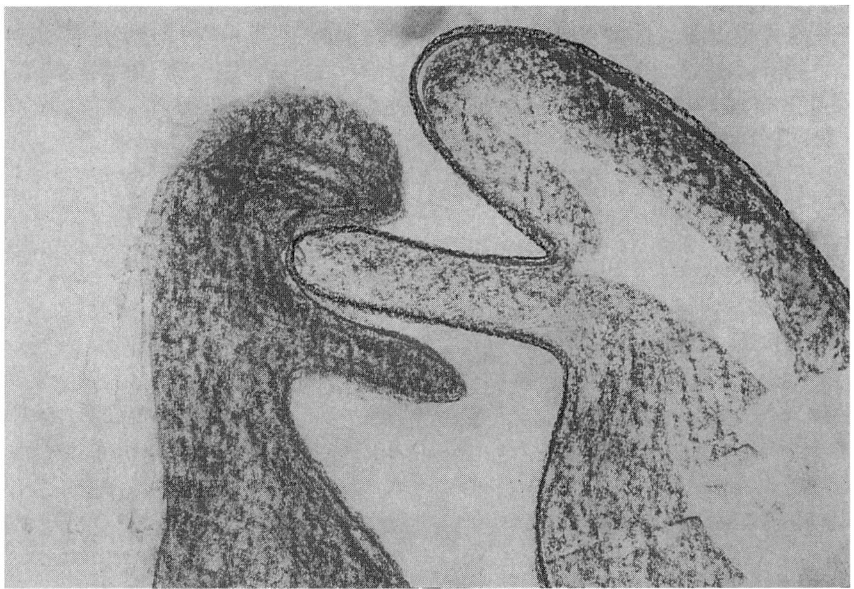

Fig. 7–10.

Therapy Session

As therapy continued it became clear that in Dave's relationships either he generally remained coolly detached, impotent, and unaffected by his peers, or overly sexualized. However, at the same time, he became overly dependent upon and attracted to certain authority figures—professors, older friends, and now his therapist.

Supervision

The helpless and hapless blue figure reclines upon an extended brown line (the therapist's graphic language for adopting analytic neutrality) (Fig. 7–11). The therapist is portrayed here as a large flower (snapdragon), which he described as oracular in that the client seemed to hang on every word of the therapist. The drawing also seemed to evoke for the intern the client's history of "melting into his mother's arms" during father's alcoholic rages. (In this session Dave had reported that his former lover had returned to attack him.)

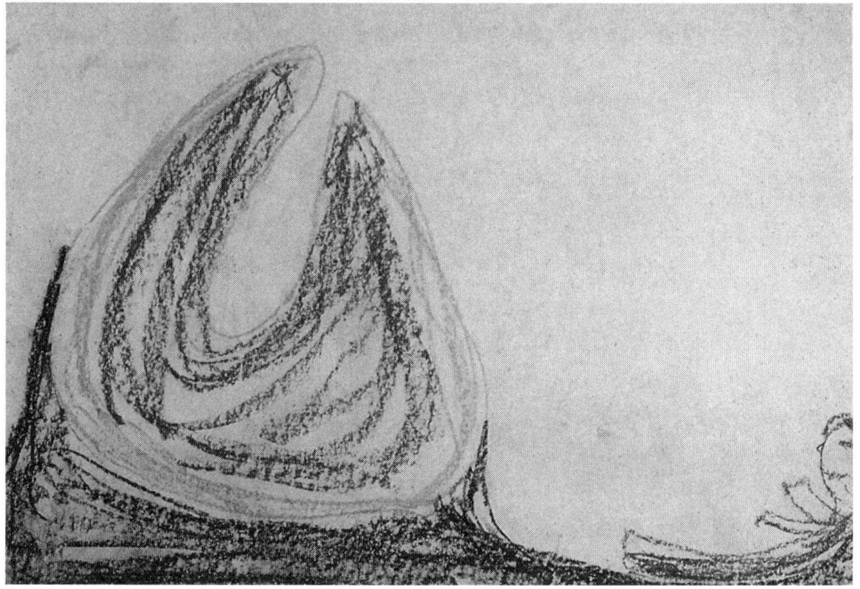

Fig. 7–11.

During our second look at this drawing, it was noted that however much the therapist saw himself as staying within an analytic stance, he was also clearly enjoying being the idealized object. He was cautioned by his supervisor neither to overidentify nor prematurely dispel this idealization. Again, this drawing is a graphic example of complementary countertransference wherein the therapist takes on the positive idealization of an omnipotent object. The supervisor suggested to the therapist to be on the alert for fears of engulfment and envy to surface in his client.

Therapy Session

The other side of the idealization—envious rage—appeared a number of sessions later (Fig. 7–12). In this session the client is critical and attacking of the therapist. In the session's drawing the blue wobbly figure on the right is the therapist, the green arrows are the client's.

Supervision

In our discussion of this drawing, it was noted that while these were aggressive arrows directed at the therapist, there was not a direct hit. For the therapist's

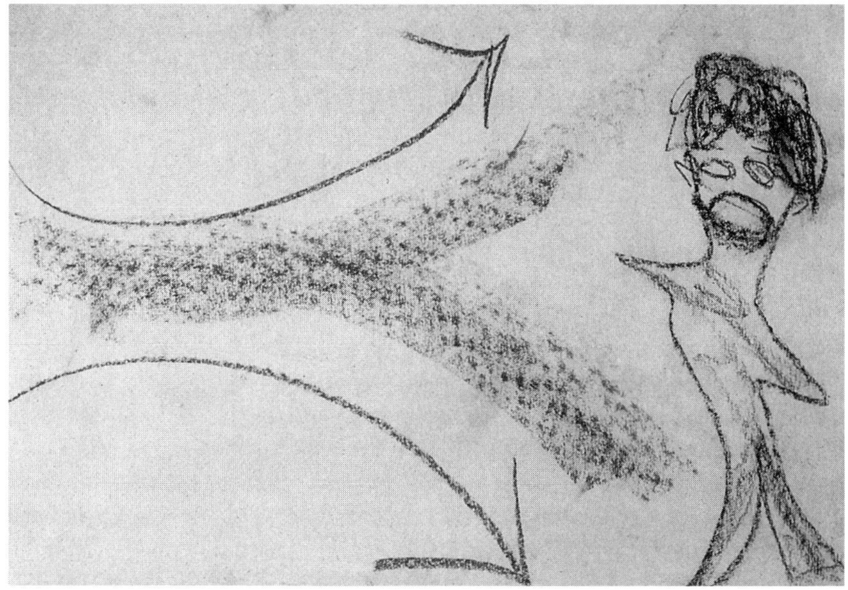

Fig. 7–12.

part, he is portrayed as wobbly but his boundaries remain intact. As illustrated here, the therapist is significantly more able than in his previous case to contain intense affect and not react outwardly. The supervisor also reframed the client's aggression as being necessary aggression in the service of the client's differentiation instead of thinking of it entirely as destructive envy. In the manner of Winnicott (1954, 1971), the therapist must survive the aggression directed toward himself so that he could eventually be discovered and made use of as a real external object as opposed to just being an internal subjective object of the client.

Therapy Session

As the therapy deepened, Dave tentatively recalled sexual advances his father made toward him in a shower when Dave was 11. He remembered wondering whether his father was homosexual, but was able to deny this from mother's accounts of their sexual satisfaction in the early years of their marriage. Apparently, she continued to confide in Dave about her sexual activities with her second husband after his natural father's death.

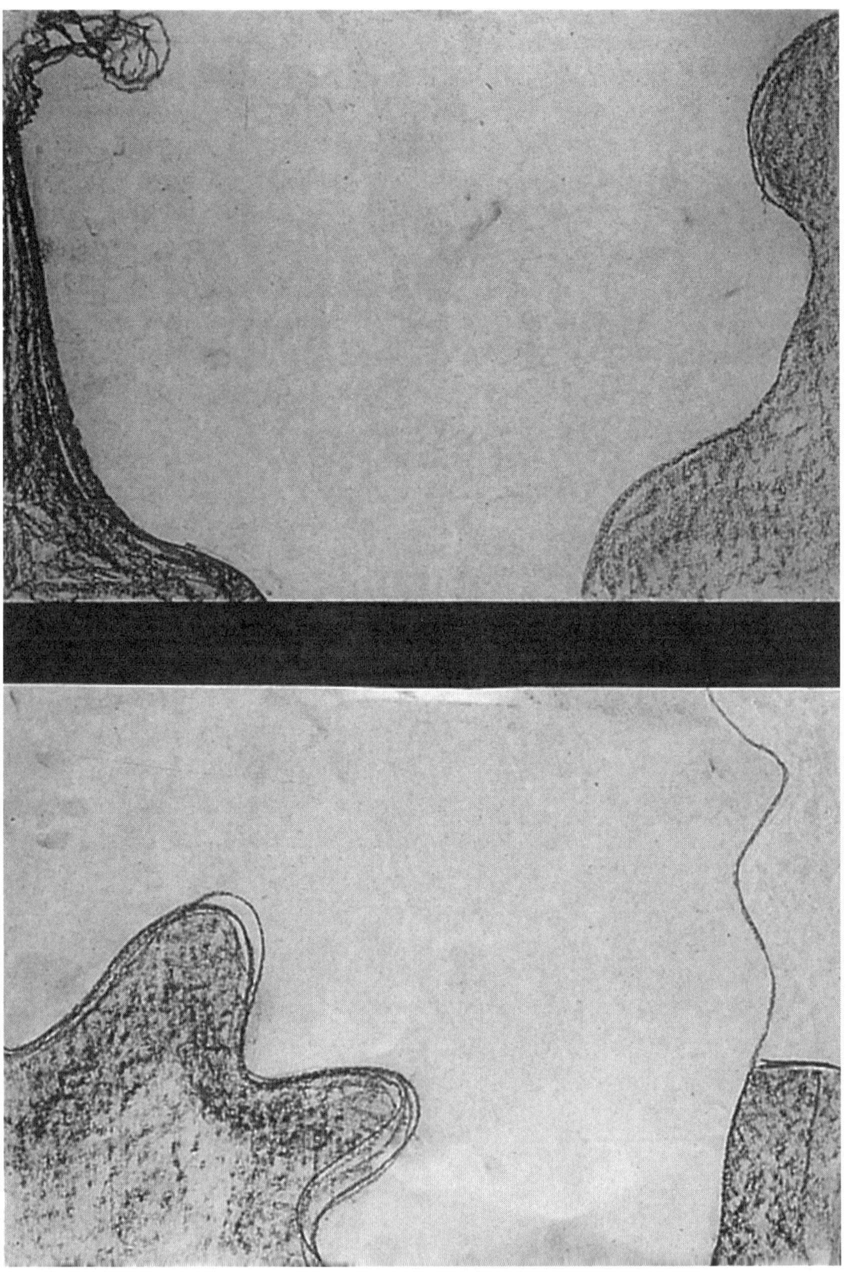

Fig. 7–13a, b.

Supervision

Two drawings of powerful projective identification processes (Fig. 7–13a and Fig. 7–13b) have been selected from later sessions, to show how the dynamics of Dave's relationship with his father and with his mother made their appearance in graphic language that was helpful for the supervision. In Fig. 7–13a the therapist describes himself as the small black figure on a cliff. Across the page on the right is a huge wave (the client) that is about to strike the shore. It was not evident to the therapist how he had drawn both himself and Dave as literally at the very edge of the paper. The brown boundary (client) raised the question of whether the client was beginning to be able to draw on the therapist insofar as this color brown had been consistently used by the intern when he was most inhabiting an analytic stance. The fact that the blue wave could be seen as an erect penis was not visible to the therapist until the second look in supervision. In this session's drawing there is a concordant countertransference. The therapist feels the sense of helplessness and fear in the face of Dave's despair, much as we might imagine Dave felt in the face of father's uncontained rages and sexuality. The pure intensity and confusion of the black figure suggested a need to attend to and listen for any arising suicidal impulses. The supervisor supported the developing work of the therapist by stressing the importance of his ongoing emotional presence and availability to Dave at this time.

In Fig. 7–13b, the therapist described himself as a brown and purple "supplicant figure" (on the left) at the feet of a blue female-looking form that had no arms, head, or feet. This time it is only the female form, which represents the client, that appears to be hugging the edge of the page. Is the figure backing away, we ask, as both intern and supervisor look together? The colors of the figure representing the therapist (brown and purple) indicate the struggle of the therapist to maintain his analytic stance (brown), while simultaneously experiencing the "primitive agony" (purple) of his client in relation to mother (Winnicott 1958). The supplicant figure has both a phallic-like and breast-like quality suggesting both Dave's gender and sexuality conflicts. The color blue fills the bottom or sexual part of the female figure; the top half is empty. In other words, the nurturing breast is empty. Here is graphically evident the effect of a narcissistically needy mother who had pressed her son into emotional caretaking.

Both of these drawings are powerful examples of the therapist learning to understand the role of projective identification and the meaning of containment in the work with more disturbed individuals (Bion 1962a,b).

Therapy Session

Late in the summer, Dave's mother came to visit him for a week. He was very much looking forward to their time together, but was dubious about her ability to control her drinking. He reported in this session that one evening, in a drunken stupor, she asked her son to make love to her. Dave was finally given outright the responsibility of setting the boundaries of intimacy in their relationship. He told her that he thought incest was improper and could not participate. She immediately recriminated and asked him to forget that she had brought it up.

One can only wonder at how Dave was able to maintain a consolidated sense of himself through this experience with his drunken mother. His sexual promiscuity, impotence, and emotional detachment all seemed a part of his strategy to guard against the threat of this union. The therapist was able to help Dave maintain a sense of integrity, both morally and psychologically, as he relived the experience in therapy. Dave clearly needed and utilized the support of this therapist, who, by this time, was safely viewed as a caring but distinct individual. (*This is the therapist's wish—a wish not actually evident in Fig. 7–14.*)

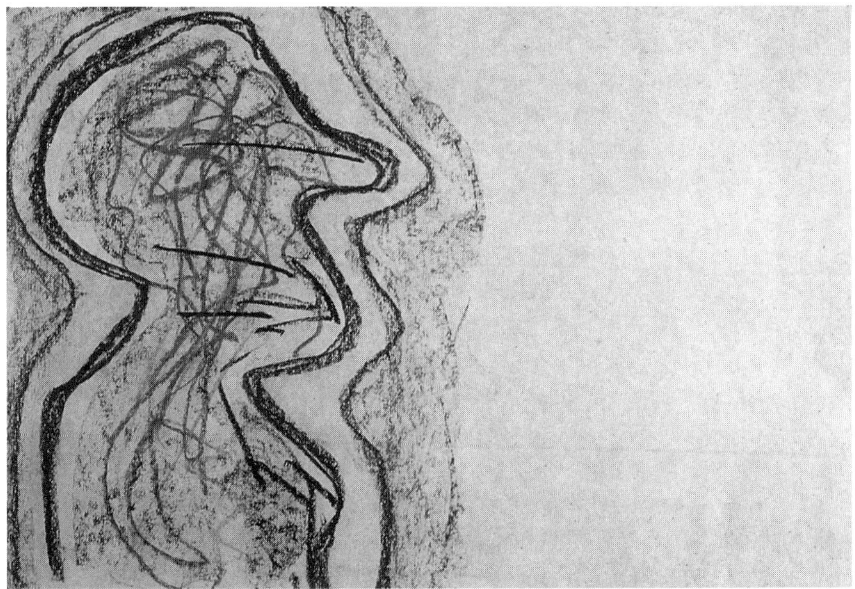

Fig. 7–14.

Supervision

The therapist described the outer brown/green profile of the head as himself. The inner profile he labeled as the client. He saw himself as "holding" the client, which indeed he was. The uncontained red fire seen in Fig. 7–8 is now within the psychic boundary of the client, while being supported or surrounded by the therapist. What was not seen by the therapist was his misinterpretation, or his wish, that the client be able to see him as more of a separate person than the client was in fact capable of at that time. In fact, the client is not drawn in a separate space, but is drawn within the boundaries of the therapist himself. The therapist is clearly wrapped around Dave. This portrayal speaks to the therapist's position at this time as being in the territory of Bion's (1962b) containment, Winnicott's (1960, 1960a) period of holding and illusion, or Stern's (1985) "self-regulating other" with his client.

The empty space on the right side of the drawing could be thought of, the supervisor suggested, as the potential space that the therapist holds in his mind for Dave's future differentiated self to take up residence. Clearly the therapist has become a reliable enough object at this point in the treatment. The therapist must now await other problematic transferences, that is, the feared sexual intrusion of the therapist's desire—that Dave's nonverbal attempts to seduce the therapist might succeed. The therapist was encouraged and was able to continue this treatment under close supervision at his next place of training. Dave became the first long-term psychoanalytic case of this intern. The treatment lasted four years.

IMPLICATIONS FOR CLINICAL AND PSYCHOANALYTIC TRAINING

In the realm of a psychoanalytic training of a verbal therapist (psychoanalysis is integral to the training of art-therapists at certain institutions), the so-called "negative space" of graphic-art language could be transformed into a "potential space," in psychoanalysis's language. The two clinical examples presented here make evident that a verbal therapist's brief and unsophisticated drawings of psychotherapy sessions can contribute in valuable ways to the development of an analytic mind. These benefits include the facilitation of case formulation within the supervisory relationship, the progressive extension of the use of the therapist's self as a clinical tool, and enhanced access to non- and preverbal psychic material that when held within the container of supervision can make its way into words and to a tangible representation of therapeutic progress.

The use of this drawing technique in clinical supervision has the potential for bringing to awareness primitive and nonverbal psychic states—those within the therapist as well as the patient. Primitive psychic states are often communicated through intense somatic and verbal evacuations, projections, and projective identifications having a coercive effect on the subjectivity of the therapist. Through a heightened but diffuse awareness, these primitive states may become clinical data to be used in facilitating the treatment. During the course of the treatment, the therapist can transfer aspects of these primitive states onto his or her drawings for verbal processing later in supervision. Initially a therapist's drawings may themselves only be an evacuation of sorts as a response to an intense transference, but as demonstrated in the two cases described, the therapist's drawings can be used by the supervisor to transmit the value of containment, leading to symbolic elaboration provided by tertiary symbolic processes—those processes lying between the workings of the image and linguistic signifiers (Green 2000). In addition, when the therapist is working with primitive mental states of mind, the drawings provide a colorful canvas in supervision for an alive exploration of the interworkings and interstices between affect and psychic representation—primary elements of the psychoanalytic discourse.

An unanticipated discovery within this drawing technique has been the finding that the therapist's initial drawing of the first session frequently functions in the same manner as that of a client's first reported dream. By this I mean that within the text of an initial dream, the core of the psychodynamic issues, which unfold subsequently in the treatment, are revealed. The same can be said for the first drawing of the therapist of his/her first session. For example, the therapist's drawings of the first sessions of the two clients—Steve and Dave—are distinctly different. They are different in how the therapist has used color, form, organization, and theme. It is not very difficult to discern from these two drawings that Steve (Case 1) functions with less psychic disturbance and impairment than Dave (Case 2). Steve is rendered in the drawing as a multicolored diamond shape with definite boundaries. The relationship between the rendering of Steve and the therapist, who is also boundaried, is somewhat tense and static—there is a sense of constricted aggression that appears here but within boundaried forms. In contrast, Dave is graphically presented as a diffuse collection of spots with no boundary containing them. The relationship between the rendering of Dave and the therapist appears simultaneously aggressive and sexualized and uncontained; the therapist's drawing of himself appears as if he has either blown the client into a collection of unboundaried bits, or is about to suck the client into himself and annihilate the client's separate dispersed identity altogether. These two drawings of first sessions evoke André Green's (1999) description of affect as a "dynamic pursuit of that, which leaving the body, returns to the body shaped by a meeting with the object" (p. 293). Even crude drawings of first sessions such as these can often give immediate access to the unconscious field of the client, of the therapist, and of the matrix of their relationship, that under ordinary conditions may take weeks, even months, to emerge in the verbal report of the therapist to his/her clinical supervisor.

There is no substantive reason that an adjunctive technique of a therapist's brief drawings of his/her analytic sessions could not be used for clinical supervision in any analytic training program, be that at a graduate or postgraduate level. Certainly for psychologists who learn the Rorschach inkblot test, such a drawing technique could easily be incorporated into training programs if a few psychoanalytically oriented art therapists could provide training and consultation on an "as needed" basis to interested analytic supervisors. Conceptual scoring categories of the Rorschach, with which psychologists are familiar, such as organization, form, color, movement, kinds of figures, perspective, shading, and so on can be applied, at least in part, to drawings as well. The addition of a period of clinical supervision where the intern or analytic candidate consistently draws his/her sessions across several cases would be well worth the effort it might take to actually integrate such a component into a clinical training curriculum.

8

Considering the Dilemmas of Training, Formation, and Authority in the Making of an Analyst[1]

> ***More than most forms of authority, analytic authority is mediated and influenced by individual consciousness. [and unconsciousness]***
>
> **(Kenneth Eisold 1998)**

Early analysts constructed and sustained their analytic authority in some measure on the basis of their idealization of analytic knowledge. The actual presence of Freud's paternal shoulders, of course, provided additional elevation. But from our current vista—the uneven landscape of postmodernism and the multiple subjectivities it includes—prescient claims "to know" correct, objectively formulated, and timely interpretations appear inflated. Such inflations reflect an identification with an Ideal ego (Freud 1914) residing in narcissistic omnipotence and Lacan's (1953) Imaginary—as opposed to an identification with an Ego ideal (Freud 1914) situated in a symbolic netting of imperfection (which, recalling our mobius, always has holes).

In narrations of early psychoanalytic institutions' travails, we find intense conflicts and actual psychic destruction. These seem to have been wrought from an "overly soldered" linkage of the idealization of analytic knowledge on the one hand, and the exercise of analytic power and authority on the other (Eisold 1998, Wallerstein 1998). Even now we experience the less than desirable psychic consequences of this linkage in residue. For instance, in some cases an individual analyst's public/didactic statements as to the prevailing norms of psychoanalytic knowledge and practice are found to be discontinuous with his/her actual clinical practice (Mayer 1996).

1. A version of this chapter was published in 2000 as "Considering Psychoanalytic Learning and Legitimacy: Another Perspective" in *Fort Da* 6:33–47.

Post-Freud generations have had to analyze the previously unanalyzed transference concerning "knowledge as power"—not only within and between psychoanalytic institutions, but also within the context of the psychoanalytic dyad itself (Benjamin 1996). This analysis (an interminable one, no doubt) has been evident in the concerted and continuing efforts by multiple analytic streams to understand what is the knowledge gained from countertransference and how the experience of countertransference can be used in the treatment (for example, see Boyer 1989, Gerson 1996, Hoffman 1991, Lacan 1953, Ogden 1994, Renik 1995, Spezzano 1996).

A palpable dynamism has been brought into psychoanalysis by the postmodern influence concerning the "psychoanalytic situation." But there is also potential catastrophic anxiety that this perspective carries with it as well. There is the potential that the ongoing and unceasing wave of deconstructionism could lead to the virtual destruction of all ego Ideals, which in turn could leave practitioners of psychoanalysis bereft of guiding standards as to what would constitute a "good enough" analytic encounter. In such a circumstance, there would remain little to inform and authorize an analytic practice.

The crux of the issue may be that substituting another (or any other) Ideal ego concerning analytic authority (e.g., healing instead of knowledge) would leave unaddressed the place and function of the Other in the context of psychic reality. Like the necessary illusion of the "ego" (which offers psychic cohesion but at another level is a misrecognition), any of a number of possible Ideal egos might serve to bind the analyst's anxiety, but may also function to close off the dynamic unconscious.

Jessica Benjamin (1997) addresses the importance of Otherness in her article "Psychoanalysis as a Vocation," by highlighting the manner in which unconscious contents of clinicians/analysts can easily be projected upon those who seek treatment. And psychoanalysis must address the function of the Other if creative exchange among the divergent strands of psychoanalysis is to occur. The Other has three aspects—aspects that need to be differentiated and yet are often not, in the psychoanalytic discourse in the United States. There is the Other as the locus of symbolic language—the structuring element for the unconscious in the human experience. There is "the other" that refers to all those internal objects that are not-me. And finally, there is the Other that refers to an other subject with a different subjectivity than my own. The Other is what marks a place for psychoanalysis apart from other forms of therapeutic treatment.

So how does one attain and hold a sense of viable analytic "authority" that does not rest primarily upon an identification with an Ideal ego of a repressed (or not so repressed) omniscient father? And how does one also account for the Other? Is there a viable residence for analytic authority in this postmodern world of multiplicity? I believe the answer is yes . . . but this residence may now more resemble a mobile home than a stable brick dwelling. Analytic authority lives within a dialectical space, between the Ideal ego of the tenets of one's chosen psychoanalytic school and the ego Ideal shared among all psychoanalytic schools: the recognition of the unconscious as the third party in any analysis—the underpinning of analytic authority.

To my mind, analytic authority is partly based upon an acquired knowledge of "theoretically and technically guided processes of interpretation, construction, etc., where certainly not all, or any, interventions will do, because there is always some actual experience of the analysand [and unique signifying elements] . . . that provide constraints . . ." (Mitchell 1998, p. 16). This acquired knowledge serves in part to bind the analyst's anxiety as well as to frame clinical thinking.

On the other hand, analytic authority is also partly based "in not knowing and not understanding, but a willingness to look at and think about the irrational, frightening and elusive aspects of human behavior" arising out of the unconscious (Bollas 1987, Eisold 1998, p. 883). Analytic authority resides "mobile-ly" rather than in a static place of a presumed knowledge of standards for psychic and behavioral health. To be the one (analyst) who knows reflects more of a modernist view. Postmodern analytic authority resides more mobile-ly in terms of its ongoing inquiry into the process of how the analyst's subjectivity contributes to the analysis, and how much this contribution should be verbally expressed within the analytic encounter.[2]

---

2. The shift from modernism to postmodernism is evoked in Lacan's description of masculine and feminine identification. A masculine position is linked more to the frame of symbolic language and its effects—here One could stand and be recognized for the group. A feminine position is less linked to the frame of language and therefore less anchored by it and more doubtful of it. Also, the feminine position is equally linked to the excess, or leftovers, from the limited reach of symbolic language—here Other-one must be recognized individually within context and it is not as if One can stand for the group. Modernism is more descriptive of a masculine position where there is more invested in the power of language to name and make knowledge. Postmodernism is more descriptive of a feminine position where knowledge gained via language is seen only as a part of a work (i.e., person) that is never complete or finished. In psychoanalysis a shift from knowing the correct interpretation (the One) to positing interpretive hypotheses drawn from the very

Finally, a postmodern analytic authority, I believe, must include a cognizance that any mutuality in the analytic relationship needs to be contextualized by an acknowledgment of the asymmetric relationship of power between analyst and analysand. As surely as the analyst must draw upon and use his/her subjectivity in the work, from whatever chosen analytic theory, the analyst must also monitor him-/herself, as self-awareness permits, "to hold and protect the analytic process to which the analysand has surrendered his/her speech and being" (Mitchell 1998, p. 29).

THE AMERICAN SCENE: WHO, HOW, AND WHAT SUSTAINS THE ANALYST'S WORK?

Who?

Who may, or may not be, an analyst has been a peculiarly North American question, for only in the United States was psychoanalysis originally established and maintained as the exclusive province of medical psychiatry. Despite Freud's (1926) support for the training of lay analysts, he nonetheless appears to have encouraged within the analyst an identification with an Ideal authority based upon an idealization of knowledge. Such encouragement may have fueled American medicine's entitled claim to psychoanalysis. As healers with elite authority, physicians have traditionally carried (or used to carry) an idealized transference. Entrance into and dissemination of psychoanalysis in the United States has been under the exclusive sway of physicians, as was assured by their initial colonization of the field. Indeed, the 1950s has been called the "golden age of psychoanalysis" precisely because of the degree of influence psychoanalysis then exercised upon psychiatric training and practice.

The enthusiastic embrace by psychiatry of an idealized identification, however, at least in part contributed to the serious challenge and devaluation of psychoanalysis during the 1960s and 1970s, a period characterized by widespread disaffection with authority and hierarchical institutions. By the 1980s, however, efforts to vanquish psychoanalysis intellectually (and/or to spoil it through envious attacks) had dissipated considerably. A

particular intersubjective matrix (the Other) of patient and analyst has occurred. This shift is perhaps most visible in the reworking of the concept and use of countertransference. (This reworking has its own problems and excesses that will need to be worked through in the future.)

desire to gain access to psychoanalytic experience and knowledge was increasingly expressed by nonmedical mental health professionals and academicians.

In 1988, The American Psychological Association executed a successful legal challenge to psychiatry's monopoly on psychoanalytic learning. This resulted in a significant broadening of the psychoanalytic playing field, by enabling nearly all mental health professionals and academic scholars to apply for psychoanalytic training if so desired.[3] Since 1988, there has been a flourishing of new analytic training programs, many attended by nonmedical participants. According to a January 1999 *New York Times* article, by 1996 there were 990 non-M.D. candidates in training at 29 institutes nationwide.

The San Francisco Bay area provides a prime example of such burgeoning and broadening interest in psychoanalytic training. Before 1980 there were only two analytic institutes extant: the San Francisco Psychoanalytic Institute (SFPI) and the C. G. Jung Institute. In subsequent years, three additional training institutes have arisen: the San Francisco Institute of Psychoanalysis and Psychoanalytic Psychotherapy (SFIPP), the Psychoanalytic Institute of Northern California (PINC), and the Lacanian School of Psychoanalysis (LSP).

How?

Among most U.S. psychoanalytic training institutions, several core elements of training have emerged. They include: (1) a personal or training analysis (there is some debate as to whether there is a difference), (2) four years of didactic seminars and case conferences, and (3) two or three supervised control analyses, case write-ups, and the completion of a written and/or public professional presentation.[4] These core elements reflect North American psychoanalysis's early insistence on establishing "quality control" to guard against what they saw as the practice of "wild analysis" elsewhere.

---

3. This was different for Jungian training. Psychologists (from the 1950s), social workers, and M.F.C.C.'s (from the 1970s) had already been admitted for analytic training among the Jungians—at least at the San Francisco Jungian Institute.

4. Interestingly, Kappelle (1996), in a 17-year study of the Dutch psychoanalytic institute selection criteria for new candidates, found the criteria to be vague, and the strongest factor to be utilized by admission committee members was intuition.

Through a special arrangement with the International Psychoanalytic Association (IPA) in 1938 (and unlike any other country), the American Psychoanalytic Association was singularly authorized to establish, oversee, and legitimize all psychoanalytic training institutions. The positive side of this special arrangement concerns the issue of quality control. But the negative side has included medical psychiatry's appropriation of psychoanalysis, and the hegemony of ego psychology as the voice of U.S. psychoanalysis (Bergman 1997, Wallerstein 1998). From a Lacanian perspective, the (traditional) medical discourse is the quintessential "master's discourse." But a master's discourse and an analytic discourse are two very different entities.

Every psychoanalytic training program, of whatever persuasion, strives to foster the internalization of analytic knowledge and authority within its candidates. But the nature of this knowledge and authority is understood differently by the different institutions, and these differences naturally influence the professional authority transmitted to its candidates.[5] One need only read the accounts of the splitting of the New York Institute to feel the fractious history surrounding the issues of analytic knowledge and authority at that institution, and, by extension, that all who pursue analytic training consciously or unconsciously carry (Eisold 1998). It is an understatement to say that the making of an analyst within any institution is fraught with myriad challenges at different levels.[6]

Siegfried Bernfeld, one of the early fathers of the San Francisco Psychoanalytic Institute, remarked that the motives for establishing a training institution often differ from those motives that serve to maintain it (Bernfeld 1962).[7] Another way of saying this is that founding motives are rarely consonant with those motivations needed to maintain institutional existence and influence in a wider community. Both founding and sustaining mo-

5. In Jungian analytic training, the emphasis on didactic seminars, writing, and presenting clinical work is perhaps second to the institution's role in facilitating and provoking the candidate's personal journey of transformation on the road to becoming an analyst.

6. Both iconoclastic and traditional avenues of learning have characterized my particular path into, and within, psychoanalysis, giving me perhaps an atypical perspective regarding psychoanalytic training. This path no doubt is determined by my own private psychic landscape. It has led me to a personal search for and finding of individual mentors/analysts/clinicians preceded, and then later paralleled, by more formalized training. Beginning with the work of Jung, moving into the British school (a special love for the Middle School), and, in more recent years, to Lacan and the French influence, I have found psychoanalysis to be a mixed media montage—a work always in progress.

7. Bernfeld ultimately resigned from the Institute, related to issues of training.

tives within an institution are, however, subject to the interplay of group dynamics. For example, the nurturing paternal motive of founding a structure that supports the flow of ideas and interpersonal connections can, via group dynamics, transfigure over time into something quite different. Jungian analyst Gareth Hill (1962) has called the end product of this devolution the "negative static masculine"—a structure that becomes hierarchical, calcified, and suffocating of creativity.

Otto Kernberg's (1996) article, "Thirty Methods to Destroy the Creativity of Psychoanalytic Candidates," is written in a humorous and provocative vein, but touches on many of the ways that institutions can and do indeed take on Hill's negative static masculine. Kernberg's list includes:

- isolate candidates within the institution
- emphasize hierarchical relations
- neglect exploring theoretical controversies
- perpetuate conflicts around training analysts
- intellectually insulate the institution itself

Kernberg's thirty ways are resonant with various historical accounts of psychoanalytic institutions, but they remain salient issues for this new generation of analytic institutions as well.[8]

What?

Following upon Kernberg's remarks, the question of what sustains analytic work beyond training arises and moves to the foreground. A significantly antianalytic element regarding "recognition" operates in the fantasies of those who seek to become "an analyst" (Grinberg 1989). "The wish for authentification of one's desire, the search for identificatory symbols, and a desire to belong to a group" are all factors of recognition that, to a greater or lesser degree, influence how one seeks psychoanalytic education and/or certification (Filloux 1996, p. 460). But "dis-identification" is an element crucial to assuming and maintaining an analytic stance over the course of an analysis, as one needs to be able to make use of and differ-

8. It is quite unlikely that such a humorous and provocative article would have even appeared in the *International Journal of Psycho-Analysis* had it not been written by the then President of I.P.A.

entiate from both transference and transference/countertransference enactments. The need to be recognized, then, and to recognize others, may jeopardize the aspiring analyst's ability to "dis-identify."

Certification and position in the institute may satisfy a "desire" for recognition insofar as desire generally is supported by fantasy. It is hoped that idealizing fantasies attached to the signifier "psychoanalyst" will be optimally disillusioned during the training process. (If analytic identification is staked upon an Ideal ego of an omniscient object, then this is not the case; see Rycroft 1993.)

Thus, whereas a desire for recognition may serve to impel one into analytic training, and whereas this same desire may resurge from time to time throughout training and beyond, it will not really serve to sustain analytic work through the years. Another kind of desire, and, I would say, even something of partial drive satisfaction, must occur in order to sustain analytic work over time. It is my experience that this satisfaction is derived from something beyond the letter of the law of certification or institute position; it is also something apart from the fantasies of one's ego. It is derived from something more akin to a drive. The pleasure of discovering and using image and word to name and interpret is the epistemological drive at work—be that framed by Freud, Klein, Bion, and so on. For Lacan, it is not so much the epistemological drive as it is a passion for deciphering that constitutes the desire of the analyst.

To my mind, there is something of a knot at the level of Winnicott's primary creativity that makes for the passion that serves in part to constitute and sustain the desire of the analyst. On the most primitive psychic level, I believe that the analyst's investment in working with psychic envelopes has both a compensatory and a creative aspect. The analyst's infantile libidinal investment in the "strangeness of verbal signifiers" is no doubt related to her/his experience of the holding function of [mother's] sonorous envelope of the voice, as well as of the signifying function of phonemes and words (Guillaumin 1990).[9] The quality of "strangeness" to the verbal signifiers arises from either insufficient infant–mother connections

9. The role of vision (gaze of mother and baby) and the image in the making of psychic envelopes is also considerable (see Lacan's article on the mirror stage). Due to this, in Lacanian psychoanalysis the work with a psychotic individual is face to face. In these cases the psychic envelope or ego is insufficiently formed so the visual contact is considered necessary. A period of face-to-face work may precede a shift to use of the couch in nonpsychotic individuals as well, but for different reasons.

or insufficient scarification of its ruptures, during the development of early psychic envelopes. It can be said that analytic work largely concerns the use and differentiation of internal and external envelopes of all kinds, at different levels, within a verbal/voice territory. The analytic session, though not solely a verbal territory, nonetheless privileges speech because it is how the meaningful relationships between inside and outside, registered in multiple sensory modalities, are recognized. It seems to me that "good-enough" analytic work is significantly sustained by repetitive, libidinally lived, compensatory and creative experiences. These experiences include, for example, silences filled with the not-yet-spoken, and at times simply unspeakable, stuff of love, hate, loss, desire, and so on. There is pleasure for the analyst in seeing and hearing a patient express in his/her unique gestures, imagery, and language, previously inchoate experiences, especially after patient and analyst have mutually emerged from a transference/countertransference wormhole. There is the rustle of aliveness, also, in being present in, and a witness to, the singularity of a person in her/his analytic process owning her/his lived history. It is these experiences that sustain us through the stressful (perhaps even persecutory) times of managed health care's challenge to analytic authority and psychoanalytic treatment (Widlocher 1998).

POSTMODERNITY, ANALYTIC IDENTITY, AND AUTHORITY

Having spoken briefly to the issues of who may seek analytic training, what training includes, and what may sustain analytic work over time, I would like finally to address the knotty matter of "legitimacy" and analytic identity. When the psychologists' successful 1988 legal suit opened psychoanalytic institute doors to non-M.D.'s, conflict and controversy surrounding a "legitimate" analytic identity—now contextualized by a postmodern sensibility—was also generated (Slavin 1990, Spezzano 1990). Is I.P.A.'s recognition of an institute necessary for analytic graduates of an institution to legitimately assume an analytic identity?

Reflecting the shift from modernity to postmodernity, there is more than one position on the question of what makes analytic identity legitimate. Jessica Benjamin (1997) noted in her paper "Psychoanalysis as a Vocation" that the Lacanian theorists were the first to address the question of what postmodernity may portend for identity. Freud's insistence on the singularity of each person's identity, marked by conscious/unconscious division, led Lacan (1964) to highlight the analyst's desire in his emphasis on the formation element rather than the training element in the making of an analytic identity and its legitimization. Looking into Lacan's concept of the desire of the analyst as it was the focus of "la passe," the three issues of analytic authority, training, and legitimacy are found to spiral one another.

Lacan's "la passe" was designed as a procedure for punctuating a legitimate transition—a passage marking one from being an analysand to becoming an analyst. This experiment in large part failed (Lacan 1967) for reasons too intricate to detail here, but the germ of Lacan's idea about "la passe" remains pertinent to the clinician's taking an analytic stance—whether or not the signifier of psychoanalyst is taken up. The "passe" procedure was an accounting of the analyst's unconscious desire. It posed the question: Around what does the desire to become an analyst turn? I say "turn" here because the desire of the analyst is not equivalent to the desire to become an analyst. No, the spirit of the passe could be framed as an attempt to use "clinical fact" as a basis for authorizing an analytic position first, identity second (Britton and Steiner 1994, Lacan 1967, Ogden 1994, Wilson 1998).[10] Such questions arise as: Has there been a felt realization that, like the Wizard of Oz, the analyst has stood in the place of the big Other, to whom one's demands, symptoms, sufferings, and desires have been spoken? Has the vulnerable, divided human being who worked with (and behind) the screen of transferences on one's behalf also been her-/himself discovered? Has a particular knowledge been gained about the truth of one's own particularities of desire? Have these discoveries been followed by a creative act—in deed or in speech? In other words, has there been an act of personal authorship? And is there an insistent passion for the unconscious and its formations (i.e., dreams, verbal slips) that pushes one toward the position of the analyst?

For Lacan there was only personal analysis, and if the analysis ended with the desire of an analyst, then retroactively it could been seen as having been a training analysis. Knowing that the pronoun "I" is preconstituted in a field of language preceding the individual, when anyone assumes the

10. A Lacanian analytic training begins with a public presentation of a palimpsest—a writing on, or editing of, a founding manuscript of a school so as to address the question of wanting to become an analyst. La passe continued in a modified form in the Lacanian School of Psychoanalysis during the period in which I was there. The initial palimpsest is retained, but the passe has been renamed the "passage"—which concerns one's personal testimony to the school members regarding her/his analytic experience.

position of an "I" on certain occasions (in this instance following an analytic encounter), it is not simply to communicate or to describe, but to make speech a performative act—that is, this act creates and/or claims an area of subjectivity for one's self. It was from this sort of psychic space that Lacan spoke of the analyst authorizing him-/herself by laying claim to the position and identity of "analyst" (Canton 1991). (It should be noted, however, that even he added later that this identification must also recognized by "some others.")

ANALYTIC TRAINING OR ANALYTIC FORMATION IN THE MAKING OF AN ANALYST

A fertile question "la passe" continues to pose to the current community of analysts is this: What does it really mean to be an analyst? Experienced practitioners are aware that merely bearing the signifier "psychoanalyst" does not guarantee the quality of clinical work, nor does it guarantee in fact that a psychoanalysis or psychoanalytic psychotherapy has taken place (despite any training institution's best efforts to implement quality control). Similarly, at the level of "clinical fact," it is also evident that successful psychoanalyses and analytic psychotherapies occur in consulting rooms of clinicians who do not carry the symbolic signifier of "psychoanalyst."[11] The fact that it was not uncommon for partners of analysts in earlier times to seek training and develop a psychoanalytic practice outside the purview of the institutes is a reminder that legitimacy in psychoanalysis has always been a relative term, as well as a term of relative desire, so to speak. Adopting the psychoanalytic method is distinct from training institutions per se.

The critical distinction to be made at the nexus of analytic training, analytic authority, and legitimacy is identifying the difference between what goes into an analytic training and what goes into the formation of an analyst. Training involves traversing a formal structure of seminars and procedures; it has a defined beginning and end. This traverse can be certified. An analytic formation is less easily (and less temporally) defined. A formation entails living through a process of being irrevocably altered in one's being by the analytic encounter. As such, it cannot be regulated by

11. Psychoanalyst Owen Renik was quoted in a *New York Times* article: "I don't care what you call yourself, if you help people feel better, word gets out. If you don't help people, I don't care how good your marketing is, you'll go down the tubes."

institutional procedures. Nor can it be guaranteed to have occurred by any symbolic certification from an institution or international organization, that is, I.P.A. (Canton 1991).

When there has been a psychoanalytic training only, and no actual formation, one's analytic identity may be deemed symbolically legitimate, but what does that mean? It could be no different from merely adding another set of letters (such as Ph.D.) to one's name. Lacan's procedure of the "passe" can be framed as a vital challenge to this kind of psychoanalytic training, whereby there is no questioning of the desire of the analyst-to-be.

When there has been an analytic formation only, without a formalized psychoanalytic training, an analytic identity may be experienced by one's self and colleagues; yet this identity will lack the symbolic legitimacy of recognition by an analytic institution. Each of these analytic identities has a kind of legitimacy in its own terms; each has a kind of currency in day-to-day professional practice.

In the broader field of legitimacy, the ethics of training speaks to the significant issue of quality control and standard of care that professions demand. Ethics related to formation, however, speak to a territory apart from, but in relation to, our symbolic institutions. This quality, in my mind, is in part evoked by Antigone's insistence that her brother's body be buried rather than left exposed to be ravaged by nature—as was decreed by Creon's laws. Her claim appealed to what prefigures social law in blood relations, and also to what is somehow beyond symbolic law—all the while remaining accountable to the law as decreed.

One (ego) ideal of a "legitimate" analytic identity contains, and is contained by, an analytic training and an analytic formation. By definition, however, ego ideals are never fully realized; there is always something missed in our aim—a gap, in other words. But it is in aiming at an ever-moving horizon that capacities are stretched, with the remaining gap nourishing creativity.

In one of his last essays, "Analysis Terminable and Interminable," Freud (1937b) describes the practice of psychoanalysis as being closer to an art than a science. This position is highlighted in bold relief by Lacan (1953), who could be said to have named an analytic ego ideal in his Rome Discourse: "The art of the analyst must be to suspend the subject's certainties until their last mirages have been consumed" (p. 43) so that the subject might make conscious decisions that are more in keeping with having a dynamic relationship with her/his unconscious desire.

In the final analysis, a legitimate analytic identity is not a static identification to be achieved, but the taking, losing, and retaking of an analytic position through time as to the legitimacy of the analytic method itself, a method that necessarily makes the analyst, as well as those who seek her/his consultation, a "subject [always] in process" (Kristeva 1982). How might psychoanalysis, within the borders of educational institutions, promote the analytic method of renewing the "subject in process," versus getting bogged down in a prescribed analytic institute curriculum?

Insofar as the unconscious is the third place that analysts of all persuasions return to with their patients, should the unconscious not be a place to return to in analytic institutions as well? If the conflictual tension between the paths of psychoanalytic training and a psychoanalytic formation is held, with elements of certainty put aside, would this facilitate the unconscious's remaining alive in any analytic curriculum? Is it be possible in the United States for an analytic identity to form partly within, and yet also beyond, institutional walls? Could there be an analytic passage similar to the tutorial model of psychoanalysis's early pioneers? Is there a place for the construction of an analytic identity that would constitute an explicitly individualized passage—a passage guided by an analyst/mentor, recognized by participating analytic institutions, authorized by one's own analytic encounter, learning, and supervised analyses? Can there be an analytic passage that is an apprenticeship?

If an apprentice were to move in and out of analytic institutions, within a singular personalized formation, could not the comings and goings of this Other offer these institutions something positive? In this period of renewal for psychoanalysis, and amid the pallor of managed health care, I would suggest there is a benefit for analytic institutions to have what Lacan called a "plus one." The "plus one" is someone who intermittently enters a preestablished working/learning group—a someone who is, by definition, not a regular member of the group. It is anticipated that the presence of the intermittent "plus one" may partially disrupt transferences forming within the group and make them less able to solidify—to make a mirage in which the unconscious has no part to play. The aim therefore of the "plus one" is to help to protect the mental, creative, and learning space of the group members by making an optimal and periodic rupture/gap that facilitates a working dialectic between conscious and unconscious processes. Could not an analytic apprenticeship function in this manner for psychoanalytic institutions?

The recent document on Standards of Psychoanalytic Education from the Psychoanalytic Consortium[12] (2001) attempts, within a diverse field of analytic training programs, to address how to minimize Kernberg's thirty destructive methods of training. Thus the conscious intention no doubt is good. Yet this document is also an unconscious repetition. It is a more benign hegemony than that which the American Psychoanalytic Association established in the 1940s, but it is a hegemony nonetheless. The education standards as described therein must be intended to apply only within the borders of the United States; there are no international bodies named as its sponsors. If this is so, why does the United States analytic community again need to split and cordon itself off from the larger international psychoanalytic community? Other questions are raised as well. What is to be gained by this splitting off from the international community other than an illusory control managed by an identification with an Ideal ego, but not an ego Ideal? Would the international community of psychoanalysts endorse the definition of psychoanalysis in this document as "a specific form of individual psychotherapy"? Would there be agreement that the aim of psychoanalysis includes "enhanc[ing] adaption"? Can numbers—session frequency or linear time—ever assure "a personal psychoanalytic experience of frequency, depth, intensity, and duration adequate to provide a deep psychoanalytic experience"? (Additional questions and issues are raised by the Consortium document, so interested readers are encouraged obtain a copy from any of the ratifying organizations.) Surely psychoanalysis is an impossible profession, when its very nature is subversive, and, yet there insists a desire for transmission, of continuing the analytic method (Safouan 2000).

Surely, it is also only realistic that both older and newer institutions will inevitably face the dilemmas detailed by Kernberg. Any sequential training, operating within an established hierarchy of authority, tends to promote infantilization, hindering candidates' ability to exercise their own authority and hindering their ability to alloy this authority with clinical responsibility, by being able to think their own thoughts within a dynamic relationship to their unconscious. Would creativity, fluid thinking, even optimal anxiety, not actually be facilitated for institutional candidates by

12. Consortium composed of American Academy of Psychoanalysis; National Membership Committee on Psychoanalysis in Clinical Social Work; Division of Psychoanalysis, American Psychological Association; and the American Psychoanalytic Association.

periodic interruptions of institute structure by the comings and goings of a few apprentices on the path of their own analytic formations? This now-and-again presence of the Other within the institution might also serve as a salient reminder of the complex psychic responsibility the candidate desires, and indeed accepts, when the signifier of "analyst" is ultimately claimed.

9

Tracing the Limits of Symbolization in Psychoanalysis

The universe is made of stories, not atoms.
(Muriel Rukeyser 1994)

When a psychoanalyst takes her/his place in one of the inextricably linked spaces of our metaphorical psychoanalytic mobius (see Chapter 2, this volume), she/he is putting her/his own psyche-soma into play to further a Symbolic process that is exquisitely, and at times excruciatingly, Real. This closing chapter concerns the issue of the Real (Lacan) and how it forwards the aim of an analytic encounter and the experience of being real (Winnicott).

It has been said that the depressive individual's interiority reflects most acutely and truthfully the level of loss /absence that must be humanly borne in order to fully inhabit a place from which to love, create, and desire. In parallel fashion, the psychotic individual's interiority, and the holes therein, might be said to reflect most acutely and truthfully the complexity and fragility of the symbolic weaving that is required to construct and hold a human psyche. To experience too much of the Real, be that in ecstasy or agony (or psychosis), is to be pushed beyond what is essentially human. The human condition by definition requires that a symbolic net be (gently, firmly, and adequately) laid over the starkness of unmediated Realness. This Symbolic netting provides the means and the time needed to break the Real up into smaller, psychically digestible pieces. (Bion's [1962b] transformation of the Real as beta elements into alpha elements for alpha function refers to this same territory.)

Joanne Greenberg—author of *I Never Promised You a Rose Garden*, a description of the treatment of her own psychosis—described this relationship of psychotic process to Symbolic net in a public presentation recently.

She said, "To have experiences, you have to have them be defined. In psychotic states there is only now, and now, and now. . . ." She observed further, "There is a rupture of metaphor in psychosis and so there is no meaning. A recovery of meaning only comes through an ability to learn." (Here the reader may pick up the clear resonance of both Bion and Lacan's ideas regarding how learning from experience is tied to the symbolic capacity to think and transform the sensuous.)

At its best, our Symbolic netting provides a container in which much of the Real can be wrapped, leaving the elements of the Real that do fall through the holes of the symbolic netting to be experienced as the ongoing pulse of the drives. At its least adequate, the Symbolic netting allows too much of the Real to fall through its holes, creating the experience of there being a lurking, ever-present disaster waiting to happen, or of the individual's having to undergo an endless series of catastrophes that must be survived. Without adequate Symbolic netting, the Real is too real—too hot, too cold, too something—for any human being to bear or psychically metabolize. Here life is survival and not living.

These comments lead to a place where the dialectical tension described in Chapters 1 and 2, between the figures of Winnicott (developmental) and Lacan (structural) and their approaches to psychoanalysis, partially resolves in their creative coupling pertaining to the polyvalency of the word "Real."

To be alive and feel real was foremost in Winnicott's (1956, 1958a) mind as to where an analysis ought to aim, because for him it constitutes the essence of being human. Feeling real resides in the experience of being saturated with the color of one's own internal objects (the Imaginary). Winnicott's investment in the analysand's being able to establish and sustain an intermediate play space has as its endpoint the richness of feeling real. Foundational to the infant/subject's being able to establish this intermediate space is minimal provision by the external object/mOther (Winnicott 1960).[1] This provision is Real (actual environmental sensory care), and Imaginary, in the manner in which the mOther draws upon her own Imaginary to fantasize about and hold her infant in reverie, and Symbolic in how mOther and father both reserve a place for the infant as a subject in the process of becoming (specifically in terms of Bion's containment—see Chapter 3, this volume).

---

1. This represents an addition to, not a negation of, Klein's elaboration of the inner object world.

Turning the kaleidoscope a bit, Lacan's (1953f, 1964) aim for an analysis also concerns the Real. The analysand in analysis has the opportunity to encounter, via the analytic discourse, the unconscious kernels of the Real as the source of her/his own desire and aliveness. S/he can also encounter how this Real has been clothed in fantasies (Imaginary). These fantasies are of course necessary, but they also obfuscate the fact that a major function of the fantasies is to obviate one's own existential angst. In fact, Lacan's definition of what it means "to be human" could be summed up in his (1953) statement, "Life has only one meaning, that in which desire is borne by death" (n.p.). To be human is to bear the gain and the loss/angst inherent to the human capacity for symbol making—a capacity that gives some degrees of freedom to shape one's life and death as one's own in a manner that no other living being can or *must* face.

How might this look in terms of the mobius metaphor of Chapter 2? If the weave of the Symbolic mobius ribbon has large gaps/holes in it, there are then many more opportunities in the everyday flow of life to trip and fall into one of these holes of the Real and experience moment/s of anxiety in which any self-reflection disappears—because the subject him-/herself disappears. How large or small the gap/hole may be will be reflected in how much time and psychic effort it takes for the subject to reach the other side of the gap, where the regularity of the weave or social/symbolic structure reestablishes his/her subjective footing. For example, a minor fall might look like "Oh, oh. . . . Okay, I am here in the job interview. I blew it on that question. Okay, now get ready for the next one." A major fall into the Real, on the other hand, might look like psychotic disorganization.

It has been said that Winnicott's potential or intermediate space and Lacan's gap or lack do not at all refer to the same psychic space. Yes and no. While theoretically speaking, this may be the case, clinically speaking it is much more useful to think of them in relation to each other as a complementary co-creation. The interlocking structure of the Real, the Symbolic, and the Imaginary, of course, precedes every mother–infant couple, making their intersubjectivity a triadic affair. And this triadic affair must turn into a lasting and good-enough relationship in order for the potential space (a space that both the infant and adult subject require in order to mine the essential gap in being carved by the symbol) to be created or sustained sufficiently.[2]

---

2. In the United States these last thirty years, more individuals with severe psychic disturbance are seeking mental health services, making considerations of the concepts of the Real and real all the more relevant to clinicians.

The two analytic encounters that follow are ones for whom my years of infant-observation training strengthened my analytic presence to make me more able to bear with disturbed states of mind. In the (first) case of Ms. O., this training also paradoxically enabled my taking an executive/maternal position in the face of her disassembling mind. Both of these analytic encounters highlight the dimension of the Real (Lacan) and the real (Winnicott) as follows: (1) the Real as severe trauma in need of further symbolization, (2) the kernels of the Real animating the unconscious fantasies of desire, and (3) the impact on the subjective experience of feeling alive and real when the accumulation of the first two experiences of the Real has been untenable. Of these two analytic encounters, only the latter, the one with Ms. S., served to mitigate the traumatic Real enough to enable her to shift her subjective position in relation to the kernels of the Real, such that she could experience feeling more real in her life.

Of the two cases that follow, the first is a presentation of a patient's encounter with the traumatic Real that effectively set a limit on the analysis and its aims.

THE CASE OF MS. O.

Ms. O. forgot the door code to enter my office building and began knocking upon the glass entry door. Since such forgetfulness may be the first communication in an initial appointment, my ear was attuned to hearing a knock. I answered the door.

Striking in her sophisticated style of dress, she replicated in sight what I had heard in her voice when she called for an appointment. In other words, she got right down to business. It was somehow not surprising to me, after having described herself as depressed and disconnected during the last year, that, having finally arrived here in my office, she was not entirely sure why she was here. Her depression had lifted shortly after making the call for an appointment.

Her life of fifty years had been marked by recurrent periods of this self-described depression/disconnection. She had almost always managed these episodes on her own, reaching out to books, nature, or meditative practices rather than to people.

Ms. O. left home at age 22 by marrying someone she did not love as a primary guilt-free means to leave her single mother, whose own depressions had been severe, recurrent, untreated, and quite debilitating to her capacity to emotionally parent her two children (i.e., children left with baby sitters during the work week and left to their own devices on the weekend when mother was often depleted and bedridden by her depressive condition).

Father had been alcoholic and a womanizer, leaving the family when Ms. O. was 3 years of age. She mentioned specifically that she had seen her father on only three occasions thereafter. (This was the moment that the number three first palpably registered within me.) Ms. O. in large part could be said to have constructed in her mind what "being an adult" was by watching TV, reading books, and the adult movies her mother would take her to see as her companion. The brittleness of this construction is conveyed by how decentered I became one day when I went to the waiting room for Ms. O. I did not recognize the woman I encountered there—without make-up, dressed in sweats—as Ms. O.

Describing herself as a "loner at heart," what long-term friends Ms. O. had, lived in other cities—a telephone cord linking them. She preferred it this way. Often excited about the possibility of a "new friendship," she said that she had found that over time it was always difficult to maintain the same level of interest in the relationship as did her friends. Although not college-educated, she was very bright and it was clear that her work had been the most consistent source of personal success. Currently she lived with a roommate (not really a friend) in a bedroom community that offered few social opportunities. Her lifelong series of monogamous relationships had begun for Ms. O. with her first marriage at age 22. She blurted out in the second session, quite unrelated to the train of thought she had been pursuing, that she had not had an orgasm since age 20. The decision to marry someone she did not love had its cost; however, it may have been the better of the two choices she was faced with—marry or stay home with a profoundly depressed mother.

Most of the above information was obtained during three preliminary sessions. At the end of these three sessions I suggested that she had a choice. She could once again go on with her life, since she was now feeling better, as she had done many times before. Or, if she wished to pursue another kind of encounter with herself, my recommendation was that she commit at least a year to her treatment, coming no less than twice a week to sessions and more frequently if possible. She was startled. This was not at all what she had expected. She had anticipated every-other-week sessions, or at most, once-a-week sessions for a few months. Though she felt surprised, she was also intrigued. She wanted to think about it so she made another appointment. By the next meeting, Ms. O. explained that she had decided to continue in the hopes she might better understand something about herself, though she was not sure what that actually meant. We began meeting twice a week.

It was during our fifth session that Ms. O. asked to use the analytic couch. She found it very difficult to stay in touch with her own experience and speak of it while she was looking directly at me. She noted that when she could on occasion tear away her gaze, words came more easily. On my part, I was finding it difficult to think when under the intensity of her gaze and wondered about my not having suggested the use of the couch. And indeed, once the initial awkwardness remitted for her (that of lying on a couch with another adult sitting out of view behind her), she did find it easier to stay with and speak from her own experience. She began to remember significant recurrent dreams and memories, and my mind felt free to wander upon the musical landscape of her words and silences. In other words, she seemed ripe for an analytic journey.

At three months into the treatment a very unusual session occurred. This followed a session in which she had spoken of several key issues: (1) how she thought of relationships as functional versus providing emotional attunement and "how not feeling good enough [about herself] plays into this," (2) how she always felt like an "outsider and got twisted into feeling underdeserving" because she came from a single parent family, (3) how they were "farmed out to babysitters and got no recognition from dad," and (4) how she used to "make up worlds to be in and make a cocoon for [her]self."

Session

Ms. O.: The last session is the first time that afterward a depression seeped over me. It was all pervasive, but subtle, and it lasted until yesterday afternoon. It was in the atmosphere all around me. First I reacted to it, but then I asked myself what was going on. I then realized it was connected to how I act so autonomously in my relationships. I realized that I had always thought it was a positive attribute. It is so fundamental to me that I now realize how BIG it is and how hard it will be to change now that we have talked about it. And I know I like things to be identified and fixed quickly, and this is not something that can be fixed on my time line—and at the same time, and being in this place, something did shift in me.

MI: A recognition of something?

Ms. O.: A woman psychic that I used to speak to once a year for about fifteen years once told me that none of the men in my life knew me or knew how to feel close to me. . . .

MI: [I speak here to how she had felt intrigued in the beginning sessions as if I might help her be able to get closer to knowing something of herself through coming closer to me through twice-a-week sessions.]

Ms. O.: [She reports three dreams, the last one having to do with my upcoming three-week vacation. We process the dream material awhile, especially about my leaving. She falls silent for a moment.] Then another thing happened. I usually call my mother every two or three weeks—more out of obligation than anything else. Since June I just haven't felt that obligation and I stopped calling.

MI: Does mom ever call you?

Ms. O.: Sometimes. . . . [She goes blank here and at first I don't realize the extent of it. Then she speaks.] I don't know what just happened. But all of a sudden I don't know where I am. This has never happened before. I can't remember what I was talking about.

MI: What do you remember?

Ms. O.: I don't know where I am except that I am here with you in this room. I know that this is my therapy appointment. But I don't even know what city I am in. I wouldn't even know how to find my car. What day is it? Where is my jacket? Did I wear a jacket? [She didn't.] I don't remember what my next appointment is. . . .

She repeats many times the questions about her jacket, her appointment times, and so on, as she sits up. After a moment she goes and sits on a chair and pulls out her palm pilot and checks her schedule of appointments. Then she realizes she doesn't know how to drive to work or where her car is parked. I excuse myself for a moment and go tell a supervisee that I will be late for our appointment. I walk with Ms. O. outside to see if anything is recognizable. She recognizes now that she is in Berkeley, but not where her car is parked. Walking around the corner with me she sees her car parked across the street. It is clear, however, that she shouldn't cross the street or attempt to drive. I ask for her keys. She hands them to me and we walk back to the waiting room, and as we are walking I ask her to wait through my next appointment in the waiting room. She agrees readily. After the supervision session, I then bring her back into my office and we talk again. She is clearer now, but not entirely so. After a few moments it seems as though she could drive, but I ask her to call when she gets to the office. She does not do this. She does call late in the afternoon and reports it took most of the afternoon in the midst of a busy schedule to return to her normal state of mind. An extra appointment is scheduled for the next day.

At the next session Ms. O. takes a seat on the other couch, saying that she wants to sit up for awhile (which she did for the period of the next three months). I accept her decision. The events of the previous session are gone over in detail and she asks me for some way to think about what happened because she has no reference point from which to think about it. I repeat the sequence of what she said and I said before she lost her bearings. I suggest she had come too close to something so terrifying that she had ejected this "something" with such force as to drag many other parts of her psyche with it. (In other words, she had fallen into the Real in a cataclysmic manner.) This construction seems to have landed in her somewhere because she then described how she had awakened herself by hearing her own "bellowing sobs." "What was striking about this dream," she said, "was that there was no story to the dream, or no scene really, just the bellowing sobs. It felt like a cleansing. Leaving me empty."

Since our next session would be following a weekend break, I offered to be available by phone. She did not call, as was expected. In the next session Ms. O. reports that the days in-between have been the hardest she has lived in years—the well of despair had been very deep. Exploring her feelings of aloneness, how she breaks links between thoughts and feelings, her belief that to ask for emotional attention is too much of a demand upon another—these concerns occupy the next three months of the analysis. Also in that period she decides to look for an apartment in the city and returns to using the couch at the end of this three-month period.

In the beginning of the seventh month of treatment, Ms. O. says, "I have to put my cat down. Losing this cat gives my life a stripped-down-to-the-core feeling, almost like a hobo hitting the road—like having no attachments." A couple of weeks later she is called back for a repeat mammogram and advised to get a biopsy. This decision, she says, raises the familiar question that has occurred throughout her life at selected moments: "Do I make a decision for life, or not?" She does go for a second medical opinion, only to be told the same thing—obtain a biopsy.

Over the next couple of weeks Ms. O. moves in and out of speaking about how "the question of life or death has always been fundamental." Ms. O. knew there would be a lump when she was first called back on her initial mammogram—much as she once knew when she was pregnant (later aborted) before the test results. Ultimately Ms. O. decides to repeat the mammogram in two months rather than doing the biopsy—saying that if cancer was found, she was not sure she could endure chemotherapy. (During these sessions Ms. O. stated strongly that she needed the analyst not to interject her own opinion on the subject. I remained silent but with difficulty, struggling against a feeling of creeping paralysis.)

At the end of the eighth month of treatment, our session begins with her lying upon the couch and being quiet for several minutes. Then she says, "The painful part is not having anything to say."

"What happens if you were to let yourself just sink into whatever you are experiencing?" I reply. She is then silent and remains so, as do I, until the end of the session. During the approximate forty-five minutes remaining of the session, my mind moves through a landscape colored by emotions of fear, despair, and tenderness. At the end of the session I simply say, "It's time." At the door, she thanks me in a soft voice.

In the next session Ms. O. asks how I could remain silent for so long and not be bored. "Because you are not boring," I respond. Another long silence follows before she begins to speak.

The next week, Ms. O. finally finds an apartment in the city that she "loves and wants," but it is expensive. Because of the treatment she has realized she has to move—to move away from isolating herself, to move to an urban center where more opportunities exist to be near, if not to meet, people. In order to rent this apartment, however, she says she must cut back on her sessions to once a week, even though I do note that this is the moment of repetition that had been anticipated—a pattern of beginning relationships intensely and then withdrawing. At the ninth month of treatment Ms. O. moves into her apartment. She is enjoying the process, decorating it the way she actually wants versus how she thinks others would want to see it. She reports stories of exploring the city.

In the tenth month Ms. O. cancels a session without explanation. In our next session it is learned that she had also cancelled last week's follow-up mammogram that she had scheduled instead of the biopsy and that she did not reschedule it. When asked why she did not reschedule it, she says, "Well, if they found something serious, I wouldn't do anything anyway."

MI: Oh, really. It sounds like you have made a decision. How did you get there?
Ms. O.: Oh, I don't know, it just has evolved somehow. I mean, I'm going to accept whatever it is (cancer or benign growth), so what do I need information for?
MI: For later, if you don't accept it anymore.
Ms. O.: I won't. I accept it.

At the end of the eleventh month of Ms. O.'s treatment, she says, " I am feeling more definitive about people and things and how I am investing my time now than I ever have before."

"Speaking of time," I answer, "I am aware that the year is ending soon and a decision-making time is approaching." She says she has been thinking of the year's end too. "I have more clarity now and this makes me aware of the fears involved in my risk-taking decisions, and not just the liberating aspects."

Ms. O. ended her treatment at the close of the contracted year. The remaining sessions were spent reviewing the year's work, what risks she had taken, what fears she experienced along the way, and what liberating aspects she gained.

Discussion of Ms. O.

Did Ms. O. find in her analytic journey what she had unknowingly sought? Since questions, uncertainties, and the trace of Ms. O.'s presence remained and were not able to be processed within the analytic encounter itself, the analyst brought the case to her weekly consultation group to discuss approximately a year later.[3]

Living within a False self, as Winnicott (1962) would say, Ms. O. expressed a desire to encounter something real at the heart of herself. She

3. Winnicott (1971) speaks of the problem of "waste" for the analyst in her/his dealings with infantile states of unthinkable anxiety.

already knew that her mother's depression was a significant factor in her own character formation and in her own tendency toward depressions. This knowledge or insight was not, however, an experienced or lived truth. The forceful psychological ejection/evacuation that occurred would suggest that it was a truth that could not be experienced by Ms. O. because the Real had been too traumatically present and Symbolically uncontained in her early life.

It could be that Ms. O. was a person with a psychotic structure that the analyst's initial hesitation to recommend the couch evidenced. If so, from a Lacanian perspective she should not have used the couch at all because use of the couch forecloses a patient's use of the analyst's gaze,[4] and therefore decompensation in the analysand may be provoked (Lacan 1953d). Perhaps this is precisely what happened. And yet because Ms. O. was able to return to using the couch and to use it to some gain, it seems more likely that Ms. O. was, from a Lacanian perspective, an obsessive[5] who fell into a psychotic wormhole related to a maternal transference evoked by the analyst's question. (The ambiance of the session encircled abandonment or loss—my leaving on vacation, her not calling mOther, her mOther not calling, the depressed mOther not hearing the infant's call—these all seemed to tumble into one another.) She had reconstituted in a few hours' time. Perhaps a psychotic part of her personality (Bion 1967) was activated by the question, "Does your mom ever call you?" by its being contiguous to her dream report of my impending three-week absence.

Ms. O. had been deeply curious that those who had loved her in her life never felt like they "really knew [her]." In turn, she had felt as if she had never been really known. What does "really" mean here? When Ms. O. left her treatment after the year's end, she left saying that she felt more known than she had ever felt before. If this was true, it was as much because of the two sessions of containing silence as it was about any interpretations that may have been spoken.

In those two sessions, Ms. O. appears to have lived her isolation in the analyst's presence as an attuned environmental presence. This did not seem to be about a child being at play alone in the presence of another (Winnicott 1958a). Rather it seems she was given a sense that she had been known at the most primary level—at the level of an infant having a Real

4. The mOther's gaze is critical to the infant's forming of, and helpful later to maintain, psychic integrity in the encounter with another.

5. The obsessive's organizing question is: Am I alive or dead?

shared sensorium with the (m)Other in which a moment-by-lived-moment together accrues toward an accumulation, and ultimate psychic construction, of a sustainable ego/self. These moments, it could be said, were experienced as very real in Winnicott's sense (in the sense of there being a relationship between the Symbolic and Imaginary in the analyst's fluctuating reverie capacity during this silence). The moments were also palpably Real in a Lacanian sense (Lacan 1960)—in the sense that there were aspects of a shared sensory experience within the room. Had Ms. O. not returned to using the couch, this experience surely would have been foreclosed.

Winnicott (1963), usually speaking the language of relatedness, nonetheless described the real self as residing in a private place of internal isolation. This isolation is total, according to Winnicott, because it is never, and cannot be, spoken. It would seem that through the analyst's sensitivities in creating an environment free of impingement, there was for Ms O. a return to the territory where her tie to the object could extend new roots and be able to take hold—in a mOther–infant matrix before maternal depression constellating mOther as dead occurred (Green 1985b). Yet when her cat died shortly thereafter, it was as though Ms. O. was killed one last time. In light of this death, the fact that her breast tissue anomaly followed, remained just that, a fact—not to be imaginatively elaborated, but to be received as a (Real) thing in itself, for whatever thing it may do to her. Those two sessions of full silence registered the need for a level and degree of psychological containment and holding that could not be realized in this treatment, or perhaps in any treatment. These moments were simply not enough to foster Ms. O.'s "try starting life over again," just one more time.

For Ms. O., there was a re-union with a certain cause of her own subjective truth—both in terms of the powerful evacuative experience and the silent periods. She said, in so many words, and nonwords, "yes" to the truth of a kind of foreclosed desire and cycle of despair that was the result of a psychological catastrophe. Of course, it is my hope that this year-long encounter facilitated a feeling that her life could exist a bit more on its own terms now (for however long her life might be), if only in her own mind (instead of in those terms as she described it—"late twentieth-century North American woman" that she had used as her guide).

The inherent paradox of living life on one's "own terms" is that one's desire is always entangled in the desire of the Other (Lacan 1951, 1953a,b,c). The arc and pattern of Ms. O.'s life—periods of flaming brightness and subsequent fadings into extinction—appeared so marked by her own infantile reception. Ms. O. had been the much desired child—a love-child. But mother quickly fell into a season of unending loss where her first, and seemingly only, love abandoned her and their child to pursue the charms of alcohol and other women.

Ms. O.'s nighttime experience of awakening herself sobbing was not really a dream in the usual sense. In fact, it was not a dream. A dream is the work of a dreamer who is working with experiences that have already found some form, that is to say, images that can then become further transformed through language in the telling of the dream. This nighttime occurrence appears more as a repetition of the traumatic Real, not dissimilar to the category of Freud's (1895a) "actual neurosis" where there is not the mediation of symbolization (Bion 1992). The unfolding of the session's events with the insistence of the number three, in prior sessions and within this session, followed by her nighttime nondream, brought forward a possible construction that somewhere in Ms. O.'s infantile life (3 months, 3 years?), she had been plunged into the Real of Winnicott's (1974) primitive agonies. The unconscious may be timeless (Freud 1915), but it knows how to count (e.g., anniversary reactions).[6]

To my mind, taking Ms. O.'s car keys reflects both the complexity and simplicity of the moment. The keys could be described in Bion's terms as a beta element. They were a Real thing, a "Thing in itself" that could not be transformed or be used by Ms. O. at that time. All the same, it was necessary that I hold the keys as a symbol for Ms. O.'s mind until she could take it back. This was done in the manner that reflected that sometimes each analyst acts in ways that are not analytic, but necessary (Winnicott 1962).

Ms. O.'s treatment reached an end, but the question remained: Was this simply an untimely ending, an artificial limit of a year-long contract introduced by me as the analyst? Did factors in my character mark a Real limit in what was actually possible for Ms. O. in this analytic encounter?[7] Or, then again, were these same proclivities what made something possible for Ms. O., while also making evident severe personal limits stemming from the etched form of her life as she had needed to construct it? Given the lack of necessary illusion (or its premature destruction), and the impingement of the Real having been so catastrophic, Ms. O. seems to have made a schizoid retreat into a minimally nascent mind as her only means to psychosomatically survive—and now her only way to continue surviv-

6. It has been noted that the insistent presence of repeated numbers holds places marked by the traumatic Real—as if it were a map coordinate.

7. Lacan (1953d,1953–1954g, 1955–1956) said that all resistance lies in the analyst.

ing. In this analytic psychotherapy, Ms. O.'s encounter with the Real concerned the Real as a cataclysmic force that she only partially psychically survived. But surviving is not living, and it is not feeling real. Ms. O. made the decision that the gradient of difference between living and surviving could not be bridged in the lifetime available to her—in this treatment or not.

THE TIME OF AN ANALYSIS

"The time of an analysis is by definition that in which trauma is brought into evidence; it is the time of the production of the trauma and consequently of its symbolic construction" (Mieli 2001, p. 268).

A time of illusion is allowed in analysis when clinically indicated. Yet, there comes a time when analytic act(s) of interpretation will bring to bear the potency of symbolic castration (see Chapter 4, this volume). With the awakening from illusion, desire and play may come, but desire hurts even as it may please. In the case of Ms. O. above, the re-created trauma brought psychic death into evidence. The symbolic construction available was partial and inadequate in that her subjective position remained essentially the same—perhaps a failure of a particular analytic dyad, perhaps a Real limit of what was psychically possible for Ms. O.

In analytic encounters where there is a subjective shift, made possible by virtue of the analysand's recreation of the trauma in the transference, again it is in the encounter with the Real that a feeling of being uniquely real and alive occurs. These encounters with the Real are the most alive opportunities for the analysand to awaken from unnecessary illusions (or destructive delusions). For some, these psychic awakenings include (for the more disturbed patient) the awakening to a wider world of symbolization itself, and to what the object/world offers to a subject in terms of being able to inhabit the depressive position. For others (the more neurotic patient), the awakening consists of the realization that a different (symbolic/oedipal) position must truly be taken up if any lived sense of creating/desiring and re-creating her/his own life is to become possible (Lacan 1959). For many analysands, several awakenings and necessary losses/separations need to be lived through, at both of these levels.

Analysts often say to one another, "Timing is everything." It is not unusual that an analyst may be able to identify important signifiers early on in an analysis, nor is it unusual that essential interpretations can be formulated early on. It requires a time of elaboration, however, as lived within the transference, before an act(s) of psychic separation or symbolic castration can actually occur for the analysand. Lacan (1953d, 1964) calls such moments "moments of conclusion." (This is used more often in terms of the end of analysis, but it can apply to other times as well.)

THE CASE OF MS. S.

It was a halting beginning of an analysis. A 44-year-old single woman, Ms. S. sought consultation as to whether she ought to move back to the state she had left only the year before, saying she now felt like "a loose rock on the side of the road" and that she was "not sure why I go on [with her life]." Mother's death the previous month was the catalyst for her present state. Ms. S. decided to remain in California—at least for another year—and to begin her second treatment. (The first treatment had been critical to enabling her to move to California.)

The degree of tenseness radiating from her body as she entered my office, session after session, registered in me via frequent moments of my involuntarily holding my breath, suddenly feeling anoxic, and needing to silently tell myself to breathe. Ms. S. often seemed as if she were encased in a steel box, rendering any of my intuitive capacities as an analyst useless. Her speech was often so cut up in its flow by the static of internal censorship and emotional blockages, that it often felt like the analytic dyad was treading carefully on thin ice or walking in an active mine field. On those occasions when the ice would crack open (i.e., a moment of contact, the admission of a feeling, an interpretation that landed, a complete miss of the analyst's words), Ms. S. would fall into an uncontrollable tremor or shaking, and often simultaneously would become freezing cold. In her relationship with her mother, love was in the form of hate. The coldness seemed to be a mark of the body's shuddering in anticipation of a physical or emotional attack after a moment of contact. After a session, such coldness could take several hours to resolve.

It was not unusual for me to find myself attempting to gauge Ms. S.'s silences so as not to be intrusive or abandoning, yet no matter what, I often found that my words seemed somehow brutalizing. Frequently, Ms. S.'s staccato silences would lead me to become permeated with a hatefulness and a tendency to want to verbally poke at her. Guilt and a kind of horror within myself would follow. The nonverbal sounds of my voice and/or soft, slow adjustments in the chair, were finally understood to offer the best registration of an attentive presence of the Other that Ms. S. could safely take in. The Lacanian analyst Alain Didier-Weill (2002) observed that "to give your voice is to give your basic note of being," and nowhere was this brought home more than with the work with Ms. S.

Ms. S. was the youngest of four children, the only daughter and "a mistake," according to mother. She described the circumstances of her delivery as having been born trapped within the placenta, which necessitated her having to be cut free by the physician. Mother, upon seeing her encapsulated baby, was (according to family myth) reported to have said, "It's a monster—not my baby." This story was frequently repeated, along with another joke/story that mother provocatively told other adults in the presence of her children—which was that if she (the mother) were standing on a dock and saw her husband and one of her children in the water drowning, and someone asked, "Who would you save?," mother would always say, "My husband," and then laugh in an inappropriate manner.

A maternal lineage of trauma appeared to span three generations in Ms. S.'s family, although it remained impossible to hypothesize as to original reasons, because her maternal grandparents had been long deceased when Ms. S. was born. (If this could have been known, it would have helped in clarifying the role or structural position Ms. S. held for her mother.) In Ms. S.'s mother's generation, only three of the nine children were ever able to leave the family home to establish separate lives and households. Ms. S.'s mother was one of these three. She married and moved out when she became pregnant by a neighborhood boy. Another of the three was the unmarried aunt whom Ms. S. loved deeply and was loved deeply by. (This aunt was no doubt her subjective salvation.)

The third sibling who managed a separate life was an aunt who figured centrally in Ms. S.'s earliest memory. Ms. S., who was 5 at the time, was told by this aunt to share a toy with her same-aged cousin. She refused. The aunt then made critical remarks about Ms. S. to her (Ms. S.'s) mother in such a way as to humiliate the mother. Shortly thereafter the aunt left, with the crying cousin in tow. Mother then dragged Ms. S. to the bathroom, saying it was time to take a bath, even though it was not the usual time for bathing. Once Ms. S. was in the tub, while washing and rinsing Ms. S.'s hair, mother began to hold Ms. S.'s head under the water. Ms. S.'s terrified fighting and screaming alarmed the neighbors next door to such an extent that they came into the unlocked apartment and pulled the mother off the child.

Living in alternating states of terror, humiliation, hate, numbness, and despair, Ms. S. spent time with the good aunt whenever possible. Mother seems to have wanted this, and at the same time seems to have been envious and jealous of the attention and love her daughter received. As for Ms. S.'s father, he was rarely home until late at night, and always gone in the morning when Ms. S. awoke for school. Father was living a downward spiral from her earliest childhood, involving himself in chronic alcoholism and gambling. Father died when Ms. S. was 12, leaving her at home with mother and one brother, who was described as mother's favorite child. Overall, she retained remarkably little memory of her childhood and adolescence.

As soon as she could be self-supporting, Ms. S. left home. Once employed, over time she found her way into the paralegal profession. (With no paternal intervention or protection from the cruelty of her mother's omnipotent Law, it is interesting that she managed to situate and devote herself to defining the Law and its outlaws.)

Most of her friendships developed at work. The few intimate (heterosexual) relationships she had were characterized by her responding to the desire of the Other, followed by feeling trapped by the man's emotional dependency, which was thinly veiled by the threat of physical violence. She relocated to California in order to leave a frightening relationship and attempt a new start on life. (Six years of once-a-week psychotherapy had enabled her to take this risk.) Even so, she still said that she didn't feel like she was "committed to [her] own life" or was "deserving of having a life," and that most of the time "life [felt] meaningless."

Over a period of seven months during the first year of work, Ms. S.'s sessions increased from once a week to three times weekly—each increase in frequency following her (unconscious) expression of a wish via either her discourse or in a dream. (Analysis per se was not immediately suggested for fear of overwhelming her.) A little over a year into the analysis, Ms. S. did two things that potentiated the unfolding transference. She took a leap forward to buy a new used car that she really liked. This meant that the car was not simply utilitarian and inexpensive, as had been all her other automobiles. This decision took some work. The car, as it turned out, was the same make as the car I drove, but a newer model. The maternal transference fears of my rejection of her gesture of love and identification, as well as fears of my envy and retaliation, were unleashed, and, bit by bit, interpreted.

Shortly after this purchase Ms. S. stretched further when she decided to accept an invitation to go on a two-week trip with a group of newly made friends. Up to this point, any small positive movement in her life had been followed by a form of psychic backlash, but this time it was to be of a different magnitude on the Richter scale of psychic-quakes. Shortly after she returned from this trip (now one and a half years into the analysis), a new and disturbing somatic symptom appeared on the analytic stage. What follows are the closing words of a session that took place one week before this symptom occurred.

Ms. S.: So I was wondering—I was thinking of last week when one day I had been on the phone all day long. And so at the end of the day I told a guy who was talking to me, "I just can't listen anymore," and he really backed up. This is not at all like my ex-boss who could listen patiently to someone go on and on. So I was going to ask how can you listen all the time to people's problems day after day, hour after hour?

MI: It seems you are asking about limits here. And maybe you are also saying you don't expect that anyone, maybe me as well, is really interested in listening to you.

Ms. S.: In a way, you responded to what I would want to ask next, but it would have been too hard to say it just then: Can you listen to me?

MI: Yes, we both are listening. "Do you know what I mean?" [This is her characteristic repetitive phrase that I am using here to address the part of her that is hopeful for, and wants, change to occur in her life.]

Ms. S.: ———Yeah, but when my negative parts take over I don't listen to myself sometimes—sometimes I don't even understand what I'm doing, or why I react as I do. Why am I barely close to another? Or more to the—or more like, I get close to a point with someone, and yet, feel pretty isolated somewhere else. All this stuff is floating around in my mind—all this stuff we have been talking about in the last two weeks—thinking about my brothers, cars, that am I just too weird to really get to have a life.———That I actually feel human and have desires, and that I don't listen to myself is a discovery———but get this—I'm happier than I've ever been, and I don't know where I'm going.

MI: Maybe it is more important that you are going, than where you are going.

Ms. S.: It was just something spontaneous just then, that when you said that, something just clicked. I don't know what it means——but there is something different about my life now, than the life I left. But I am not sure how to describe it or put it into words. There are some people I can feel. If I analyze my friends in terms of who I usually can't wait to talk to—it is Susan most of the time. If we hit it good for both of us—we really have fun talking—I don't know what I'm getting to—maybe it is just that I know better who I love and who I don't love, than I did before.

MI: And that seems like a good place to stop today. Until tomorrow then.

The transference love and identification in evidence here soon came under a massive psychosomatic psychic attack—or, hate followed. A rash and itch appeared on her hands and pains began in her chest when she breathed. She became fatigued and winded easily. It was actually several weeks before she spoke about these new symptoms because in her mind she minimized and ridiculed herself for being such a "cry baby." She had not even consulted a physician as yet.

Over a couple of months multiple medical tests ensued—CAT scan, pulmonary work-up, and so on. In a second several months, the tests broadened to include a lung biopsy and an ultra-sound. All these tests yielded diagnoses to be considered, but none that could really be named. She had to reduce her hours at work. Finally she was told that there was thickening in her lung tissue within certain areas, causing a stiffness—a lack of plasticity in her lungs. It was an inflammation without infection that could be from any number of causes, the doctors said. Pulmonary tests revealed that her lungs were not providing her as much oxygen as is required. In the analysis at this time, she spoke of how she couldn't ever take a bath even though she imagined it might feel good, because she could never sit in a tub. An association followed—how she thinks that it was her crying that pushed her mother over the edge.

As medical and analytic appointments continued, her symptoms become more precisely described, but not diagnosed: inflammation in the interstitial areas of her lung (the necessary open spaces were collapsed). This condition may or may not have been there all along—which left it unclear as to why the symptoms would manifest now.

Near the end of a session during this time Ms. S. said, "I ran into a friend yesterday and she hugged me. I liked it, but I could feel myself instinctively and automatically pull back." Then she was silent, a heaviness in the air accumulated. She broke the silence with, "I don't want to die like this." And I said, "I don't want you to either." The session ended.

After this session she began to actually feel her depression. Somatic pain began to transform into psychic suffering. She began to talk about when, as an adult, she didn't talk to her mother for two years. She noticed she "can't stand being corrected if I think I'm right," and connected it to how similar it was to how her mother would be. "It is the mother in myself," she said. "I mean, my mother almost killed me because I didn't want to share my toy—what is that!" She noted moments of enjoying some of the solitude and rest that her weakened condition had demanded. With some anxiety, she decided to put her former residence in another state up for sale.

Over the next three months, several medications were tried—no new inflammation occurred but none went away, and her symptoms continued to wax and wane. It was during these months that she returned to speaking about the trip she had taken with her new friends and the "new" used car she had bought. She also noted that the opening of love had brought her more fluid speech. Bit by bit, the collapsed interstitial spaces were being reconstructed with words, weaving a net around her of not "sharing" with the analyst, her buying a newer model of a car like mine, and her feeling loving (as to her aunt versus her mother). She understood that all these elements had had the effect of collapsing her into being a monster who didn't deserve to live. The mOther's desire was for Ms. S. to not live, but if she was going to live, then at least live without need or desire. She was betraying the mOther. The monster was drowning, suffocating. Perhaps she needed anOther doctor to help cut her loose, to open some breathing room? Perhaps it may even be hard to accept her own discovery—that she is "human," which is ordinary—and not extra-ordinary like a monster. Perhaps the Other (in this sense the other being me as a real other person as well as the analyst's place of symbolization—Lacan's Other) wants (desires) her to live, not die.

During the subsequent few months, an observing third was born in the new space in Ms. S.'s mind. She even began to muse upon a newly emerging curiosity—Why does she remember certain things and not others, like the bathtub incident, and why did her mother make her feel so afraid all the time? Follow-up testing of her lung capacity revealed that the oxygen level had now improved significantly. The thickening in her lungs appeared to be a little less. No one could tell her if it would improve any further. Gradually one medicine was discontinued, and then another. She got stronger and stronger.

In the end, the physicians could not really say for sure that the medicine was what made the difference in her condition. In the end I could not really say for sure the analysis alone made the difference. But in the interstitial space between the two spheres of intervention (medical and psychoanalysis), something new happened, shifting Ms. S. into another psychic location—from monster to human being. It could be said that Ms. S.'s psyche returned her to the place where her body as soma had been inadequately symbolized in the Imaginary (Lacan 1953). One's body is only one's own after it has been psychically constructed. Perhaps Winnicott (1945) would say that Ms. S.'s return to the body, via her lung symptom, was in the effort to further integrate her body and mind, to make each more inextricably a part of the other, or psyche-soma.

Ms. S. had begun to be able to relate to the part of herself that could unconsciously fill her words, attitudes, and behavior with a potent negativity. She became able to bring an observing third to the "mother or dark part of herself." She began to alternate between hating herself for her humanness and forgiving herself through being human. As a by-product, a degree of compassion for others began to sprout. She said one day in session, "After all, I am only human—and perhaps, I am beginning to imagine, even others may be human too."

Something new began for Ms. S. here. From an object relations perspective, a psychic separation from a toxic fusion with an internal mother had begun with the analyst's being discovered and beginning to be used as a new object (Winnicott 1969a). Another way of saying this is that only with the discovery of another subject is an adequate limit placed upon the domination of one's self by illusion or delusion or fantasy—be that a good fantasy or a bad one—and the path to taking up a position of desire becomes possible.

In Lacan's (1964) terms Ms. S. took a necessary step toward the "crossing of her fantasm" (p. 273), but this crossing was, as yet, incomplete. She was awakening from an unnecessary, even a destructive, illusion (almost delusion) in which she had lived her entire life. But if Ms. S. had remained identified with the analyst (i.e., buying the same-make car), she would simply have been trading one ego illusion or fiction for another. Thus, however clinically indicated a time of a benign necessary illusion may be in any given case, it is equally necessary that this be followed by a psychic awakening or dis-illusionment.

Lacan adds substantively to Winnicott's artful rendering of creative destruction and the discovery of the object. He does so by bringing the complexity of sexuality onto the analytic stage, as well as the concept of jouissance and its link to the death drive, with desire's link to the necessary acceptance of limits to the experience of pleasure. Lacan observes that one's own experience of jouissance must take place in the context of limits in order to be experienced as pleasure.

To this point in the analytic work, Ms. S. had yet to fully assume her symbolic or psychic/oedipal position as a human being that is sexed and sexual. For although something new happened, the question remained, If she is not a monster, who is she? What is it to be a female? What does it mean to be a woman? And how is she to be a sexually desirous human being? (In terms of the mobius metaphor, to cross one's fantasm would be to trace the edge of the mobius until one returns to the same place one started. It takes two times around the edge to get back to the same exact point of beginning. Ms. S. at this point had only gone around once.)

Several months after the resolution of her lung symptoms (or around the third year of the analysis), Ms. S. began to actively explore within the analysis her sexual history and the implications of having been born a daughter rather than a son to a mother who never wanted another child, much less a daughter. This turn in her discourse was eventually accompanied by an opening to the thought that perhaps she as a woman—different from her mother and more like what her aunt would like to have been—"could deserve to have some life of her own." This manifested in her purchase of a "new" car. (It was a car her analyst would not buy, but nonetheless certainly did arouse my aesthetic appreciation and a modicum of envy.) This "new" (neither used nor previously owned) beautiful, sexy, and petite convertible was a car she could say she "really, really wanted." Yet not surprisingly, she was also "scared to get it." Once she had the car, however, Ms. S. would spontaneously, in the months to come, blurt out from time to time, "I just love that car!" We both heard this as a call to herself—as a subject with her own desire—to become more present, because it most often occurred when she would begin speaking about moving into an new arena in her life in which she felt frightened, but also desirous of something. The aesthetic implied by her car's selection pointed toward a place beyond human language. In a strange way, this was her own Symbolic call to the Real within herself to yield to her something more—a call manifest in the car itself as her "object a" (see Chapter 4, this volume).

Ms. S.'s out-of-state property finally sold—which put both her feet in California. At three and a half years into her analysis, Ms. S. began dating a man she had been friends with for over a year. As her experiences unfolded within this relationship, missing memories (both positive and negative) were evoked and provoked, and links began to be made and cut, between the past of her girlhood, her adolescence, her sexual history, and her present. The constellated oedipal triangle between Ms. S., her boyfriend, and me facilitated Ms. S.'s further elaboration of her sexuality and feminine identification (i.e., features of identification with her real aunt as well as features of an imagined aunt who might have wanted to act, or might have acted in such-and-such ways, had she been able to).

As Ms. S.'s analysis has progressed, the (m)Other who demanded, hated, feared, and raged could be left to die; the mother who was not these ways could be given compassion, if not forgiveness. Ms. S.'s position vis-à-vis the world of work is the area in which she continues her work in the analysis, as it is now moving toward a moment of conclusion.

Discussion of Ms. S.

A significant contribution of Lacan to the concept of transference repetition is his notion of there being a co-creative relationship between the two registers of the Symbolic and the Real. Bringing meaning to an enacted repetition through a transference interpretation may bring the analysand more "under-standing" in terms of how he/she has been living/"standing within" an illusion or an Imaginary script, but this may not necessarily result in the analysand's actual movement to a different subjective standing in his/her life. For this, the analysand has to encounter the Real and make a new signifying mark that then seeds imagination, so to speak, in order to experience her-/himself as more real in Winnicott's terms.

Each person has a unique signifying chain, which is to say, each person has a set of primary letters/signifiers that have constituted his/her pathway to symbolization, and that have been involved in his/her making of a symbolic identity that is unique. Some of these primary letters/signifiers encircle the gap or space separating this individual's coming into being at his/her beginning point of primal repression. Thus, the repetition of these particular letters and words is a repetition of certain meanings; but at the same time, their repetition evokes the very conditions of a surplus-jouissance associated with the occasion when difference and loss were first carved into his/her being (see Chapter 4, this volume).

Within a transference repetition, therefore, something new is possible, though not always realizable. Repetition of this surplus-jouissance creates the occasion of a return to those points of original inscription of a person/subject's unique markings by the symbol itself.

The Lacanian analyst Serge Leclaire (1998) would go so far as to say that a unique formula of jouissance consisting only of letters could be written for each one of us. This same unique marking, paradoxically, also denotes the limit of the symbol's marking/mapping of each person's subjectivity—with what lies beyond, existing in the realm of the unspeakable, but the experientially real, Real. It is this aspect or element of jouissance contained within the repetition that has to be encountered in an alive way in the analysis. Repetition, then, constitutes an echo of both we/me and me/not me and I and you, all simultaneously.

We see, therefore, that something "new" can take place when there has been an adequate suffusion of jouissance/energy into the analysand's past inscriptions (words/signifiers) during the development of the Imaginary transferences. This adequate suffusion creates conditions ripe for a subjective revelation that in turn can produce a subjective shift.

With the addition of a new signifier, there is a retroactive (or après coup), symbolic reorganization of the set of primary signifiers that structures this person's life (Green 2001). A life is narrated anew. Another way of saying it would be, through the analytic work there is a deconstruction of a particular unifying ego construction (in the Imaginary) and a different reconstruction is made (Boothby 1991).

The meeting of the Symbolic and the Real within the analysand—via the analyst's acts—can result in a psychic shift because something is carved out of the Real by a new Symbolic signifier. In this process the analysand's subjective position in her/his life can move (Mieli 2001). As a result, an Imaginary script that has been living within a timeless zone in the analysand's psyche is brought into living (and dying) time.

Many theoretical discussions focus the analyst's attention upon the question of what would be the same in Ms. S.'s repetition with me. Yet there is something else as well that does not receive sufficient attention except within the Lacanian field. There is paradox in repetition. There is a sameness, but it is also repeating a moment when the basic quota of difference was first established, or was attempting to be established, in the psychic economy of the person/subject. These moments represent a person's/

subject's entering the Symbolic order of language, where difference is initially rooted; from that point forward, the sensory experience and the psychic trace of that experience are different and the human infant as a human subject becomes a split being (Julien 1994, Lacan 1964). Primary repression sets the coordinates of Real jouissance and the points of psychic fixation that an individual's future repressed representations will be drawn toward.

A shift in a subject's standing in his/her life denotes an act of creation vis-à-vis an analysand's hitting coordinates of the Real, so to speak. A particularly potent paradox here is that the Real is both the limit and the cause of his/her own desire. Hitting this Real limit, the analysand with his/her own Symbolic function then invests him-/herself in a new symbolic identification in relation to this Real limit. This process can happen due to the fact that one signifier in the primary chain can be replaced with another (Nasio 1992). This new signifier (or signifiers) need(s) to have some link with the original set of primary signifiers, for this original set holds the most potent juice or jouissance that is the alive remainder of the earliest co-creative meeting(s) between the Real and the Symbolic that yields satisfaction. And this original set has to have been brought to life within the (Imaginary) transference, providing the suffusion of jouissance spoken of a moment ago, to maximize the analytic act and be resonant with the basic knotting of this particular human being within the Real, Symbolic, and Imaginary. In the case of Ms. S., the signifier "monster" was able to be replaced with "human."

A shifting moment for the subject may be a "moment of conclusion" at the end of an analysis—which is an act of self-authorization (this is what is most often cited by Lacan). But there are other such shifting moments. For instance, in the case of Ms. S. when an "analytic symptom" arises in the analysis, opportunity opens. Such an analytic symptom is a new somatic symptom occurring within the analysis that is not a part of the panoply of presenting symptoms (Apollon 1998). Such a symptom may arise when the analysand's words/signifiers reach a point where they fade as containers/mediators of the analysand's experience. Despite this fact, still the analysand must speak. Timing is ripe, then, for the possibility for a subjective shift in the analysand—if the analytic dyad can make the most of it together. Life as it has been for the analysand has a possibility to transform in the direction of life as it could become. When things go well, the analysand can, in an act of "performative speech," be heard (by him-/herself), affirmed and punctuated by the Other's response (analyst's act).

The analysand's subjective standing vis-à-vis his/her own life and time is able to shift toward feeling more real as the Imaginary world of inner object relations is further articulated via a discovery and use of a new object (the analyst). These are paradoxical moments in the analysis, in that, as the basis for this shift, the analysand encounters the Real as the limit of the symbolization, only to use the symbol/signifier once again to make or carve something new for him-/herself out of the Real.

In such territory the analyst's words are important not only to form interpretations, but also to serve as the locus of recognition of the unconscious subject of desire when it speaks—as in "Yes, you are here, and heard" (Lee 1990). For example, when the analysand (according to the best hypothesis, intuition, etc. of the analyst) is able to become conscious, through speaking, of a truth previously unconscious or disavowed, the analyst might lean forward with intentional affective presence and simply say, "Yes," or something like, "Are you listening?" If the analyst is in resonance with the subject, there will be an effect—registered in the moment, or later. If not, the analysand is apt to ignore the comment or make a query, "What do you mean?" These two functions of the analyst's words—to recognize and to turn the analysand's ear toward his/her own unconscious speaking—were particularly salient for Ms. S. because the areas and ways in which the analyst could interpretively speak were severely restricted for quite awhile. When Ms. S.'s somatic symptom was provoked by her betrayal of her position within the Imaginary script/fantasy in relation to the desire of the mOther—the desire of the mOther that she be dead, invisible, and love only mother nonetheless—it still took time to accrue the analytic leverage to facilitate a subjective shift.

IN CONCLUSION: ANALYSIS AND THE LIMITS OF SYMBOLIZATION

Both Ms. O. and Ms. S. exhibited circumstances wherein the Real was dramatically and traumatically insistent in its call for further symbolization, so that it might be cut it down to digestible size. Cutting the traumatic Real down to size would be necessary before either Ms. O.'s or Ms. S.'s individual seeds of the Real (animating desire) could have been really heard by them (or by me as the analyst). In both of these cases, such Winnicottian aspects as environmental provision, attunement, and a quality of present waiting to give recognition to a spontaneous gesture, were aspects of my analytic position. An additional aspect of that position was Lacan's (1953a, 1955–1956) notion that in the neurotic, it is a question of being or how to take a position vis-à-vis desire that occupies him/her. While it is most often true that obsessional characters turn out to be male, in the cases of Ms. O. and Ms. S. the obsessive's question "Am I dead or alive?" was the organizing question for both.[8] Each of these individuals filled the gap where desire might be with compulsive activity of one sort or another so as always to postpone its arrival. Ms. S. in particular made it extremely difficult early on for the analyst to speak at all, lest the Other express a desire that would be heard as an unrefusable demand. Moreover, for Ms. S., sexual difference and its Symbolic elaboration in gender was secondary indeed to whether it was permissible at all to breathe and be alive. Here Lacan's structural linkages of the Real, the Symbolic, and the Imaginary aided me in recognizing and accepting the somatic symptom as the nodal opportunity in terms of the timing and effect of my acts as an analyst.

In the case of Ms. O., the analytic encounter was a limited one—at least for this particular analytic dyad. Words not only faltered and crashed in their capacity to bear her experience across the space between, but words and letters became concretized Things speaking and breathing a catastrophe that had to be avoided at all costs. Ms. O.'s psyche-somatic integrity disassembled in the analytic discourse, and though she reconstituted her psychic integrity, it remained as the mark of a Real limit to the treatment's outcome.

With Ms. S., however, the Real of the traumatic circumstances of her birth, repeated in the attempted drowning when she was 5, and the subsequent verbal abuse in her childhood, were able to be brought within a Symbolic net via the analyzing of a manifest undiagnosable psychosomatic lung symptom. Where it was not possible with Ms. O. to have a retroactive reorganization of her life's narrative (signifying chain), it was for Ms. S. The ongoing presence of her loving aunt probably made the difference in her having the capacity to make use of the analyst in a way that Ms. O. could not. The place of Ms. S.'s sexual drives could be located once the physical breaking-through of her primitive anxieties was more symboli-

8. The obsessive is most often male, related to a sense of being "too loved/desired" by the mOther, thus unconsciously fearing retribution from an archaic father. In the case of Ms. O., she appeared to have been very loved early on, whereas in the case of Ms. S., love appeared from birth to come from her aunt, putting mother in the archaic paternal position, with father absent via alcoholism.

cally contained and reinscribed within a different identification, leaving her desire structured and free to move outward.

Another way of describing the process of Ms. S. is to say that she experienced how in fantasy she was keeping herself in a position of being the "object a" for the mOther (i.e., a plug for the lack in the mOther by serving as the receptacle for all mOther's unwanted parts). As long as Ms. S. was in this position for the (m)Other, she could hold onto an illusion that (1) the Other is not lacking (the Other here as Symbolic network itself, which we know has holes) or "some others have access to an All or completeness, I don't get to have," and (2) I don't have to deal with the implications of my own lack, the desire it holds, and the responsibility it carries. Therefore, Ms. S. had to put a hole in her own fantasy by taking herself out of that position for the mOther, so that she could experience the gap (and potential space), and take on the responsibility for her own life—its loves and desires.

CLOSING

Finally, the analytic encounters of Ms. O. and Ms. S. speak, I believe, to how words will always reach their point of failure in analysis. But when and how words reach this failure is often decisive for the analysis and its outcome. In the story of Ms. O., the failure of the analyst's Symbolic function to contain infantile experience and to facilitate the re-Imaginarization of her psychic body was of huge consequence. Desire in its fullest "absent presence" could not have been adequately elaborated for Ms. O. without more work at the level of the Imaginary and necessary illusion. In the case of Ms. S., a viable analysis was possible despite a history of substantial childhood trauma, very likely because there had been foundation of care and minimal Symbolic intervention by her aunt. The cases of Ms. O. and Ms. S. both illustrate the fact that without the mOther's adequate Symbolic mediation of infantile need, the Imaginary body constructed by the infant remains inadequate and illusion becomes delusion. When the Imaginary inner object world is populated under these conditions, the child is handicapped in his/her capacity to traverse the oedipal passage. He/she is compromised in his/her capacity to establish an identity/psychic position from which desire can be experienced and from which she/he can feel real and alive.

Thus the "talking cure," cloaked in the masculine as representative of the Symbolic function, inevitably moves each analysand to encounter the Real in him-/herself, something that is more associated with "the feminine" (Lacan 1972a).[9] The complementary and clinically useful difference between these two analytic perspectives is that each arrives at a similar destination—from two different directions. Winnicott emphasizes that the Real of provision and necessary illusion must precede the individual's capacity to feel real. Lacan begins with the primacy of the Symbolic as the precondition for any necessary illusion to occur, but emphasizes how the analytic discourse must bring each analysand to the limit of the Symbolic (word as signifier) in order to encounter the Real within her-/himself as the cause of her/his being.

In the final analysis, I believe that the passionate engagement between these two psychoanalytic perspectives can serve to remind all psychoanalytic practitioners that there is a supplemental pleasure/jouissance to be experienced in addition to that derived solely from the exercise of one's Symbolic capacities, and from the fruits that such exercise may produce. I propose in this work that the talking cure enables each one, in her/his own way, to embrace the ongoing oscillation of one's psychic "particles to waves" and "waves to particles," while at the same time living in the gap—the potential space—between necessary illusion and speakable desires.

---

9. Not the maternal but the feminine.

Afterword

Fantasies try to assess how body parts coalesce with some cause of love that one might call the soul.
(Ragland 2001)

The term *parallactic space* of psychoanalytic practice has been the term I have used to describe my sojourn as a squiggle game that I have attempted to orchestrate for the reader, between the analytic figures of Lacan and Winnicott. Like all squiggle games, whose end is open-ended and may be determined by either player, this engagement continues. Where I have been in the preceding pages will no doubt continue to inform, but will also be different from where my analytic practice will be by the time you, the reader, are reading these last pages. Psychoanalysis is a practice, after all.

On the face of it, the figures of Winnicott and Lacan guide the analyst's work in different ways, yet I have found that the oscillation between their two positions aims at the heart of the human condition—that is, how each individual uniquely becomes, or falters in becoming, a symbolically mapped, sexed and sexual, playful, creative, and desirous being.

The British psychoanalyst Ronald Britton, summarizing neo-Kleinian criteria for a successful outcome or end of an analysis, articulated the following endpoints: (1) "relationship with self has improved (i.e., includes more, accepts more, contains more), (2) greater awareness of relationship to reality, internal and external, (3) capacity to mourn/to suffer loss and to recover from loss, (4) diminution in latent paranoia and depressive anxiety, and (5) increased capacity for thinking and self-reflection" (Scarfone 2002, p. 456). It isn't that I disagree with these statements as much as I am left with a question by them: Where is the joy/jouissance of play and sexuality—the aliveness of simply being human? I am reminded of a story told to me by an older analyst about Winnicott's presenting a case before the British Society. At the end of his presentation one of his colleagues said, "But Donald, she is still a prostitute." And he said, "Yes, but she is a happy prostitute."

Freud (1937b), reflecting upon the limits of analysis, admitted in one of his last papers that interpretation is not always sufficient to resolve symptoms or to shift someone's subjective position. Words or signifiers are sometimes simply not enough, especially if these words symbolize more of the Imaginary world of object relations, but do not touch upon the Real of the subject. As Freud discovered, it is helpful for the analysand to develop insight about the Imaginary transferences he/she sets up in his/her external life (including with the analyst). But understanding alone is often not sufficient for change to occur. To shift the analysand, subjectively speaking, something else is needed. Understanding is not enough because a measure of jouissance (held by the Real of the subject) is knotted within his/her repetition—and has to be taken into account. From my perspective it has been Winnicott and Lacan who have provided complementary and supplementary avenues into this territory and out.

Because Winnicott is more familiar to many clinicians, I want to say that the theoretical structure Lacan offers, via his Borromean knot of the Real, Symbolic, and Imaginary registers, is the most complete map of human subjectivity for guiding the analyst's acts, and their intention, that I have found in psychoanalytic theory. And while the Lacanian field may find this next statement impious, his map of human subjectivity can be brought into relationship with the Other—some of those other streams of psychoanalytic thought—in a clinically fruitful way. Psychoanalysis is a process, and subject to the art of its own change.

If the analyst makes room for the appeal of love (as both Winnicott and Lacan do), it is in part due to the fact that analyst first accepts this love for the one who is imagined to know, and then, over time, frays this love, so that the analysand's timeless fantasy(ies) of completeness/wholeness can be gradually revealed to him/her, ultimately to be taken up by the analysand her-/himself as her/his own to deal with in the presence of the analyst as witness (Leclaire 1998a). This is love by the analyst for her/his analysand, given as an active gift (Lacan 1953)—a gift fueled by the desire of the analyst (Lacan 1960) for reading both the text of the discourse and the texture of the analysand as a human being, who has come to speak and be heard.

It has been my experience on the sojourn of this squiggle game, as I have called it, within my own psyche-soma as analyst, that a primary aim of analysis is to facilitate in the analysand the ability to experience a kind of jouissance in movement. This movement is an ongoing oscillation between the psychic transformations occurring within the analysand (via symbolization), and the ripples of these transformations' effects in the movement of her/his desire as it moves her/him to engage with the world. But in order to be able to lend him-/herself to this process without too much psychic confusion or catastrophe, three minimal conditions must either have been met in earlier development or be met within the analysis—conditions that I have found possible via the creative coupling of Winnicott and Lacan (with a little help from Bion).

The first condition is that the coordinates of both space and time must exist with some stability (coordinates that are missing or profoundly askew in the psychotic individual). Thus, toward this end, a time of necessary illusion (in infancy or within the analysis) ensures that the working materials or symbolic elements will be available when the early infantile subject emerges. When there is a Real person/object present to hold and to be a Symbolic net, the act of falling—an act precipitated by the infantile subject's being cut/separated from the encapsulation of the sensory/autistic-contiguous world in the womb—is cushioned by the presence of an Other able to greet him/her in a way that a necessary illusion is fostered.

The second condition that must met be met occurs subsequently, when the infant initiates the act of cutting her-/himself away from a maternally co-constructed illusion, and metaphorically falls away. In infancy or in the analysis, there must be someone truly there, thereby enabling the subject's own partially spun symbolic safety net to catch her-/himself (see Chapters 5 and 6). Under such good-enough conditions, the Symbolic net into which the subject has now fallen (and within which he/she must make and locate her-/himself) can become a trampoline, a bridge, a hammock, and so forth—a something that supports movement of various kinds, while also preventing catastrophic falls.

The third condition needed to sustain a psychic position is one emphasized by Lacan's revision of Oedipus, and concerns the subject's symbolic/oedipal identification as a necessary component organizing and stabilizing personal subjectivity. A person/subject must take up a primary position (identification) within the constituent Symbolic net itself—either as a masculine (threads) or as a feminine subject (spaces between the threads) in order to take a place in the world that may or may not reflect the sexed body of the individual. This identification is also linked with (but is not necessarily in a complementary relation—that is, a masculine-identified female subject may still be heterosexual) his/her sexual orientation. This oedipal identification is also in an ongoing interaction with social/symbolic meanings ascribed to cultural ego and gender ideals. Finally, this identification functions as an orienting template for each individual, exerting a retroactive organizing influence upon the conscious and unconscious oscillations at play within one's mind, or between two minds at play.

Although it may be said in different words by different streams of psychoanalysis, it is our job as analytic practitioners (analyst or therapist) to midwife an analysand's process of being able to (1) bear his or her etched losses (which may involve substantial work at the intersection of the Symbolic and the Imaginary as well as the intersection of Symbolic and Real), and (2) accept that symbolic limits are the facilitating agents of one's aliveness in a unique pattern of Eros and aggression in the movement of desire. It is perhaps in this sense that the analyst aims toward no-thing or nothing but a place—a place where the analysand's jouissance is viably partitioned because her or his desire is psychically constituted and thus can be claimed. In one partition lives the jouissance/enjoyment contained in and evoked by signifiers of the symbolic webbing that holds him or her and relationships; in the other partition lives the jouissance/enjoyment held by the Real object(s) that cause us to desire and seek satisfaction.

Said in another way, passion is a semiotic affair written upon the palimpsest of the mOther's body. Analysis aims to yield a certain (savoir) knowledge of this unconscious palimpsest, that "one's capacity to care [and to desire] is rooted in the past, but that—until the moment of death—it will always be subject to retroactive re-articulations" (Silverman 2000, p. 50). The crucial substance of living close to the arc of one's desire, or "being unto death" and the ethic it implies, then, is not, as Lacan is sometimes misunderstood to mean, a prescription to pursue unlimited and disconnected satisfaction/jouissance—for this is only a characterization of the death drive. Rather, it is an experienced truth that the symbol, mediated by our family circle and cultural context, offers to each one of us a unique etching, and that the assumption of one's desire unto death is the active embrace of this fact. In the writing of the sentence that will constitute one's life, its meaning will only begin to be known after the period of death to that sentence that is my (your) life, arrives. Therefore, death as that last and enclosing absence must be sought in its particularity as one's very own limit lived, rather than a biological limit one cannot survive.

In the time of Ms. S.'s life (see Chapter 9), she was 44 years old when she committed herself to her analysis. In retrospect, it became clear that time had been really pressing upon her when she said toward the end of her analysis, "Analysis has been the hardest thing I've ever done. But then by that point in my life [when she decided to begin analysis], it was live or die—there was little point in continuing just to survive."

"Indeed."

On September 11, 2001, in every consulting room in the United States, patients and their analysts were forced to deal with having both been unexpectedly slammed into the traumatic Real. This Real was of a different kind than is usually experienced within the analytic matrix. It was a shared experience of the traumatic Real coming from a third place, not a co-production via the vehicle of transferences. Hour after hour, day after day, my patients' sense of overwhelm was nibbled at through verbal associations to past traumas and wonderings about the future. Each person searched within, and sought from others, symbolic framings (i.e., religious, political, economic), that might help to process or cut the traumatic Real of this unthinkable attack and its destruction down to a more comprehensible size.

Linear time was disrupted that week. Segments of hours would flow in a familiar rhythm, only to be cut again, leaving personal identities floating about, as if simultaneously I, and the individuals in my practice, were suddenly in space suits—tethered by cords to a spacecraft—in view of each other but unable to speak or make contact. Yet at other times, the simple experience of there being two sentient breathing bodies in one room, who wanted to speak to each other, seemed a medium supportive enough to enable speech to return.

During one of my last appointments of the week, Ms. Y. (see Chapter 4), who was well into the termination phase of her work and speaking of her recent work project in theater, complained petulantly that I wasn't saying anything. I replied that indeed that was true. I had found it very difficult to think the entire week. I said that I had been following her, but perhaps she felt my resting within myself as being too absent from her. A silence was followed by her speaking of thoughts pertaining to the ending of her analysis, words surrounded by a texturing of poignant loss, mild protest, and reluctant acceptance of limits—hers, mine, analysis in general.

In this palpable silence with Ms. Y. was a shared rediscovery of how within human experience the Real, the Symbolic, and the Imaginary co-create the singularity of each human subject. This singularity is always absolute and irrevocable. On the other hand, our silence also held the poignancy attached to a now "shared and lived truth" that we, as two separate individuals, were experiencing also in that moment a depth of intimacy in tandem with our irrevocable differences. This intimacy was possible only because psychic separation and the acceptance of certain limits had become finally bearable by Ms. Y.—at least most of the time—which is all any one of us ever manages anyway. But it is good enough.

References

Anzieu, D. (1985). *The Skin Ego*. Madison, CT: International Universities Press.
——— (1990). Formal signifiers and the ego-skin. In *Psychic Envelopes*, ed. D. Anzieu, pp. 1–26. London: Karnac.
Apollon, W. (1998). Unpublished seminar notes from Summer Training in Quebec City, Canada.
Aron, L. (1995). The internalized primal scene. *Psychoanalytic Dialogues* 5(2):195–237.
Benjamin, J. (1991). Father and daughter: identification with difference: a contribution to gender heterodoxy. *Psychoanalytic Dialogues* 1(3):277–299.
——— (1995). *Like Subjects, Love Objects*. New Haven, CT: Yale University Press.
——— (1997). Psychoanalysis as a vocation. *Psychoanalytic Dialogues* 7(6):781–802.
——— (1998). *Shadow of the Other: Intersubjectivity and Gender in Psychoanalysis*. Florence, KY: Taylor and Francis/Routledge.
Bergman, M. (1997). Historical roots of psychoanalytic orthodoxy. *International Journal of Psycho-Analysis* 78(1):69–86.
Bernfeld, S. (1962). On psychoanalytic training. *Psychoanalytic Quarterly* 31:453–482.
Bick, E. (1968). The experience of the skin in early object relations. *International Journal of Psycho-Analysis* 49:484–486.
Bion, W. R. (1956). Development of schizophrenic thought. *International Journal of Psycho-Analysis* 37:344–346.
——— (1957). Differentiation of the psychotic from the non-psychotic personalities. *International Journal of Psycho-Analysis* 38:266–275.
——— (1958). On hallucination. *International Journal of Psycho-Analysis* 39:341–349.

——— (1959). Attacks on linking. *International Journal of Psycho-Analysis* 40:308–315.
——— (1962a). A theory of thinking. In *Second Thoughts*, pp. 110–119. New York: Jason Aronson, 1967.
——— (1962b). *Learning from Experience*. New York: Basic Books.
——— (1963). *Elements of Psychoanalysis*. London: Karnac, 1984.
——— (1967). *Second Thoughts*. London: Karnac.
——— (1970). *Attention and Interpretation*. London: Tavistock.
——— (1992). *Cogitations*. London: Karnac.
Bollas, C. (1987). *The Shadow of the Object: Psychoanalysis of the Unthought Known*. London: Free Association Books.
——— (1992). Psychic genera. In *On Being a Character*. London: Routledge.
Boothby, R. (1991). *Death and Desire: Psychoanalytic Theory in Lacan's Return to Freud*. New York: Routledge.
Bott-Spillius, E. (1990). *Melanie Klein Today: Developments in Theory and Practice*. New York: Routledge.
——— (2001). Freud and Klein on the concept of phantasy. *International Journal of Psycho-Analysis* 82:361–374.
Boyer, B. (1978). Countertransference experiences with severely regressed patients. *Contemporary Psychoanalysis* 14(1):48–72.
——— (1989). Countertransference and technique in working with the regressed patient: further remarks. *International Journal of Psycho-Analysis* 70(4):701–714.
Britton, R. (1989). The missing link: parental sexuality in the Oedipus complex. In *The Oedipus Complex Today*, ed. J. Steiner, pp. 83–101. London: Karnac.
Britton, R., and Steiner, J. (1987). The missing link: parental sexuality in the Oedipus complex. In *The Oedipus Complex Today*, pp. 83–102. London: Karnac.
——— (1994). Interpretation: Selected fact or overvalued idea? *International Journal of Psycho-Analysis* 75(5–6):1069–1078.
Buber, M. (1958). *I and Thou*, trans. R. G. Smith. New York: Charles Scribner's Sons.
Burch, B. (1993). Heterosexuality, bisexuality, and lesbianism: rethinking psychoanalytic views of women's sexual object choice. *Psychoanalytic Review* 80(1):83–99.
Butler, J. (1990). *Gender Trouble: Feminism and the Subversion of Identity*. New York: Routledge.
———(1993). *Bodies That Matter: On the Discursive Limits of Sex*. New York: Routledge.
Canton, L. (1991). *The experience of the "pass" as a condition to becoming an analyst*. Paper given at the 1991 conference of the Federation of Psychoanalytic Training Program, San Francisco, CA.
Chodorow, N. (1994). *Femininities, Masculinities, Sexualities: Freud and Beyond*. Lexington: University Press of Kentucky.

Concina, M. (2002). *Panic attack and chronic fatigue syndrome*. Presentation given at the Apres Coup Psychoanalytic Association, New York, April 6.

Cooper, A. (1989). Infant research and adult psychoanalysis. In *The Significance of Infant Observational Research for Clinical Work with Children, Adolescents, and Adults*, ed. A. Goldberg, et al., pp. 79–89. Madison, CT: International Universities Press.

Copjec, J. (1994). Sex and the euthanasia of reason. In *Read My Desire: Lacan against the Historicists*, pp. 201–236. Cambridge, MA: MIT Press.

Crick, P. (1997). Mother–baby observation: the position of observer. *Psychoanalytic Psychotherapy* 11(3):245–255.

Dean, T. (2000). *Beyond Sexuality*. Chicago: University of Chicago Press.

——— (2001). *Homosexuality and Psychoanalysis*, ed. T. Dean and C. Lane. Chicago: University of Chicago Press.

de Lauretis, T. (1994). *The Practice of Love: Lesbian Sexuality and Perverse Desire*. Bloomington, IN: Indiana University Press.

Diamond, M., and Sigmundson, H. (1997). Sex assignment at birth: long-term review and clinical implications. *Archives of Pediatric and Adolescent Medicine* 151:298–304.

Didier-Weill, A. (2002). *The voice and the ethics of psychoanalysis*. Presentation given at the Apres Coup Psychoanalytic Association, New York, March 2.

Dor, J. (1999). *Clinical Lacan*. Northvale, NJ: Jason Aronson.

Dreger, A. (1998). Ambiguous sex—or ambiguous medicine—in the treatment of intersexuality. *Hastings Center Report* 28(3):24–35.

Eisold, K. (1998). The splitting of the New York Psychoanalytic Society and the construction of psychoanalytic authority. *International Journal of Psycho-Analysis* 79:871–885.

Elise, D. (2002). The primary maternal oedipal situation and female homoerotic desire. *Psychoanalytic Inquiry* 22(2):209–228.

Elliot, A., and Spezzano, C. (1996). Psychoanalysis at its limit: navigating the post-modern turn. *Psychoanalytic Quarterly* 65:52–83.

Fajardo, B. (1988). Constitution in infancy: implications for early development and psychoanalysis. In *Learning from Kohut*, ed. A. Goldberg, pp. 91–100. Hillsdale, NJ: Analytic Press.

Felman, S. (1987). *Jacques Lacan and the Adventure of Insight*. Cambridge, MA: Harvard University Press.

Filloux, J. (1996). A difficulty of psychoanalytic training: recognition. *Topique: Revue Freudienne* 26(61):457–466.

Fink, B. (1995). *The Lacanian Subject: Between Language and Jouissance*. Princeton, NJ: Princeton University Press.

——— (1997). *A Clinical Introduction to Lacanian Psychoanalysis: Theory and Technique*. Cambridge, MA: Harvard University Press.

Fonagy, P. (1996). Commentary on "The Irrelevance of Infant Observations for Psychoanalysis." *Journal of the American Psychoanalytic Association* 44(2):404–422.

Forbes, S. (1977). Bion and the future of psychoanalysis. *Samiksa* 31(1):51–79.

Foucault, M. (1976). *The History of Sexuality, Vol. 1: An Introduction*, trans. R. Hurley. New York: Vintage.

Freud, S. (1895). Project for a scientific psychology. *Standard Edition* 1.

——— (1895a). The psychotherapy of hysteria. *Standard Edition* 2.

——— (1900). The interpretation of dreams. *Standard Edition* 4 and 5.

——— (1905). Three essays on sexuality. *Standard Edition* 7.

——— (1911). Two principles of mental functioning. *Standard Edition* 11.

——— (1914). On narcissism: an introduction *Standard Edition* 14.

——— (1915). The unconscious. *Standard Edition* 14.

——— (1915a). Repression. *Standard Edition* 14.

——— (1917). Introductory lectures on psychoanalysis. *Standard Edition* 16.

——— (1918). From the history of an infantile neurosis. *Standard Edition* 17.

——— (1919). A child is being beaten: a contribution to the study of the origin of sexual perversions. *Standard Edition* 17.

——— (1920a). Beyond the pleasure principle. *Standard Edition* 18.

——— (1920b). Homosexuality in a woman. *Standard Edition* 18.

——— (1922). Two encyclopedia articles. *Standard Edition* 18.

——— (1923). The ego and the id. *Standard Edition* 19.

——— (1924). The economic problem of masochism. *Standard Edition* 19.

——— (1924a). The passing of the oedipal complex. *Standard Edition* 19.

——— (1926). The question of lay analysis. *Standard Edition* 20.

——— (1930). Civilization and its discontents. *Standard Edition* 21.

——— (1931). Female sexuality. *Standard Edition* 21.

——— (1937a). Constructions in analysis. *Standard Edition* 23.

——— (1937b). Analysis terminable and interminable. *Standard Edition* 23.

——— (1940). An outline of psychoanalysis. *Standard Edition* 23.

Friedman, R., and Downey, J. (1998). Psychoanalysis and the model of homosexuality as psychopathology: a historical overview. *American Journal of Psychoanalysis* 58(3):249–270.

Gerson, S. (1996). Neutrality, resistance, and self-disclosure in an inter-subjective psychoanalysis. *Psychoanalytic Dialogues* 6(5):623–645.

Green, A. (1985a). The analyst, symbolization and absence in the analytic setting. In *On Private Madness*, pp. 30–59. New York: Routledge.

——— (1985b). The dead mother. In *On Private Madness*, pp. 142–173. New York: Routledge.

——— (1998). The primordial mind and the work of the negative. *International Journal of Psycho-Analysis* 79(4):649–665.

——— (1999a). *Fabric of Affect in Psychoanalytic Discourse*. New York: Routledge.

——— (1999b). On discriminating and not discriminating between affect and representation. *International Journal of Psycho-Analysis* 80:277–316.

——— (2000). *Chains of Eros: The Sexual in Psychoanalysis*. London: Rebus.

——— (2001). *Life Narcissism, Death Narcissism*. London: Free Association Books.

——— (2002). *Time in Psychoanalysis: Some Contradictory Aspects*. London: Free Association Books.

Grinberg, L. (1989). Integrity and ethics in "becoming a psychoanalyst." In *The Psychoanalytic Core: Essays in Honor of Leo Rangell*, ed. H. Blum and D. Weinshel, pp. 353–367. Madison, CT: International Universities Press.

Grotstein, J. (1984). A proposed revision of the concept of primitive mental states, II: borderline syndrome; Section 3: disorders of autistic safety and symbiotic relatedness. *Contemporary Psychoanalysis* 20(2):266–343.

——— (1990). Nothingness, meaninglessness, and chaos in psychoanalysis, Part 1. *Contemporary Psychoanalysis* 26(2):257–290.

——— (1991). Nothingness, meaninglessness, and blackholes, III: self and interactional regulation and the background presence of primary identification. *Contemporary Psychoanalysis* 27(1):1–33.

Guillaumin, J. (1990). The psychic envelopes of the psychoanalyst: some suggestions for applying the theory of psychic envelopes to the study of the psychoanalyst's functioning. In *Psychic Envelopes*, ed. D. Anzieu, pp. 147–190. London: Karnac.

Hansen, Y. (1996). *Tolerating the unknown: a dimension of infant observation*. Presentation given at the Psychoanalytic Center of California's Primitive States of Mind Conference, Los Angeles.

Harari, R. (2001). *Lacan's Seminar on Anxiety: An Introduction*. New York: Other Press.

Harris, M. (1976). The contribution of mother–infant interaction and development to the equipment of a psychoanalyst or psychoanalytic psychotherapist. In *Collected Papers of Martha Harris and Esther Bick*, ed. M. Harris and W. Harris, pp. 225–239. Perthshire, Scotland: Clunie.

Hill, G. (1992). *Masculine and Feminine: The Natural Flow of Opposites in the Psyche*. Boston: Shambhala.

Hinshelwood, R. (1994). *Clinical Klein: From Theory to Practice*. New York: Basic Books.

Hoffman, I. (1991). Discussion: toward a social-constructivist view of the psychoanalytic situation. *Psychoanalytic Dialogues* 1:74–105.

Ireland, M. (1993). *Reconceiving Women: Separating Motherhood from Female Identity*. New York: Guilford.

Isaacs, S. (1948). The nature and function of phantasy. *International Journal of Psycho-Analysis* 29:73–97.

Jacobson, J. (1993). Developmental observation, multiple models of the mind, and the therapeutic relationship in psychoanalysis. *Psychoanalytic Quarterly* 62(4):523–552.

Joseph, B. (1981). Defense mechanisms and phantasy in the psychoanalytical process. In *Psychic Equilibrium and Psychic Change: Selected Papers of Betty Joseph*, ed. M. Feldman and E. Bott-Spillius, pp. 135–144. London: Routledge, 1989.

Julien, P. (1994). *Jacques Lacan's Return to Freud: The Real, the Symbolic, and the Imaginary*, trans. D. Simiu. New York: New York University Press.

Kappelle, W. (1996). How useful is selection? *International Journal of Psycho-Analysis* 77(6):1213–1232.

Keats, J. (1817). From a letter to George and Thomas Keats, December 21, 1817. In *The Norton Introduction to Literature: Poetry*, ed. J. P. Hunter, pp. 477–478. New York: Norton, 1973.

Kestenberg, J. (1977). Psychoanalytic observation of children. *International Review of Psycho-Analysis* 4(4):393–407.

Kernberg, O. (1996). Thirty methods to destroy the creativity of psychoanalytic candidates. *International Journal of Psycho-Analysis* 77:1031–1040.

Kramer, E. (1979). *Childhood and Art Therapy*. New York: Schocken.

Kristeva, J. (1982). *Desire in Language*. Oxford: Basil Blackwell.

——— (1984). *Revolution in Poetic Language*. New York: Columbia University Press.

——— (1989). *Black Sun*. New York: Columbia University Press.

——— (1996). *Time and Sense: Proust and the Experience of Literature*. New York: Columbia University Press.

——— (2000). *The Sense and Non-sense of Revolt: The Powers and Limits of Psychoanalysis*. New York: Columbia University Press.

——— (2001). *Melanie Klein*. New York: Columbia University Press.

Kumin, I. (1996). *Birth of the Other*. New York: Guilford.

Lacan, J. (1951). Some reflections upon the ego. *International Journal of Psycho-Analysis* 34:11–17.

——— (1952–1953). *Seminar I*. Cambridge: Cambridge University Press.

——— (1953). The neurotic's individual myth. *Psychoanalytic Quarterly* 48(3): 386–425.

——— (1953a). The function and field of speech and language in psychoanalysis. In *Ecrits*, pp. 30–113. New York: Norton, 1977.

——— (1953b). The mirror-stage, source of the I-function, as shown by psychoanalytic experience. *International Journal of Psycho-Analysis* 30:203.

——— (1953c). The agency of the letter in the unconscious or reason since Freud. In *Ecrits*, pp. 146–178. New York: Norton, 1977.

——— (1953d). On a question preliminary to any possible treatment of psychosis. In *Ecrits*, pp. 179–225. New York: Norton, 1977.

——— (1953e). The signification of the phallus. In *Ecrits*, pp. 281–291. New York: Norton, 1977.

——— (1953f). The Freudian thing. In *Ecrits*, pp. 114–145. New York: Norton, 1977.
——— (1953–1954g). *Seminar II*. Cambridge: Cambridge University Press.
——— (1955). Seminar on "The Purloined Letter." In *The Purloined Poe, Lacan, Derrida, and Psychoanalytic Reading*, ed. J. Muller and W. Richardson, pp. 28–54. Baltimore, MD: John Hopkins University Press, 1988.
——— (1955–1956). *Seminar III: The Psychoses*, ed. J. Miller, trans. R. Grigg. New York: Norton.
——— (1959–1960). *Seminar VII: The Ethics of Psychoanalysis*. New York: Norton, 1992.
——— (1960). The subversion of the subject and the dialectic of desire in the Freudian unconscious. In *Ecrits*, pp. 292–325. New York: Norton, 1977.
——— (1964). *Seminar XI. The Four Fundamental Concepts of Psychoanalysis*. New York: Norton, 1978.
——— (1965). *Seminar XIII. From Lecture Notes of Dr. Andre Patsalides*, Lacanian School of Psychoanalysis.
——— (1967). Proposition of 9 October 1967 on the psychoanalyst of the school. Analysis 1:1–13.
——— (1972a). *On Feminine Sexuality: The Limits of Love and Knowledge*, ed. J.-A. Miller, trans. B. Fink. New York: Norton, 1999.
——— (1972b). *Encore: Seminar XX*. New York: Norton, 1998.
——— (1973). *Television: A Challenge to the Psychoanalytic Establishment*, ed. J. Copjec, trans. D. Hollier, R. Krauss, and A. Michelson. New York: Norton, 1990.
Laplanche, J. (1995). Seduction, persecution, revelation. *International Journal of Psycho-Analysis* 76:663–682.
Laplanche, J., and Pontalis, J. (1973). Fantasy and the origins of sexuality. In *Formation of Fantasy*, ed. V. Burgin, J. Donald, and C. Kaplan, pp. 5–34. London: Methuen, 1986.
Leclaire, S. (1998). *Psychoanalyzing: On the Order of the Unconscious and the Practice of the Letter*. Stanford, CA: Stanford University Press.
——— (1998a). *A Child is Being Killed: On Primary Narcissism and the Death Drive*. Stanford, CA: Stanford University Press.
Lecours, S., and Bouchard, M.-A. (1997). Dimensions of mentalization: outlining levels of psychic transformation. *International Journal of Psycho-Analysis* 78:855–876.
Lee, J. (1990). *Jacques Lacan*. Amherst: University of Massachusetts Press.
Lemaire, A. (1977). *Jacques Lacan*. London: Routledge & Kegan Paul.
Little, M. (1951). Counter-transference and the patient's response to it. *International Journal of Psycho-Analysis* 32:32–40.
——— (1990). *Psychotic Anxieties and Containment: A Personal Record of an Analysis with Winnicott*. Northvale, NJ: Jason Aronson.

Loewald, H. (1979). The waning of the Oedipus complex. In *Papers on Psychoanalysis*. New Haven, CT: Yale University Press.

Lowenfeld, H. (1941). Psychic trauma and productive experience in the artist. *Psychoanalytic Review* 1:116.

Matthis, I. (2000). Sketch for a metapsychology of affect. *International Journal of Psycho-Analysis* 81(2):215–227.

Mayer, E. L. (1996). Changes in science and changing ideas about knowledge and authority in psychoanalysis. *Psychoanalytic Quarterly* 65(1):158–200.

McDougall, J. (1989). *Theatres of the Body*. New York: Norton.

——— (1990). *Plea for a Measure of Abnormality*. Philadelphia, PA: Brunner/Mazel.

——— (1995). *The Many Faces of Eros: A Psychoanalytic Exploration of Human Sexuality*. New York: Norton.

Meltzer, D. (1978). *The Kleinian Development*. Perthshire, Scotland: Clunie.

——— (1988). *The Apprehension of Beauty*. Perthshire, Scotland: Clunie.

Mieli, P. (1993). Femininity and the limits of theory. *Psychoanalysis & Contemporary Thought* 16(3):411–427.

——— (2001). On trauma: a Freudian perspective. In *Storms in Her Head: Freud and the Construction of Hysteria*, ed. M. Dimen and A. Harris, pp. 265–280. New York: Other Press.

Miller, L. (1999). Infant observation as a precursor of clinical training. *Psychoanalytic Inquiry* 19(2):142–145.

Milner, M. (1957). *On Not Being Able to Paint*, 2nd ed. Oxford, England: International Universities Press.

——— (1993). The role of illusion in symbol formation. In *Transitional Objects and Potential Spaces: Literary Uses of D. W. Winnicott*, ed. P. Rudnytsky, pp. 13–39. New York: Columbia University Press.

Mitchell, J., and Rose, J. (1982). *Feminine Sexuality: Jacques Lacan and the Ecole Freudienne*. London: Macmillan.

Mitchell. S. (1998). The analyst's knowledge and authority. *Psychoanalytic Quarterly* 67(1):1–31.

Mitrani, J. (1992). On the survival function of autistic maneuvers in adult patients. *International Journal of Psycho-Analysis* 73:549–559.

Money, J. (1988). *Gay, Straight, and In-Between: The Sexology of Erotic Orientation*. London: Oxford University Press.

Muller, J. (1996). *Beyond the Psychoanalytic Dyad: Developmental Semiotics in Freud, Pierce and Lacan*. New York: Routledge.

——— (2000). The origins and self-serving functions of the ego. In *The Subject of Lacan: A Lacanian Reader for Psychologists*, ed. K. Malone and S. Friedlander, pp. 41–61. Albany, NY: State University of New York Press.

Nasio, J. (1992). *Five Lessons on the Psychoanalytic Theory of Jacques Lacan*. Albany: State University of New York Press.

——— (1998). *Hysteria from Freud and Lacan*. New York: Other Press.

Naumburg, M. (1950). *Schizophrenic Art: Its Meaning in Psychotherapy*. New York: Grune & Stratton.

Nobus, D. (2000). *Jacques Lacan and the Freudian Practice of Psychoanalysis*. New York: Routledge.

Ogden, T. (1987). The transitional oedipal relationship in female development. *International Journal of Psycho-Analysis* 68(4):485–498.

——— (1989). *The Primitive Edge of Experience*. Northvale, NJ: Jason Aronson.

——— (1994). Analyzing the matrix of the transference. In *Subjects of Analysis*, pp. 137–166. Northvale, NJ: Jason Aronson.

——— (1996). Reconsidering three aspects of psychoanalytic technique. *International Journal of Psycho-Analysis* 77(5):883–900.

——— (1997). Analyzing forms of aliveness and deadness. In *Reverie and Interpretation*, pp. 21–63. Northvale, NJ: Jason Aronson.

——— (1997a). The perverse subject of analysis. In *Reverie and Interpretation*, pp. 65–104. Northvale, NJ: Jason Aronson.

——— (1997b). Reverie and interpretation. In *Reverie and Interpretation*, pp. 155–198. Northvale, NJ: Jason Aronson.

——— (2001). Re-minding the body. *American Journal of Psychotherapy* 55(1):92–104.

Parens, H. (1996). Infant observational research and psychoanalysis. *Journal of Clinical Psychoanalysis* (1):107–111.

Patsalides, A. (1992). Unpublished from 1992 *Seminar Notes*. Berkeley, CA: Lacanian School of Psychoanalysis.

Piontelli, A. (1992). *From Fetus to Child: An Observational and Psychoanalytic Study*. New York: Routledge.

Quinodoz, J. (1989). Female homosexual patients in psychoanalysis. *International Journal of Psycho-Analysis* 70:55–63.

Racker, H. (1968). *Transference and Counter-transference*. London: Hogarth.

Ragland, E. (1987). *Jacques Lacan and the Philosophy of Psychoanalysis*. Chicago: University of Illinois Press.

——— (1991). The sexual masquerade: a Lacanian theory of sexual difference. In *Lacan and the Subject of Language*, ed. E. Ragland-Sullivan and M. Bracher, pp. 49–80. New York: Routledge.

——— (2001). Lacan and the homosexual: "a love letter." In *Homosexuality and Psychoanalysis*. ed. T. Dean and C. Lane, pp. 98–119. Chicago: University of Chicago Press.

Renik, O. (1995). The ideal of the anonymous analyst and the problem of self-disclosure. *Psychoanalytic Quarterly* 64:466–495.

——— (1999). To the couch: a revival for analysis. *New York Times*, Section F, page 1, January 12.

Rukeyser, M. (1994). The speed of darkness. In *Muriel Rukeyser*, ed. J. Heller, p. 207–244. New York: Norton.

Rycroft. C. (1993). Why analysts need their patients' transferences. *British Journal of Psychotherapy* 10(1):83–87.

Safouan, M. (2000). *Jacques Lacan and the Question of Psychoanalytic Training*. New York: St. Martin's Press.

Scarfone, D. (2002). Controversial discussions: the issue of differences in method. *International Journal of Psycho-Analysis* 83:453–457.

Scharfman, M. (1989). The therapeutic dyad in the light of infant observation research. In *The Significance of Infant Observational Research for Clinical Work with Children, Adolescents, and Adults*, ed. A. Goldberg et al., pp. 53–64. Madison, CT: International Universities Press.

Schaverien, J. (1999). Art within analysis: scapegoat, transference and transformation. *Journal of Analytical Psychology* 44(4):479–510.

Schore, A. (1994). *Affect Regulation and the Origin of the Self: The Neurobiology of Emotional Development*. Mahwah, NJ: Lawrence Erlbaum.

——— (2000). Attachment and the regulation of the right brain. *Attachment and Human Development* 2:23–47.

——— (2001). The effects of relational trauma on right brain development, affect regulation, and infant mental health. *Infant Mental Health Journal* 22: 201–269.

——— (2001a). Minds in the making: attachment, the developing brain, affect regulation, and infant mental health. *Infant Mental Health Journal* 22: 7–66.

Searles, H. (1979). *Counter-transference and Related Subjects*. New York: International Universities Press.

Segal. H. (1957). Notes on symbol-formation. *International Journal of Psycho-Analysis* 38:391–407.

——— (1994). Phantasy and reality. *International Journal of Psycho-Analysis* 75:395–401.

Sharpe, E. (1940). Psycho-physical problems revealed in language: an examination of metaphor. In *Collected Papers of Ella Sharpe*, ed. M. Brierley, pp. 155–169. New York: Brunner/Mazel.

Silverman, K. (1992). *Male Subjectivity at the Margins*. New York: Routledge.

——— (1996). *Threshold of the Visible World*. New York: Routledge.

——— (2000). *World Spectators*. Stanford, CA: Stanford University Press.

Silverman, M. (1989). The first year after birth. In *The Course of Life, Vol. 1: Infancy*, ed. S. Greenspan et al., pp. 321–358. Madison, CT: International Universities Press.

Slavin, J. (1990). Authority and identity in the establishment of psychoanalytic training: questions regarding training models. In *Tradition and Innovation in Psychoanalytic Education: Clark Conference on Psychoanalytic Training for Psy-*

chologists, ed. M. Meisels and E. Shapiro, pp. 99–202. Hillsdale, NJ: Lawrence Erlbaum.

Solms, K., and Solms, M. (2001) *Clinical Studies in Neuro-Psychoanalysis*. New York: Other Press.

Sowa, A. (1999). Observing the unobservable. *Fort Da* 1:12–27.

Spezzano, C. (1990). A history of psychoanalytic training for psychologists in the United States. In *Tradition and Innovation in Psychoanalytic Education: Clark Conference on Psychoanalytic Training for Psychologists*, ed. M. Meisels and E. Shapiro, pp. 63–75. Hillsdale, NJ: Lawrence Erlbaum.

——— (1996). The three faces of two-person psychology: development, ontology, and epistemology. *Psychoanalytic Dialogues* 6:591–598.

——— (1998). The triangle of clinical judgment. *Journal of the American Psychoanalytic Association* 46(2):365–388.

Stern, D. (1985). *The Interpersonal World of the Infant*. New York: Basic Books.

The Psychoanalytic Consortium (2001). *Standards of Psychoanalytic Education*.

Travarthen, C., and Hubley, P. (1981). *Psychology of Infants: Scientific Foundations of Pediatrics*, 2nd ed., ed. J. Davis and J. Dobbing. London: Heinemann.

Trowell, J. (1996). Thoughts on countertransference and observation. Introduction in *Countertransference in Psychoanalytic Psychotherapy with Children and Adolescents*, ed. J. Tseiantis et al., pp. 37–49. Madison, CT: International Universities Press.

Tustin, F. (1981). *Autistic States in Children*. London: Routledge.

——— (1986). *Autistic Barriers in Neurotic Patients*. New Haven and London: Yale University Press.

——— (1990). *The Protective Shell in Children and Adults*. London: Karnac.

Tuters, E. (1988). The relevance of infant observation to clinical training and practice: an interpretation. *Infant Mental Health Journal* 1:93–104.

Wallerstein, R. (1998). The IPA and the American Psychoanalytic Association: a perspective on the regional association agreement. *International Journal of Psycho-Analysis* 79:553–564.

——— (1998a). *Lay Analysis: Life inside the Controversy*. Hillsdale, NJ: Analytic Press.

Widlocher, D. (1998). Quality control, condensed analysis and ethics. *International Journal of Psycho-Analysis* 79:1–12.

Wilson, M. (1998). Otherness within: aspects of insight in psychoanalysis. *Psychoanalytic Quarterly* 67(1):54–77.

Winnicott, D. (1945). Primitive emotional development. In *Through Paediatrics to Psycho-Analysis*, pp. 145–156. New York: Basic Books, 1975.

——— (1947). Hate in the countertransference. In *Through Paediatrics to Psycho-Analysis*, pp. 194–203. New York: Basic Books, 1975.

——— (1949). Mind and its relation to the psyche-soma. In *Through Paediatrics to Psycho-Analysis*, pp. 243–254. New York: Basic Books, 1975.

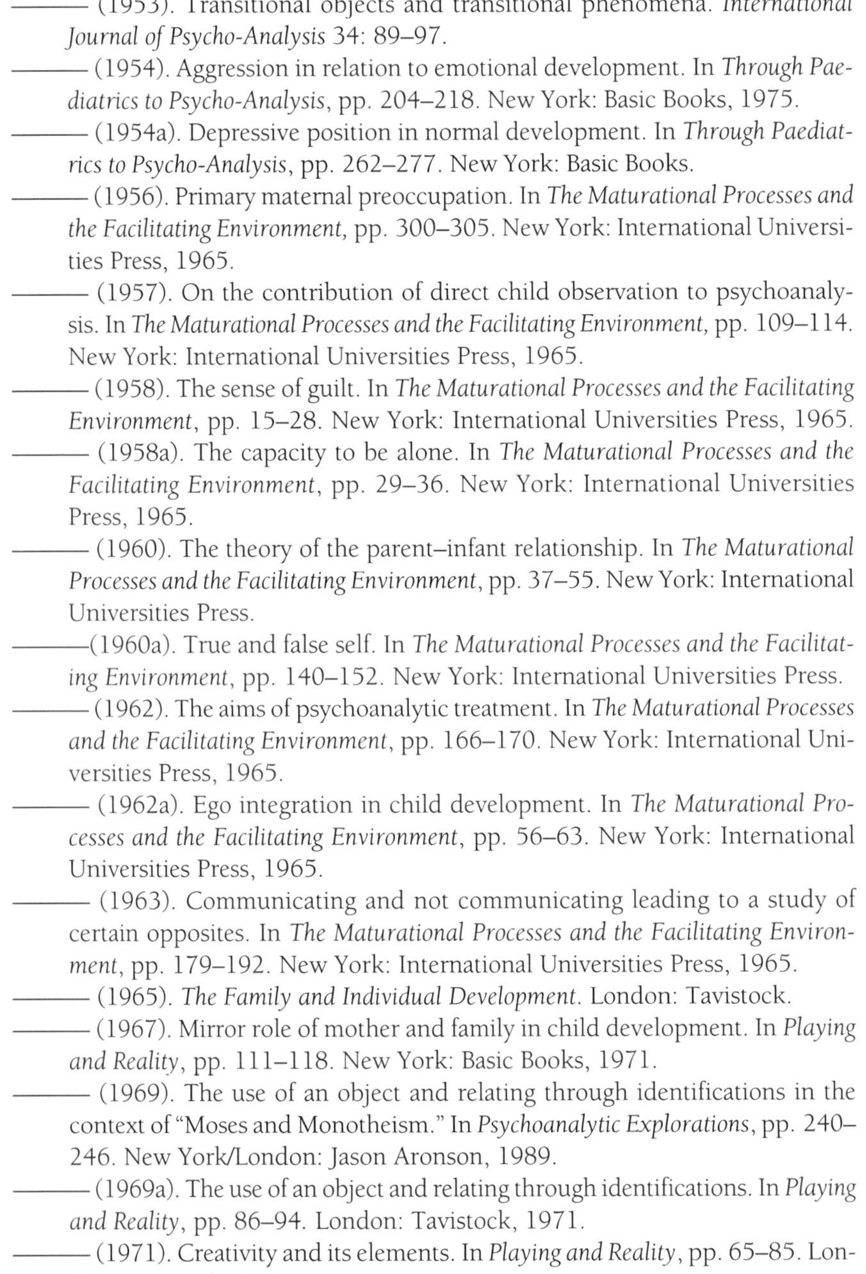

——— (1951). *Through Paediatrics to Psychoanalysis*. London: Hogarth.

——— (1953). Transitional objects and transitional phenomena. *International Journal of Psycho-Analysis* 34: 89–97.

——— (1954). Aggression in relation to emotional development. In *Through Paediatrics to Psycho-Analysis*, pp. 204–218. New York: Basic Books, 1975.

——— (1954a). Depressive position in normal development. In *Through Paediatrics to Psycho-Analysis*, pp. 262–277. New York: Basic Books.

——— (1956). Primary maternal preoccupation. In *The Maturational Processes and the Facilitating Environment*, pp. 300–305. New York: International Universities Press, 1965.

——— (1957). On the contribution of direct child observation to psychoanalysis. In *The Maturational Processes and the Facilitating Environment*, pp. 109–114. New York: International Universities Press, 1965.

——— (1958). The sense of guilt. In *The Maturational Processes and the Facilitating Environment*, pp. 15–28. New York: International Universities Press, 1965.

——— (1958a). The capacity to be alone. In *The Maturational Processes and the Facilitating Environment*, pp. 29–36. New York: International Universities Press, 1965.

——— (1960). The theory of the parent–infant relationship. In *The Maturational Processes and the Facilitating Environment*, pp. 37–55. New York: International Universities Press.

———(1960a). True and false self. In *The Maturational Processes and the Facilitating Environment*, pp. 140–152. New York: International Universities Press.

——— (1962). The aims of psychoanalytic treatment. In *The Maturational Processes and the Facilitating Environment*, pp. 166–170. New York: International Universities Press, 1965.

——— (1962a). Ego integration in child development. In *The Maturational Processes and the Facilitating Environment*, pp. 56–63. New York: International Universities Press, 1965.

——— (1963). Communicating and not communicating leading to a study of certain opposites. In *The Maturational Processes and the Facilitating Environment*, pp. 179–192. New York: International Universities Press, 1965.

——— (1965). *The Family and Individual Development*. London: Tavistock.

——— (1967). Mirror role of mother and family in child development. In *Playing and Reality*, pp. 111–118. New York: Basic Books, 1971.

——— (1969). The use of an object and relating through identifications in the context of "Moses and Monotheism." In *Psychoanalytic Explorations*, pp. 240–246. New York/London: Jason Aronson, 1989.

——— (1969a). The use of an object and relating through identifications. In *Playing and Reality*, pp. 86–94. London: Tavistock, 1971.

——— (1971). Creativity and its elements. In *Playing and Reality*, pp. 65–85. London: Tavistock, 1971.

——— (1971a). *Playing and Reality*. London: Tavistock.

——— (1972). On the basis for self in the body. *International Journal of Psycho-Analysis* 1(1):7–16.

——— (1974). Fear of breakdown. *International Review of Psycho-Analysis* 1:103–107.

Wolf, P. (1996). The irrelevance of infant observation. *Journal of the American Psychoanalytic Association* 44(2):430–446.

Young-Bruehl, E. (2000). Beyond "The Female Homosexual." *Studies in Gender & Sexuality* 1(1):97–124.

Index